STEVE McCURRY
ANIMALS

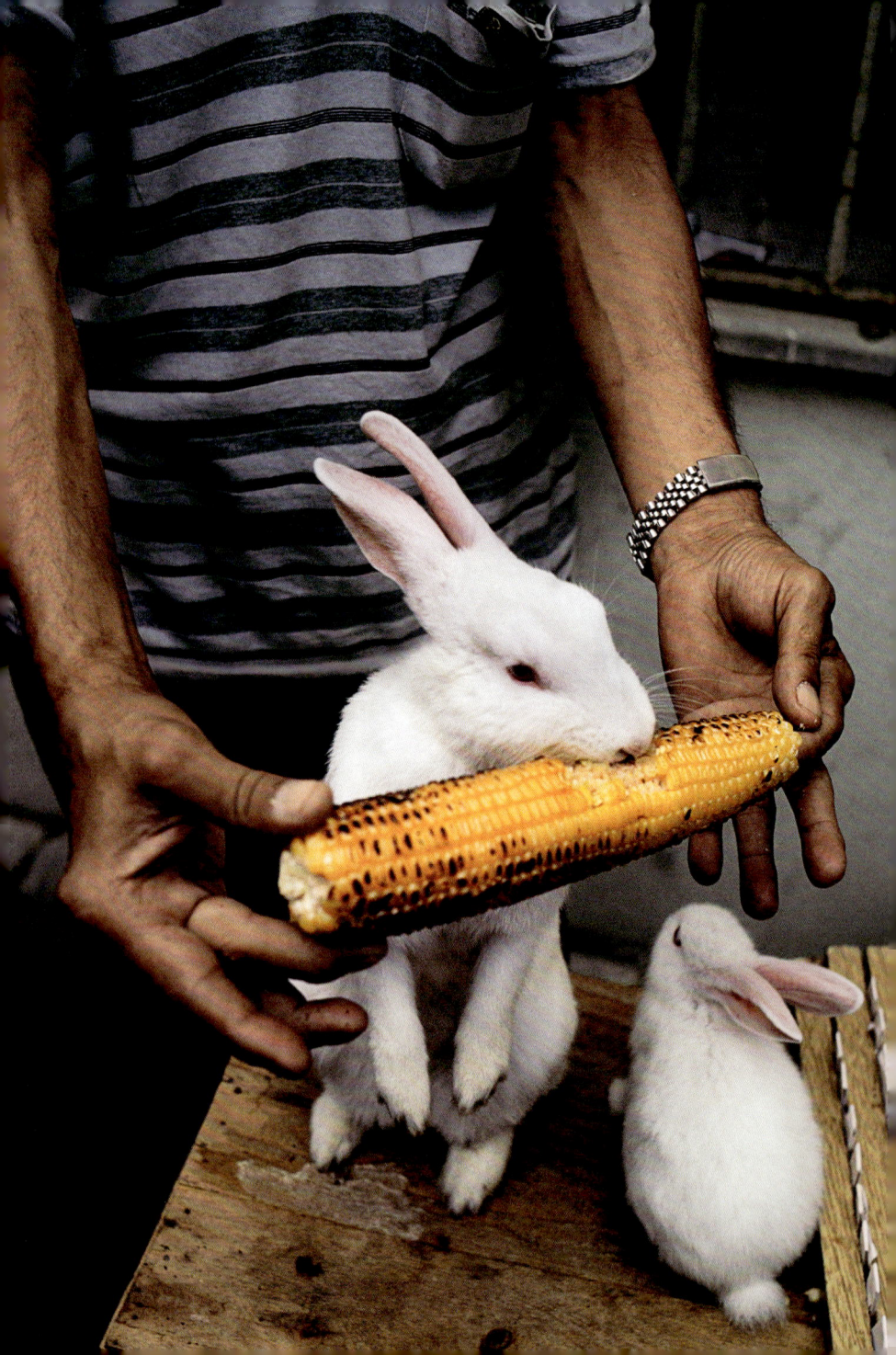

STEVE McCURRY ANIMALS

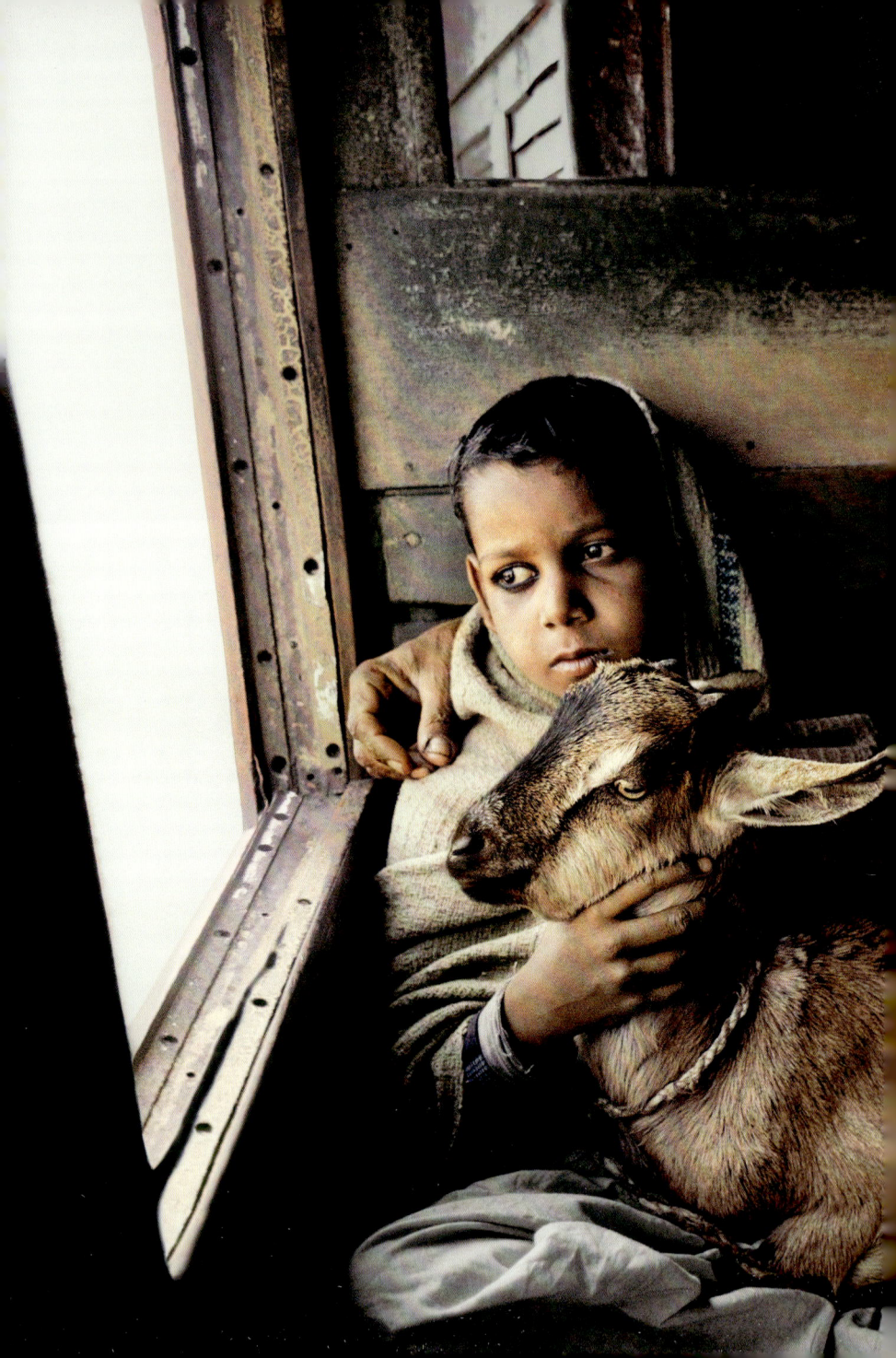

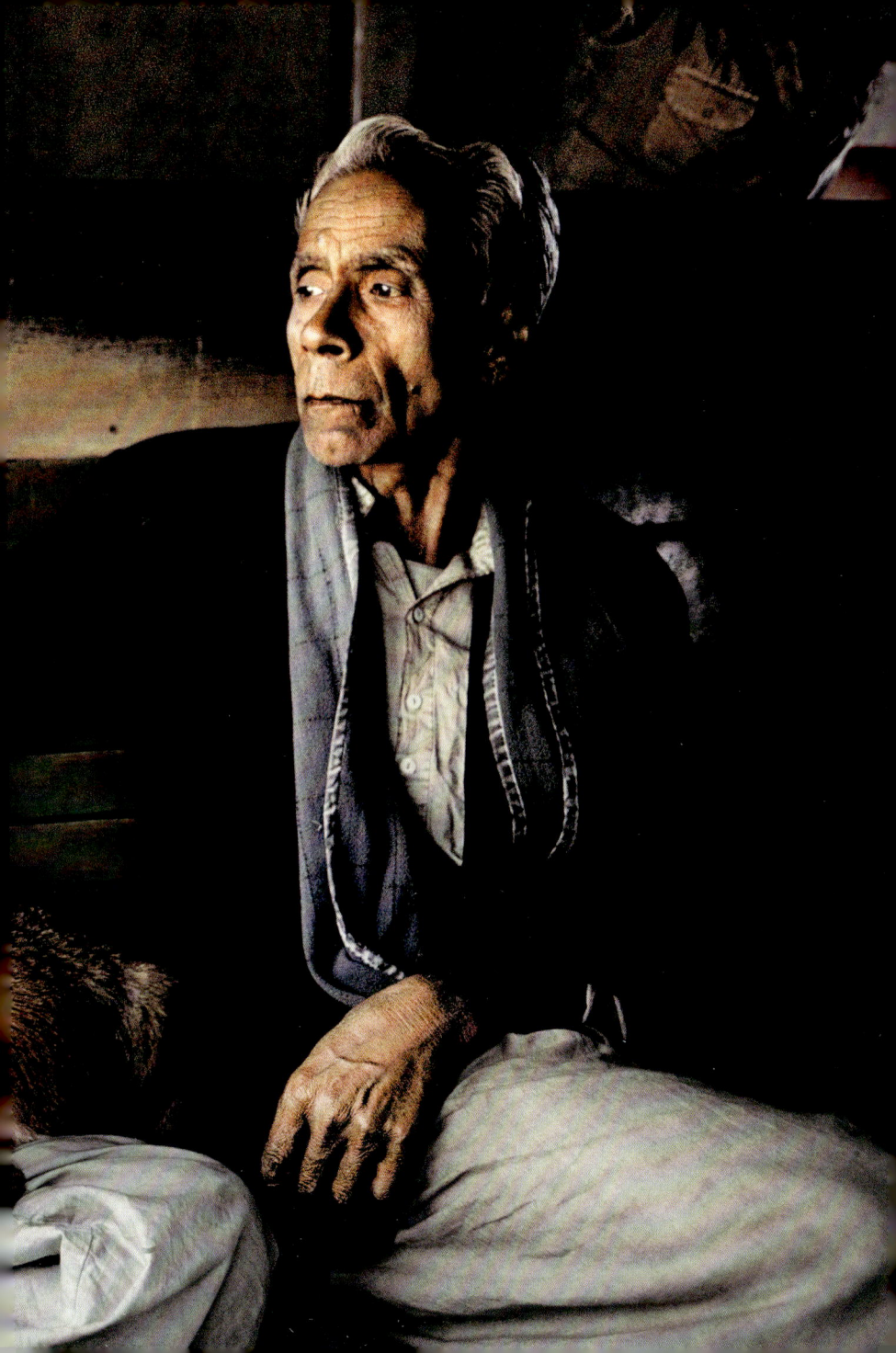

"As a college student and an aspiring artist, I was drawn to a handful of iconic photographers, but Elliott Erwitt was one whose work drew me in with every frame I saw and studied.

The first photography book in my collection was Erwitt's book *Son of Bitch*, a compilation of dog portraits given to me by my sister. At first, I was astonished that a photographer of his stature had a large body of work on dogs, but after beginning my career on the Indian subcontinent and in Afghanistan, I had encounters with many animals and began photographing them as I photographed portraits of the people nearby.

Four decades later, I have made thousands of photographs of animals, and the pictures in this book are some of the most memorable. Perhaps Elliott's book foreshadowed my career-long interest in paying tribute to the creatures that share this planet."

STEVE MCCURRY

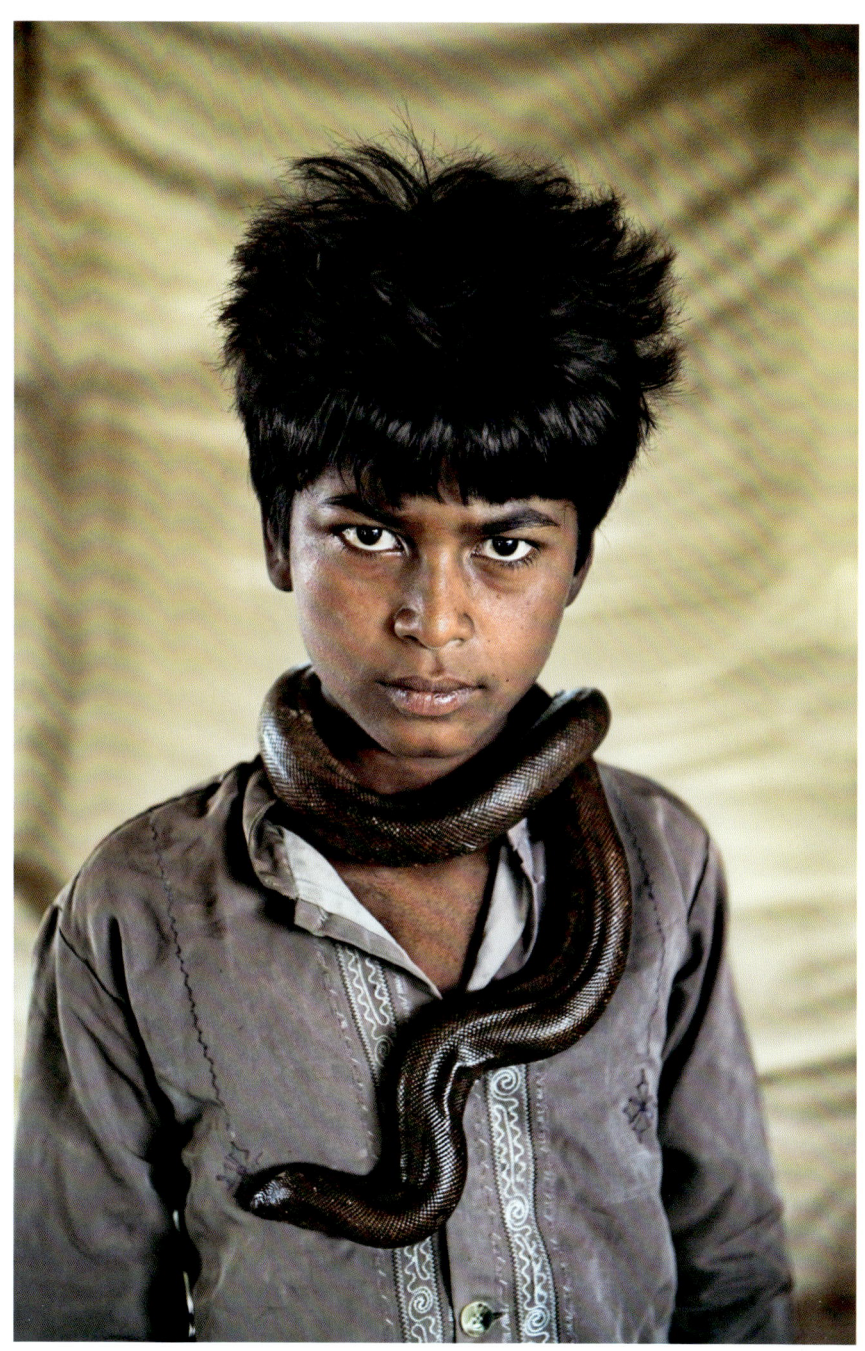

GUJARAT, INDIA, 2009

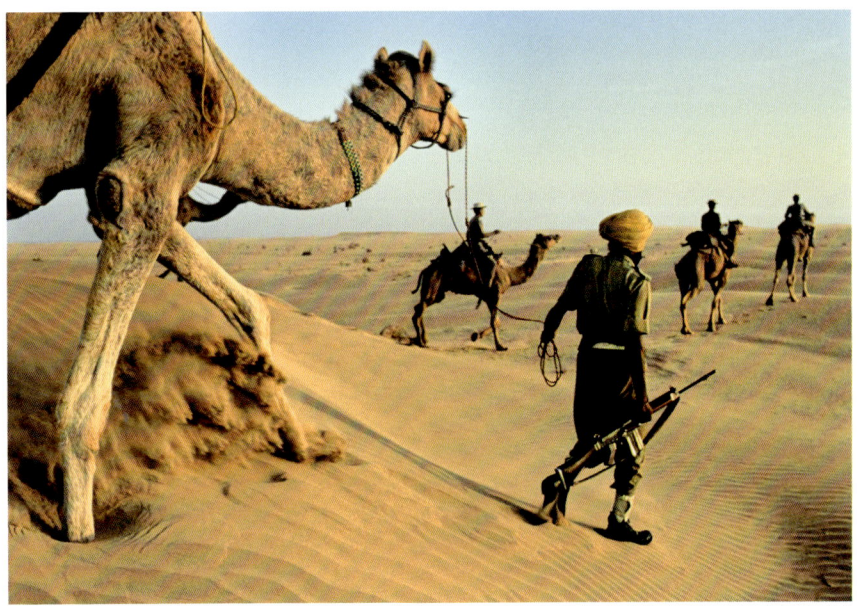

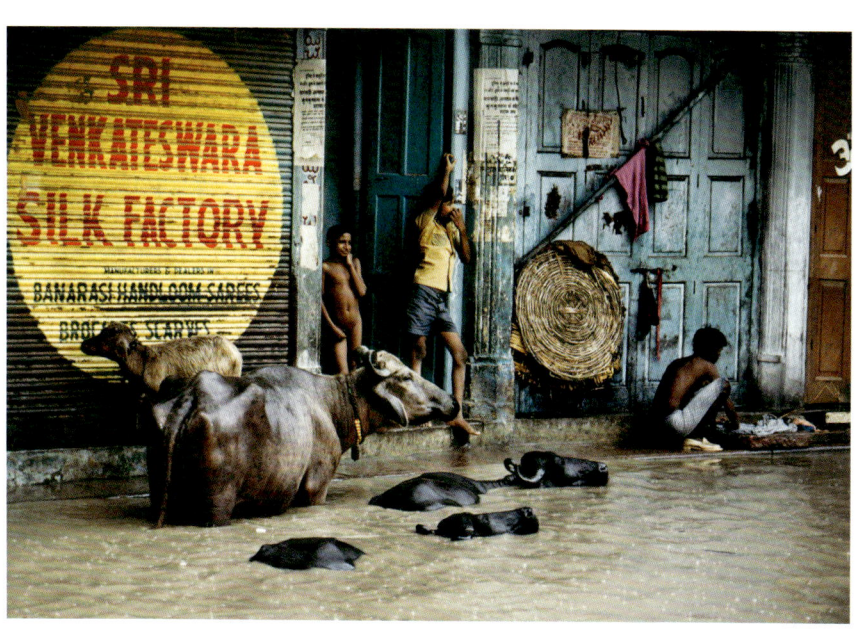

VARANASI, INDIA, 1983

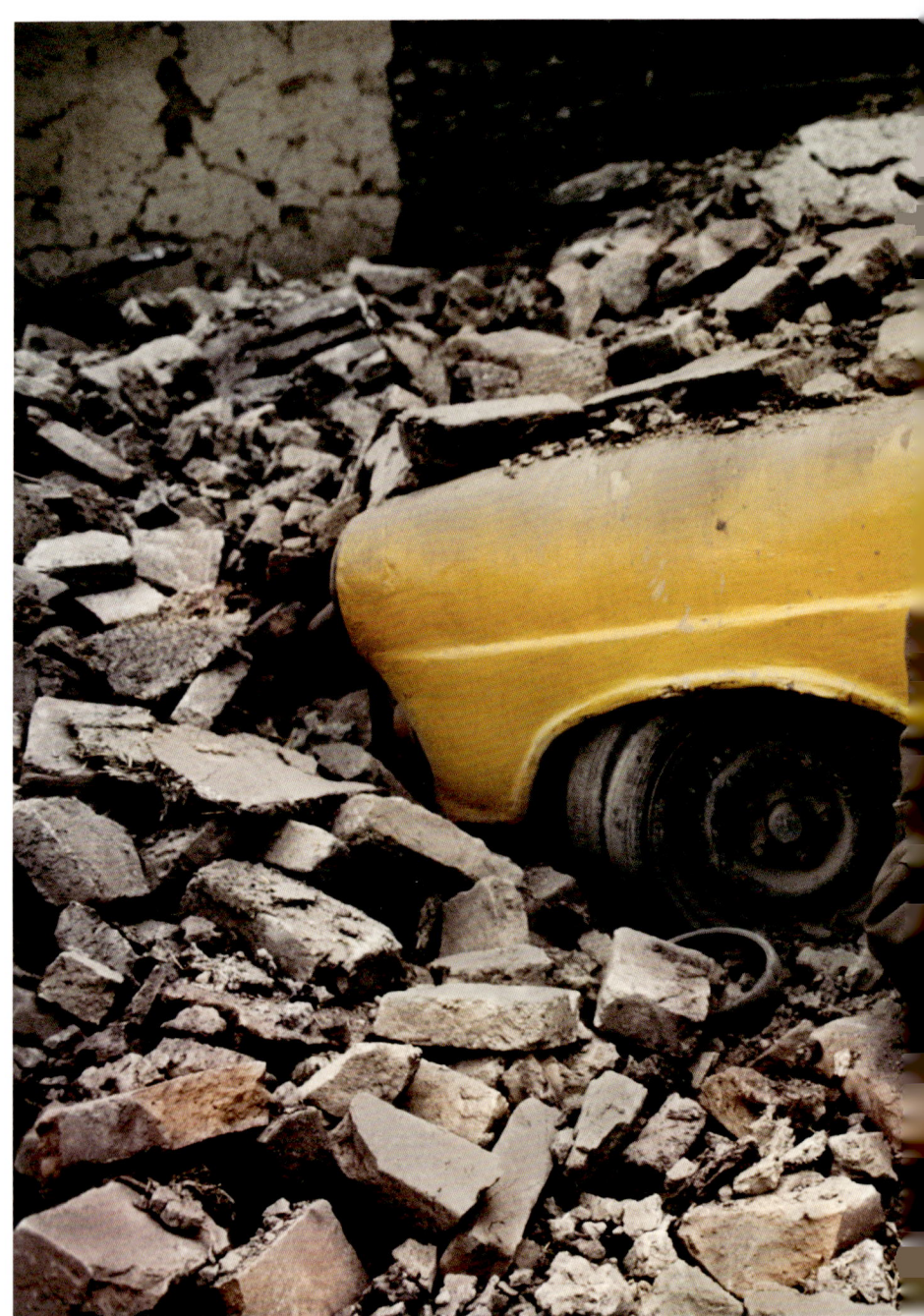

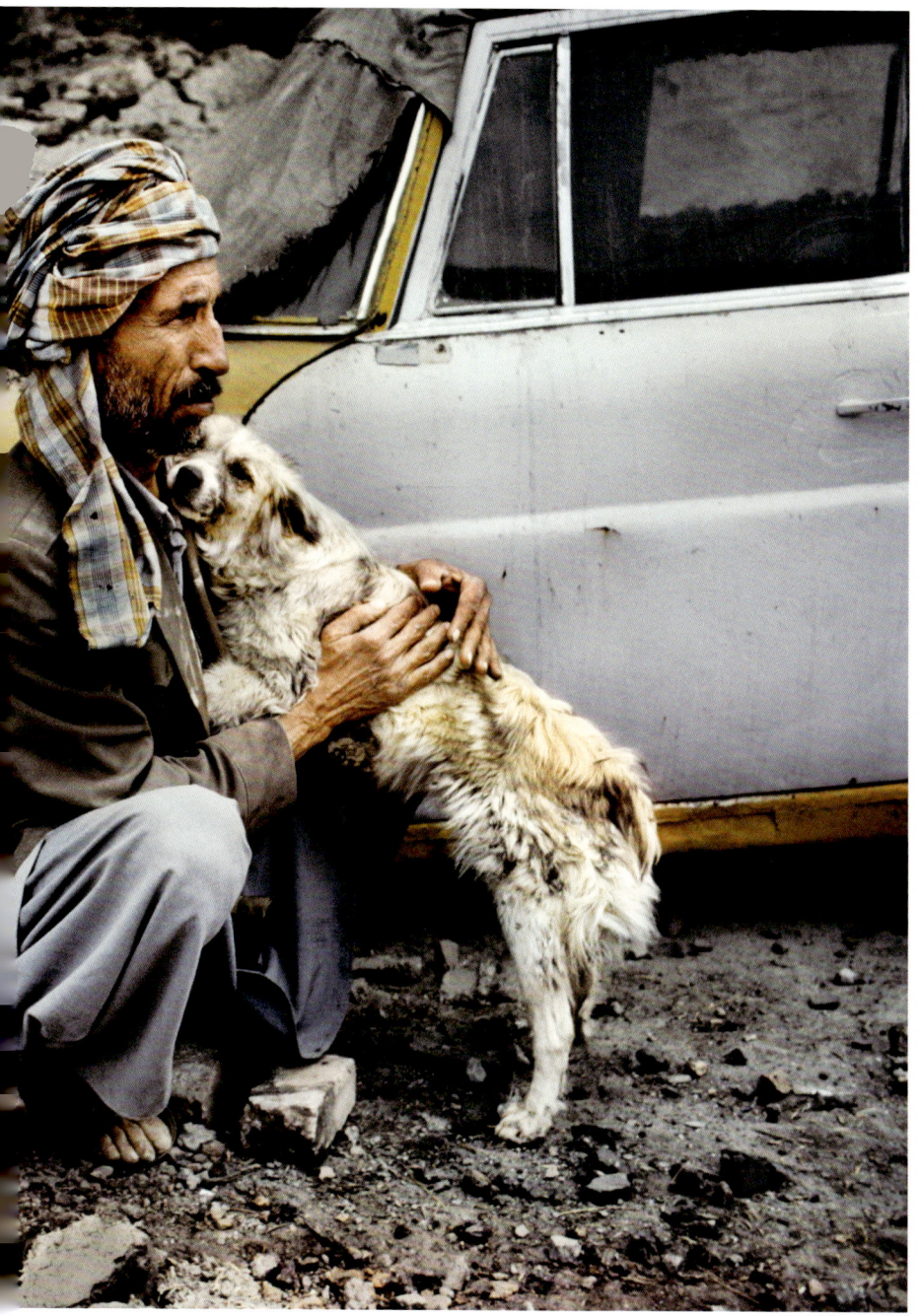

PAGES 10-11 Kabul, Afghanistan, 1992. This man ponders the future with his dog next to his taxi, which was destroyed when the building collapsed during shelling in Kabul, Afghanistan.

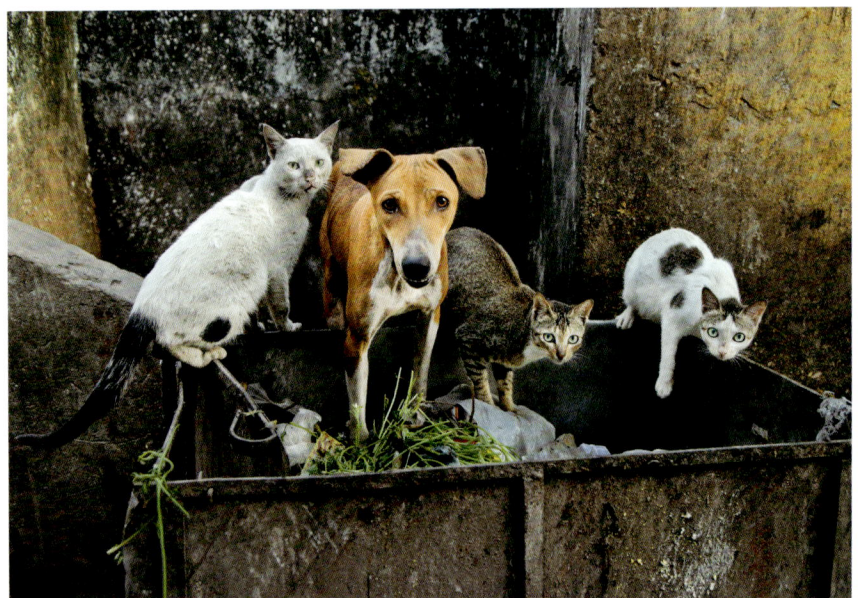

KOLKATA, INDIA, 2013

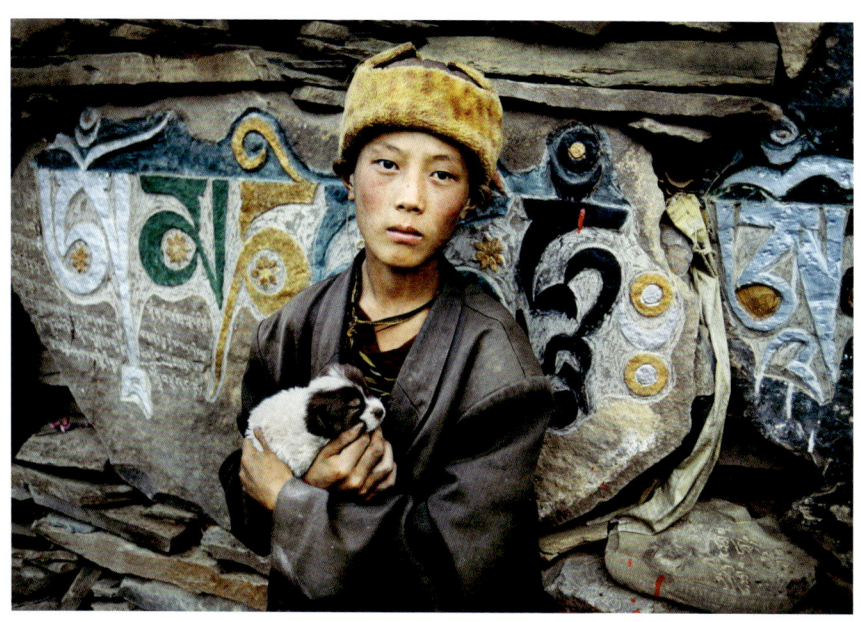

LITANG, TIBET, 2001

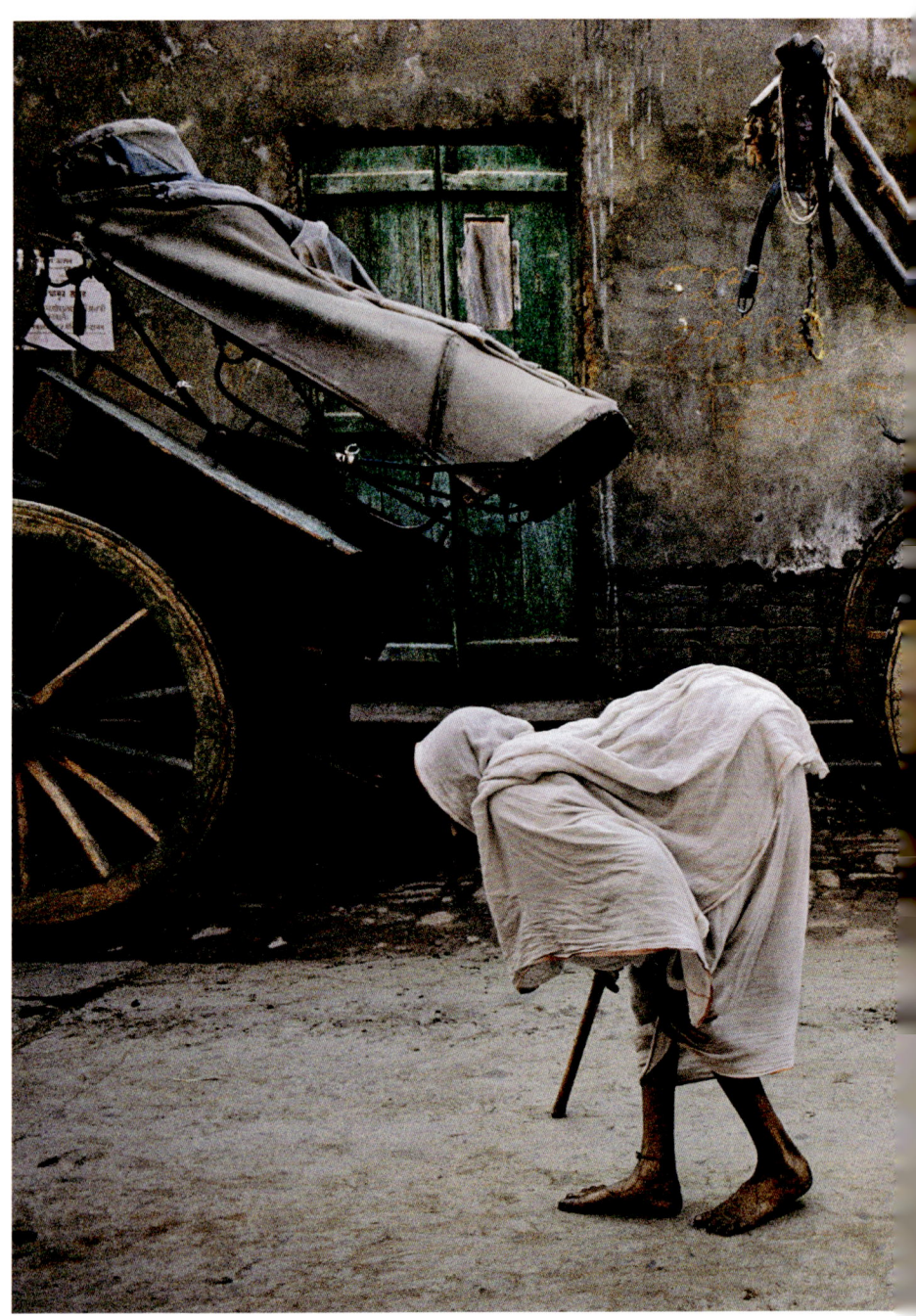

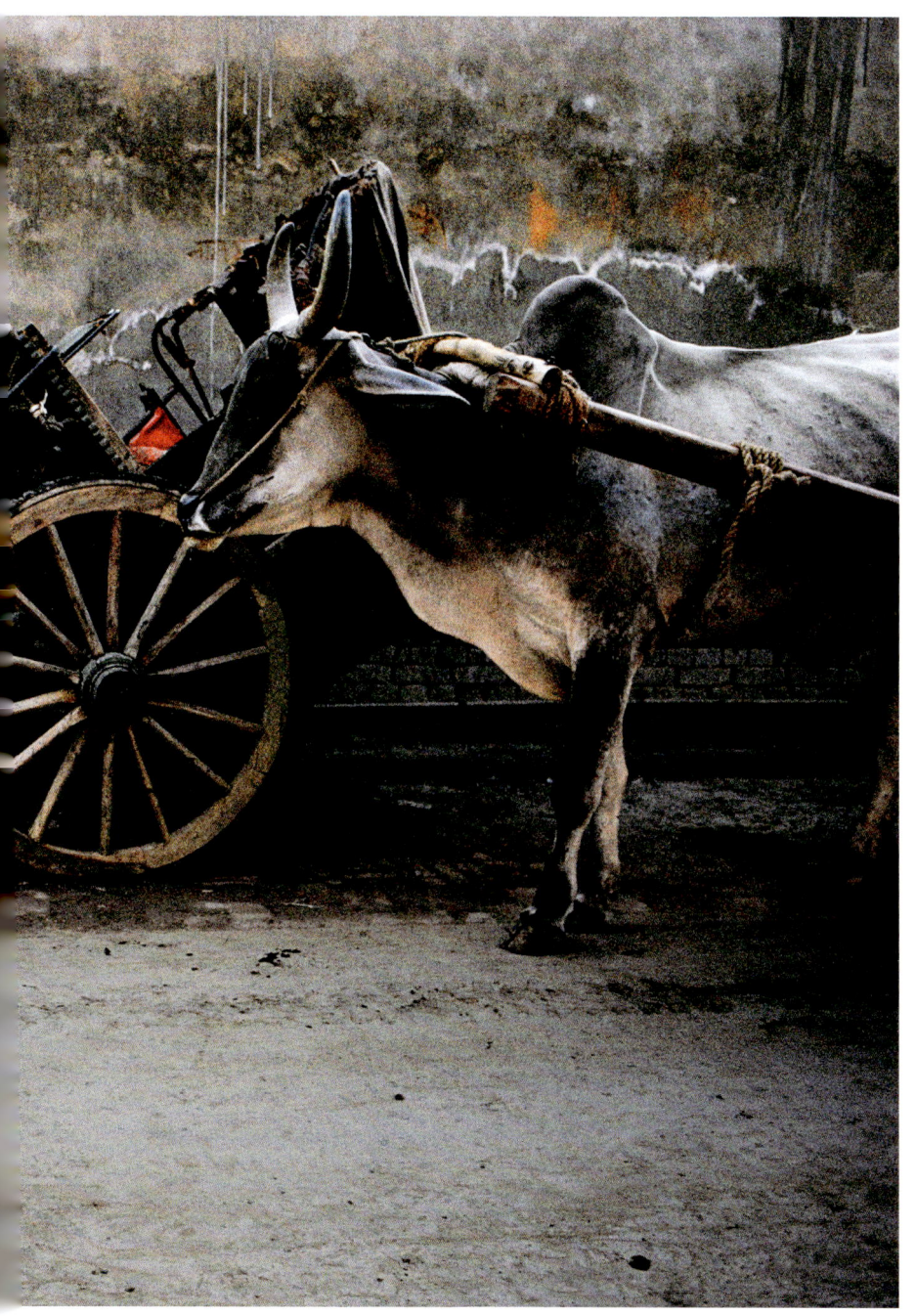

PAGES 14-15 Vrindavan, India, 1995. I was walking down the street in Vrindavan, India. I caught sight of a woman walking with great difficulty. I started following her, and eventually she noticed me and we started talking. She explained that her husband died when she was 14, leaving her a widow; she had been living in an ashram for 70 years. I found her to be very inspiring – someone who'd had bad luck in her life, but who had a wonderful sense of humor and a very giving personality.

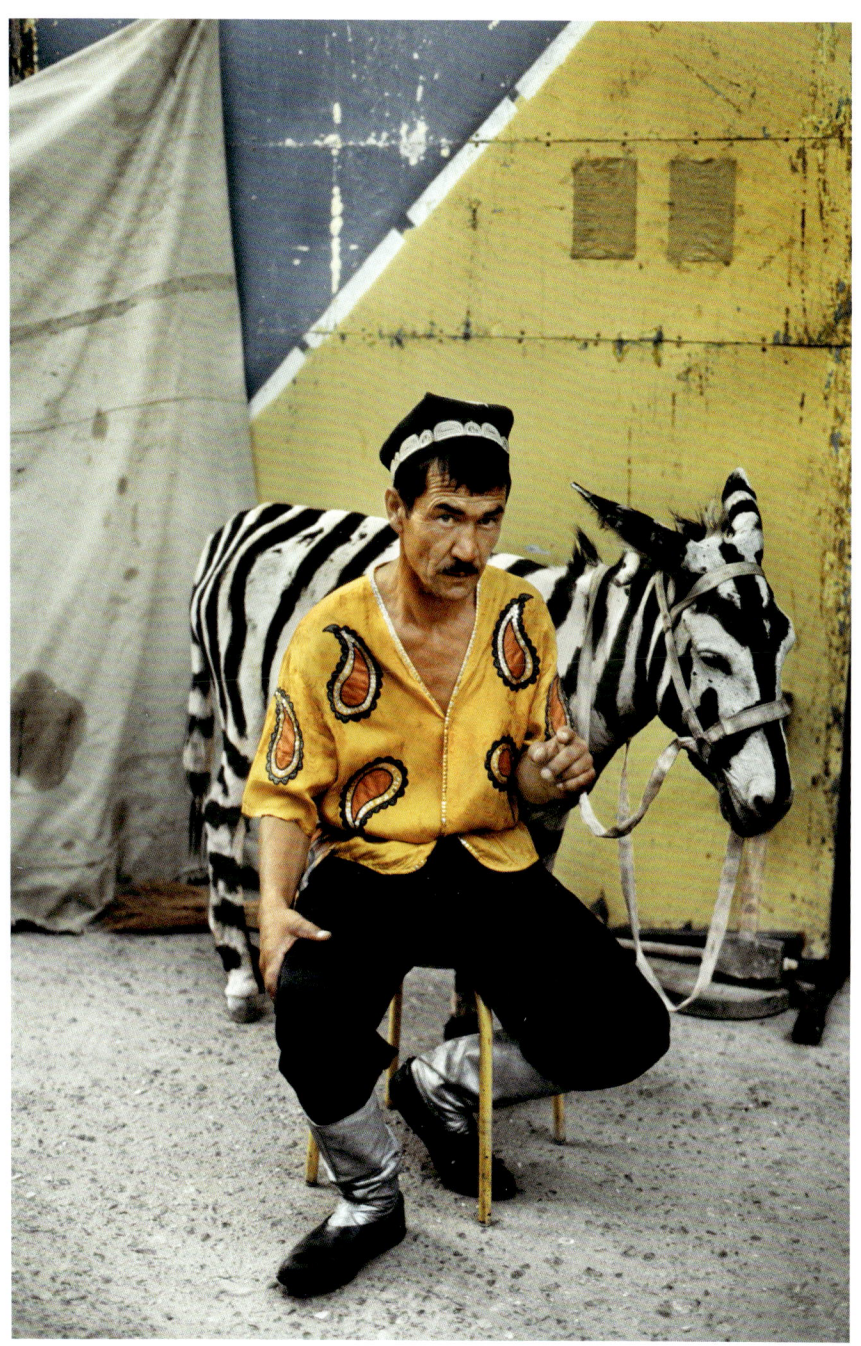

TASHKENT, UZBEKISTAN, 2005

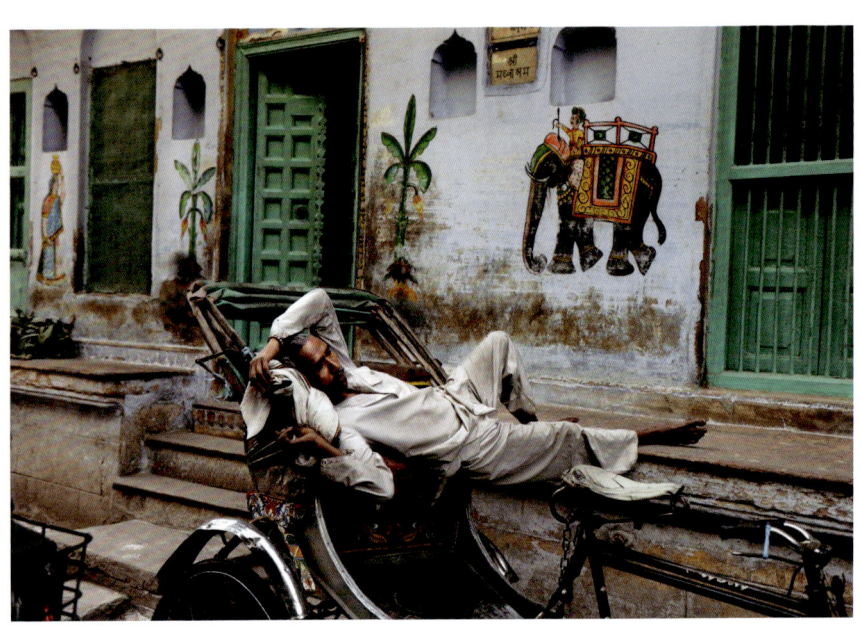

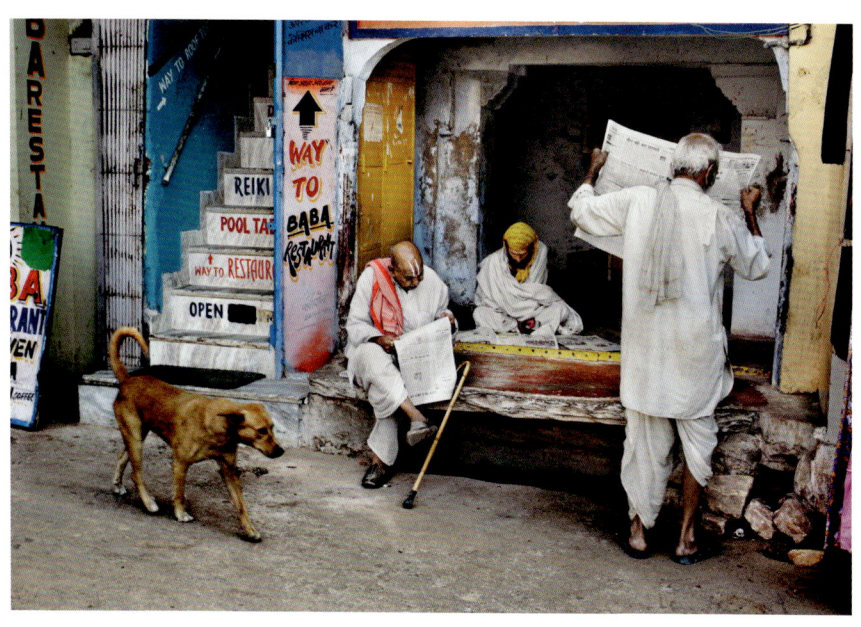

PUSHKAR, INDIA, 2009

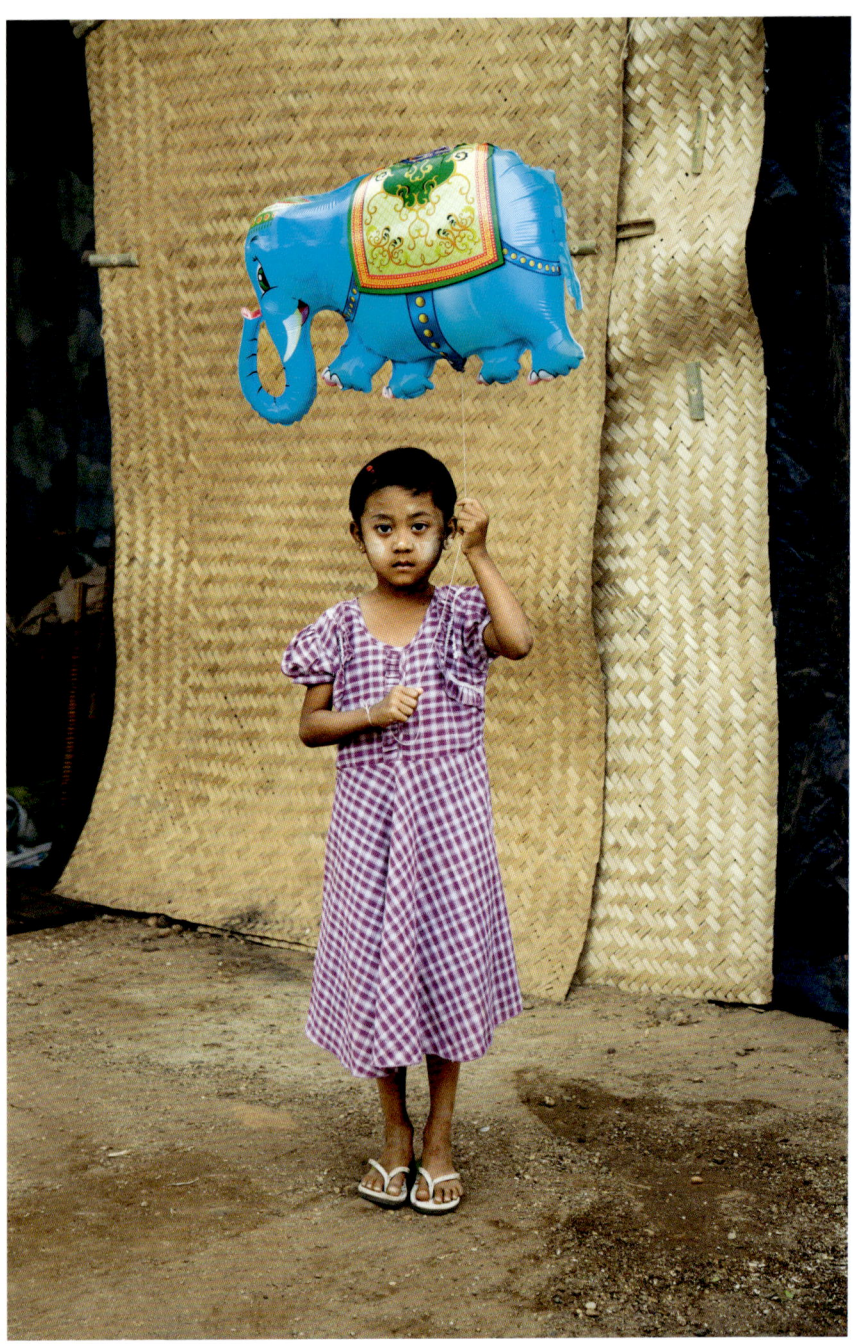

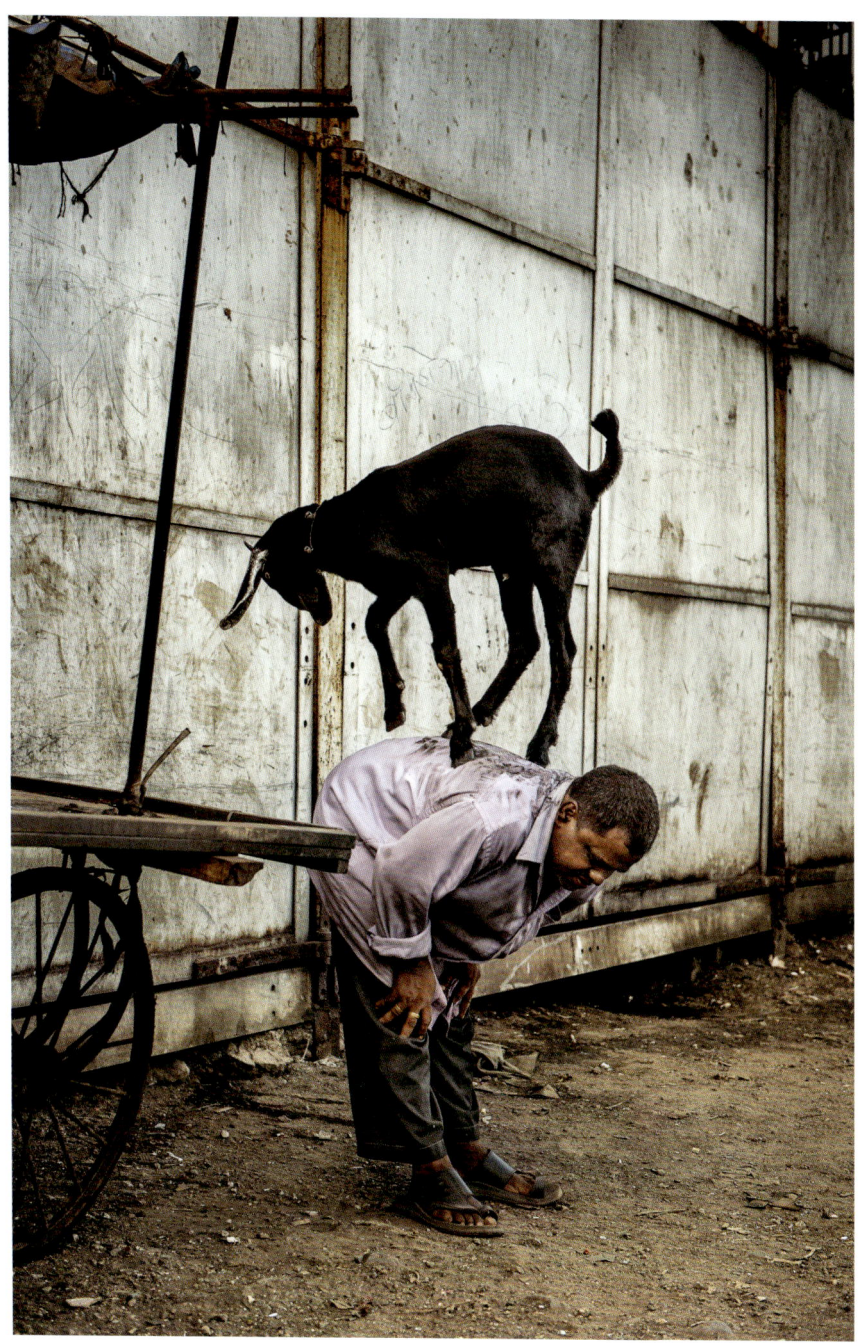

MUMBAI, INDIA, 2010

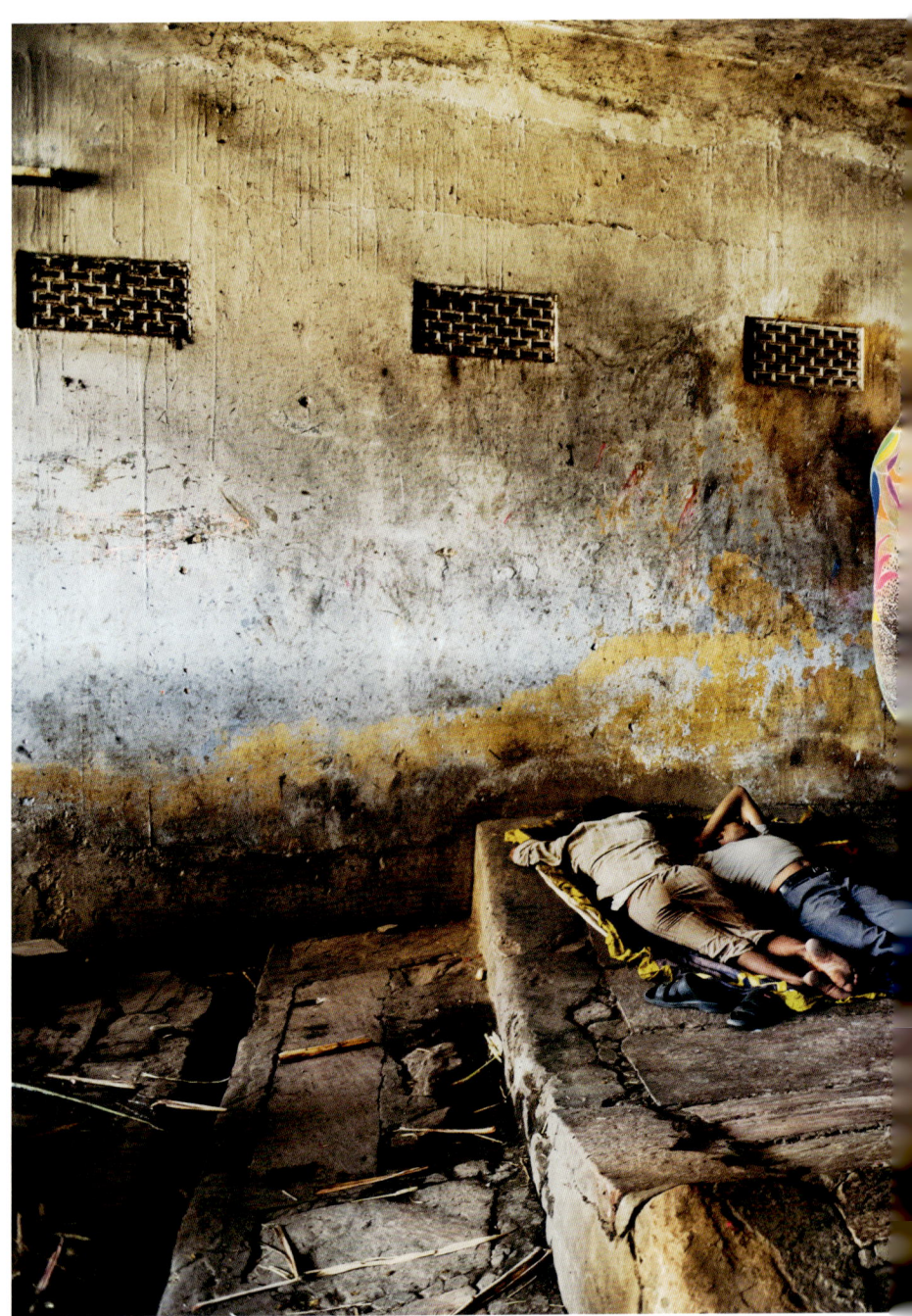

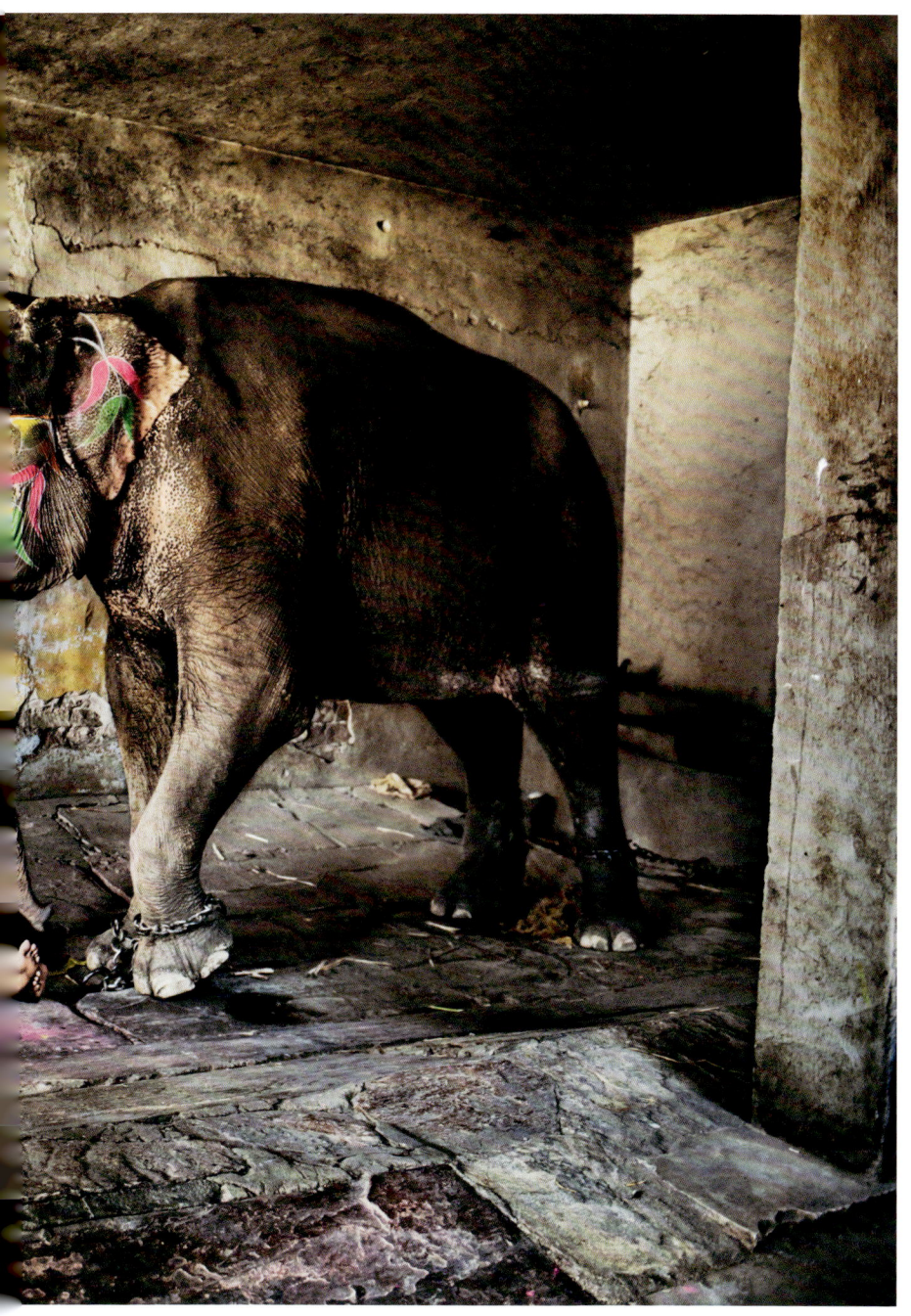

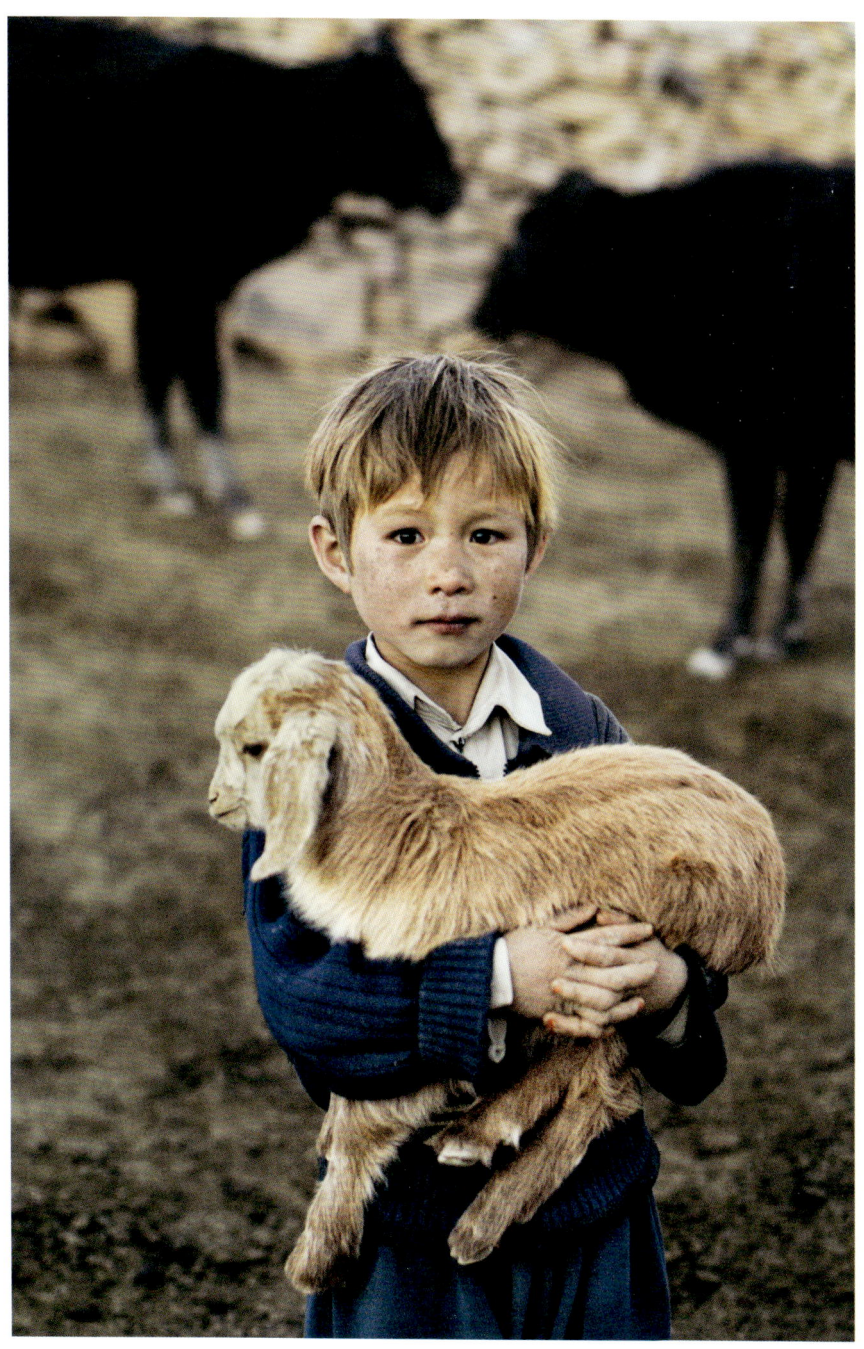

BAMIYAN PROVINCE, AFGHANISTAN, 2006

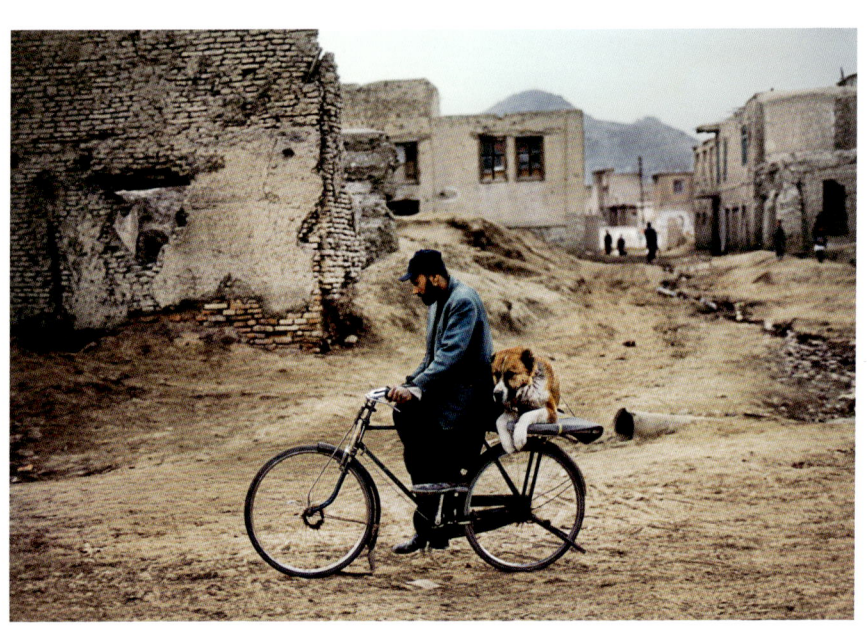

26   KABUL, AFGHANISTAN, 2003

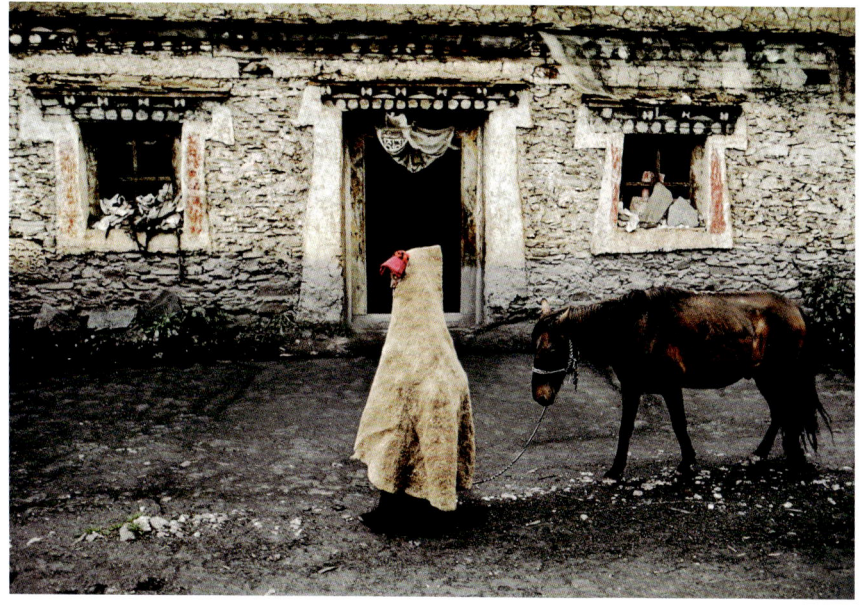

A pilgrim circumambulates a monastery in the village of Tagong
on the Tibetan plateau. It is customary for Tibetan Buddhists to walk
around a sacred object or place as part of their devotional practice.

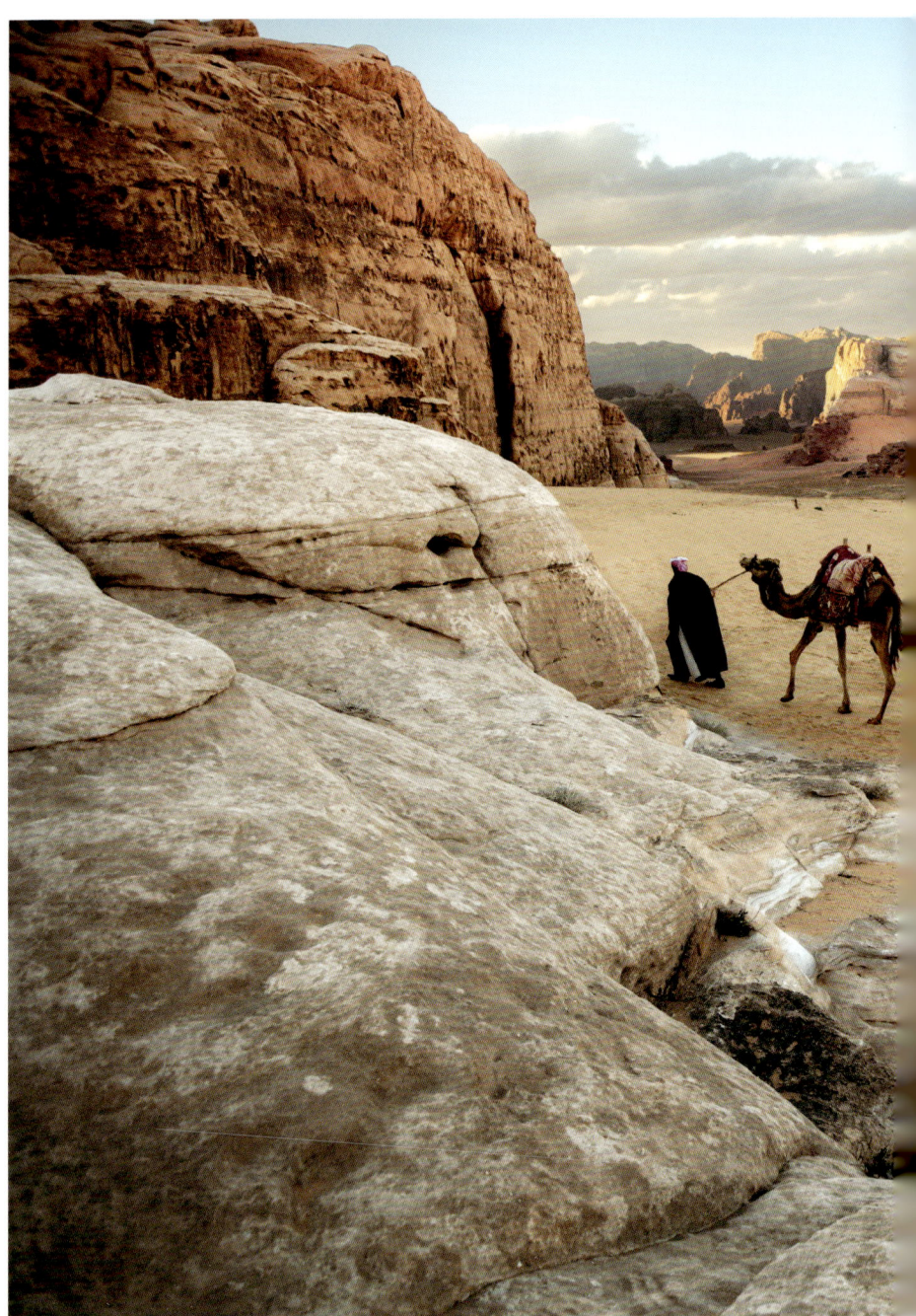

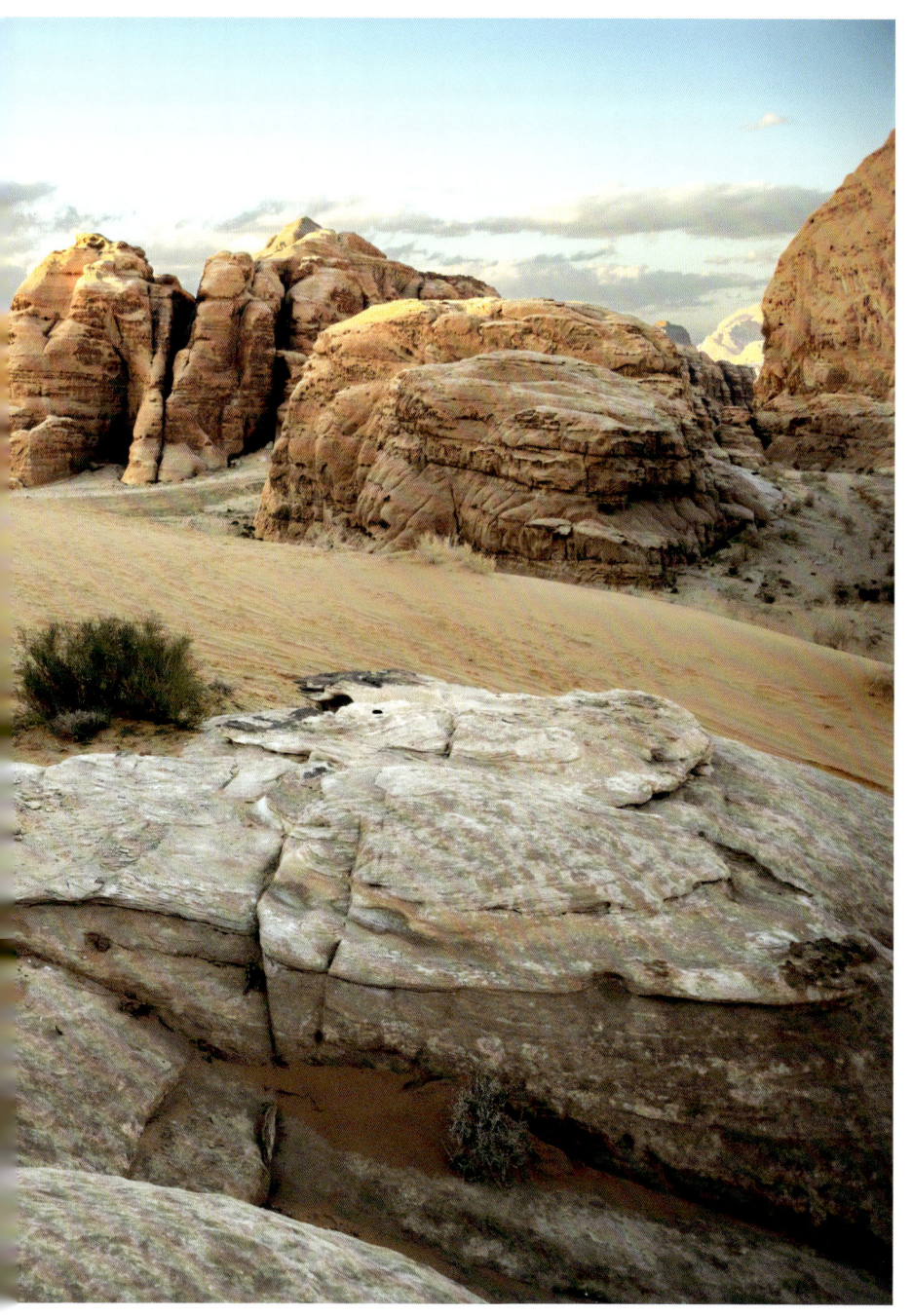

"Be like the bird who, pausing in her flight awhile on boughs too slight, feels them give way beneath her, and yet sings, knowing that she hath wings."

VICTOR HUGO

I remember as a teenager learning about a voyage that Charles Darwin took on HMS *Beagle*. For five years, the expedition allowed him to explore the coast of South America and islands including the Galápagos. His spirit of adventure and enormous curiosity impacted everything he did for the rest of his life. My trips to the Galápagos were different than any travels in my entire life. It was a rare experience to photograph the unique animals in their habitat, which in many ways has been unchanged since Darwin's time.

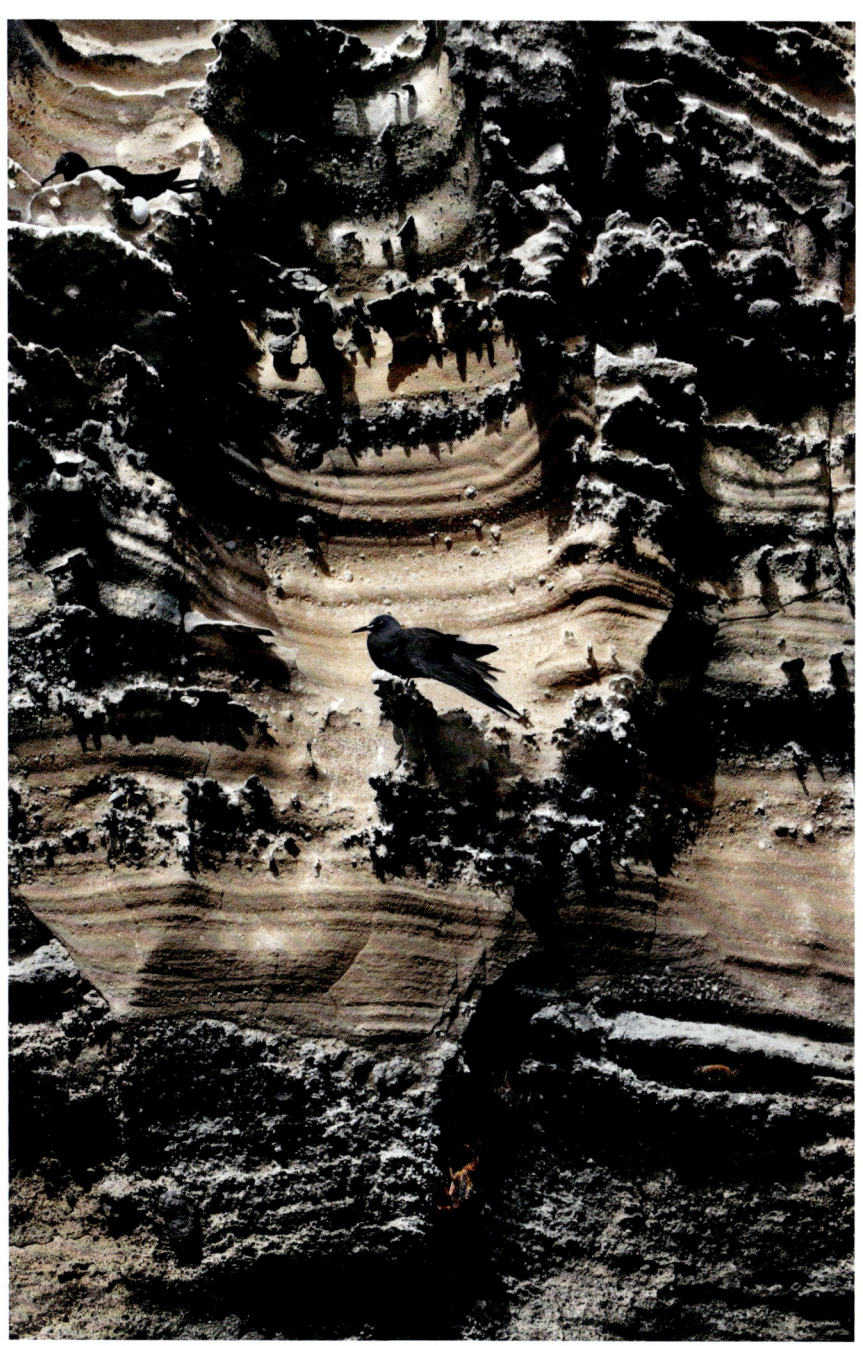

GALÁPAGOS, ECUADOR, 2019

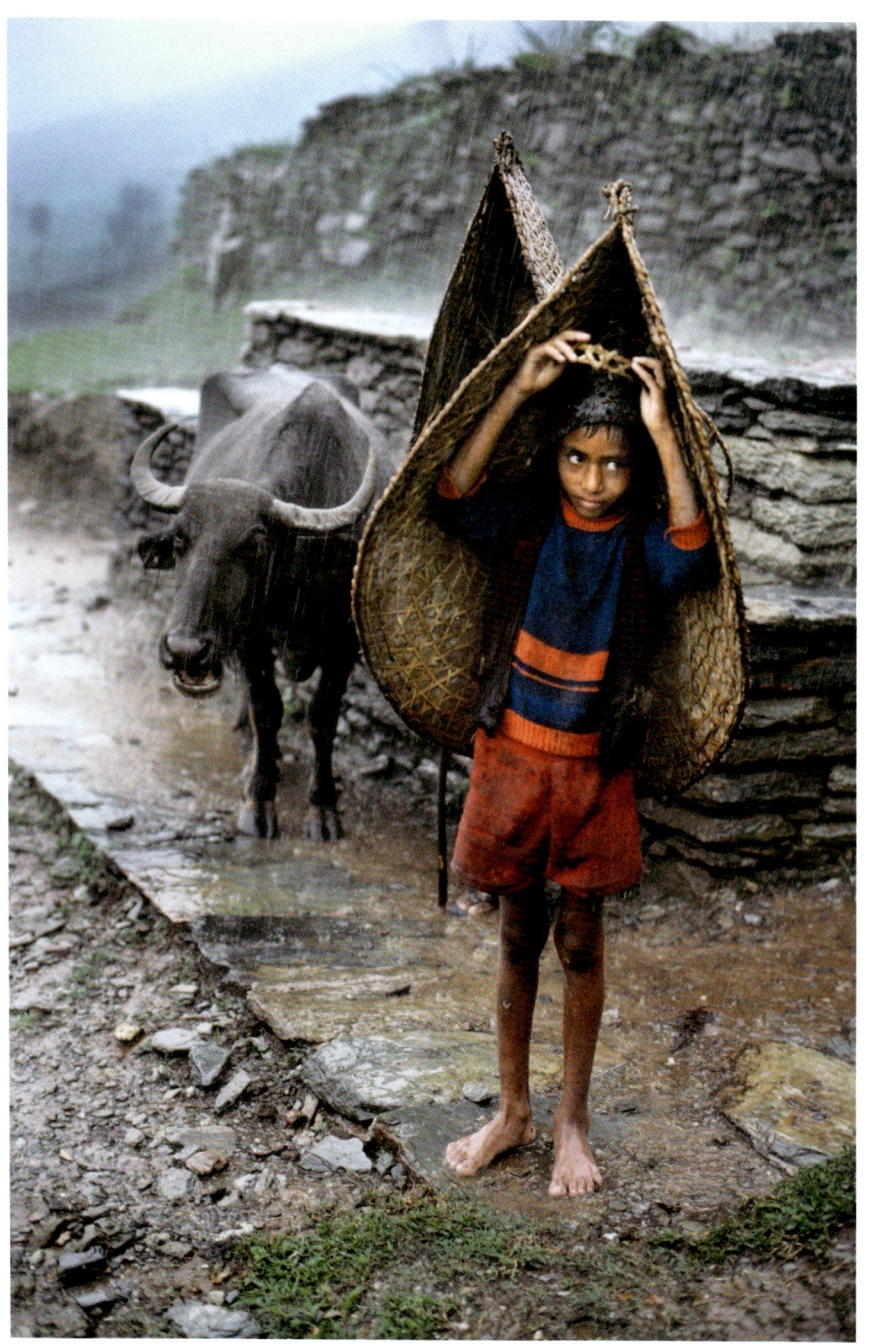

POKHARA, NEPAL, 1984

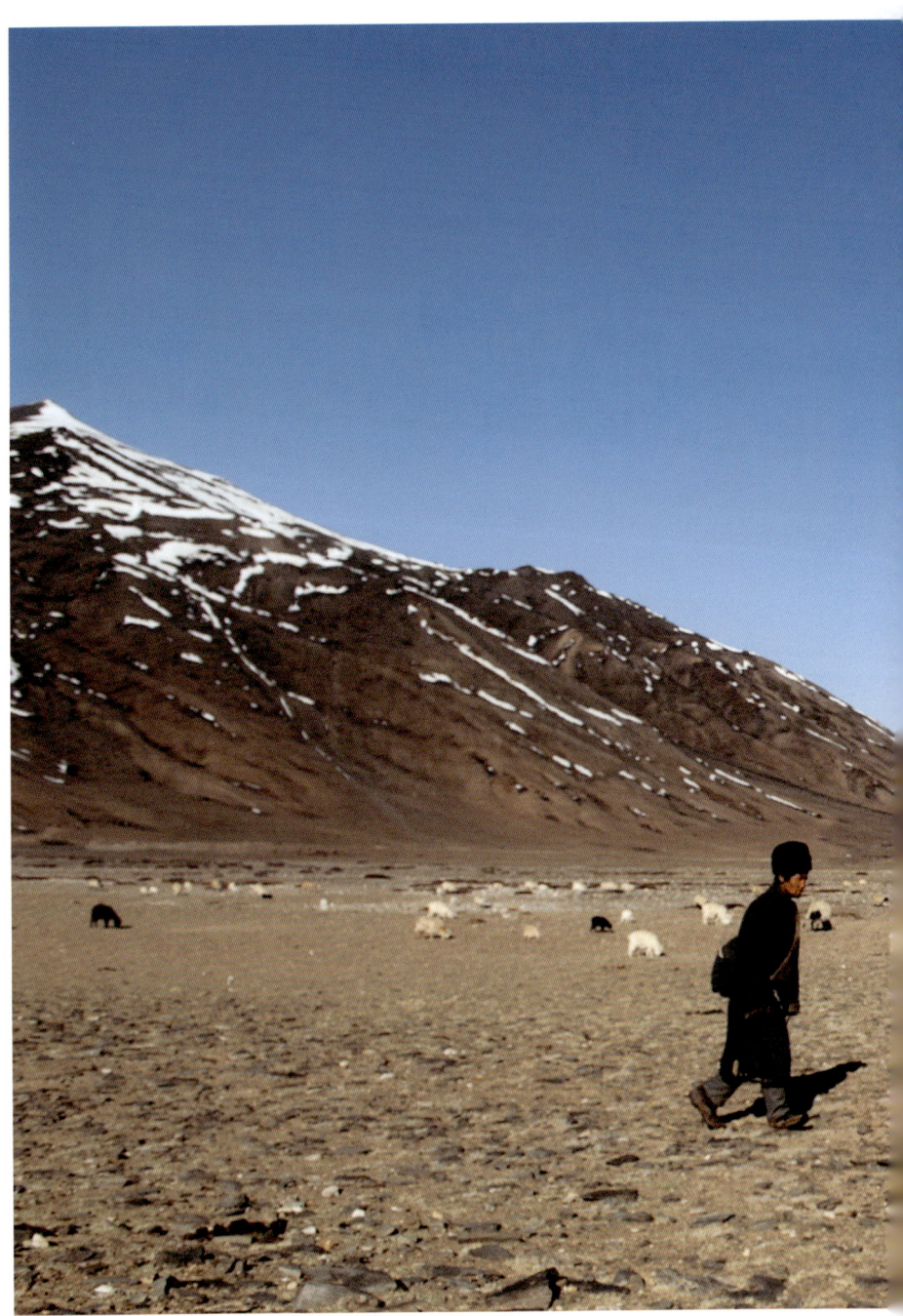

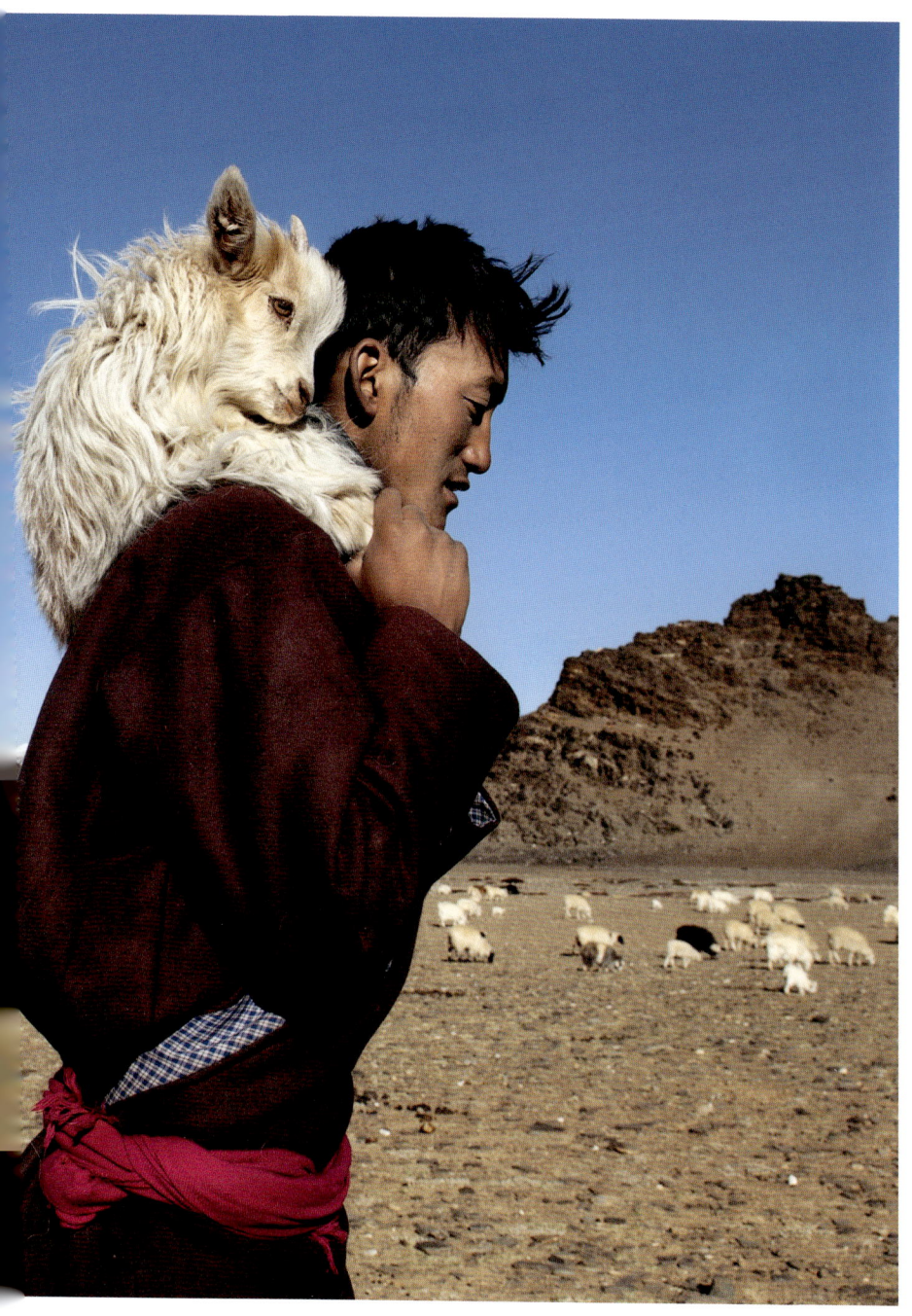

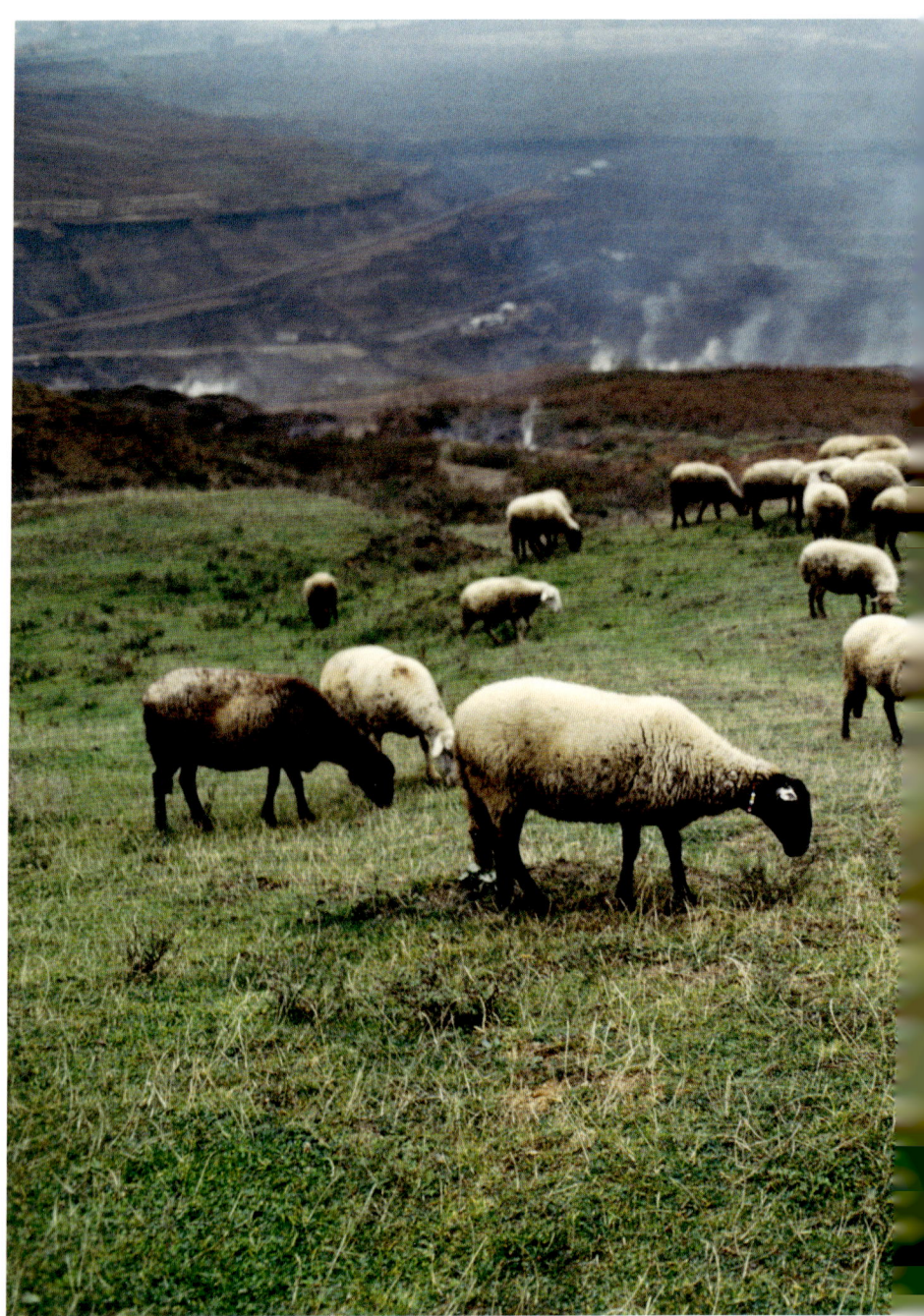

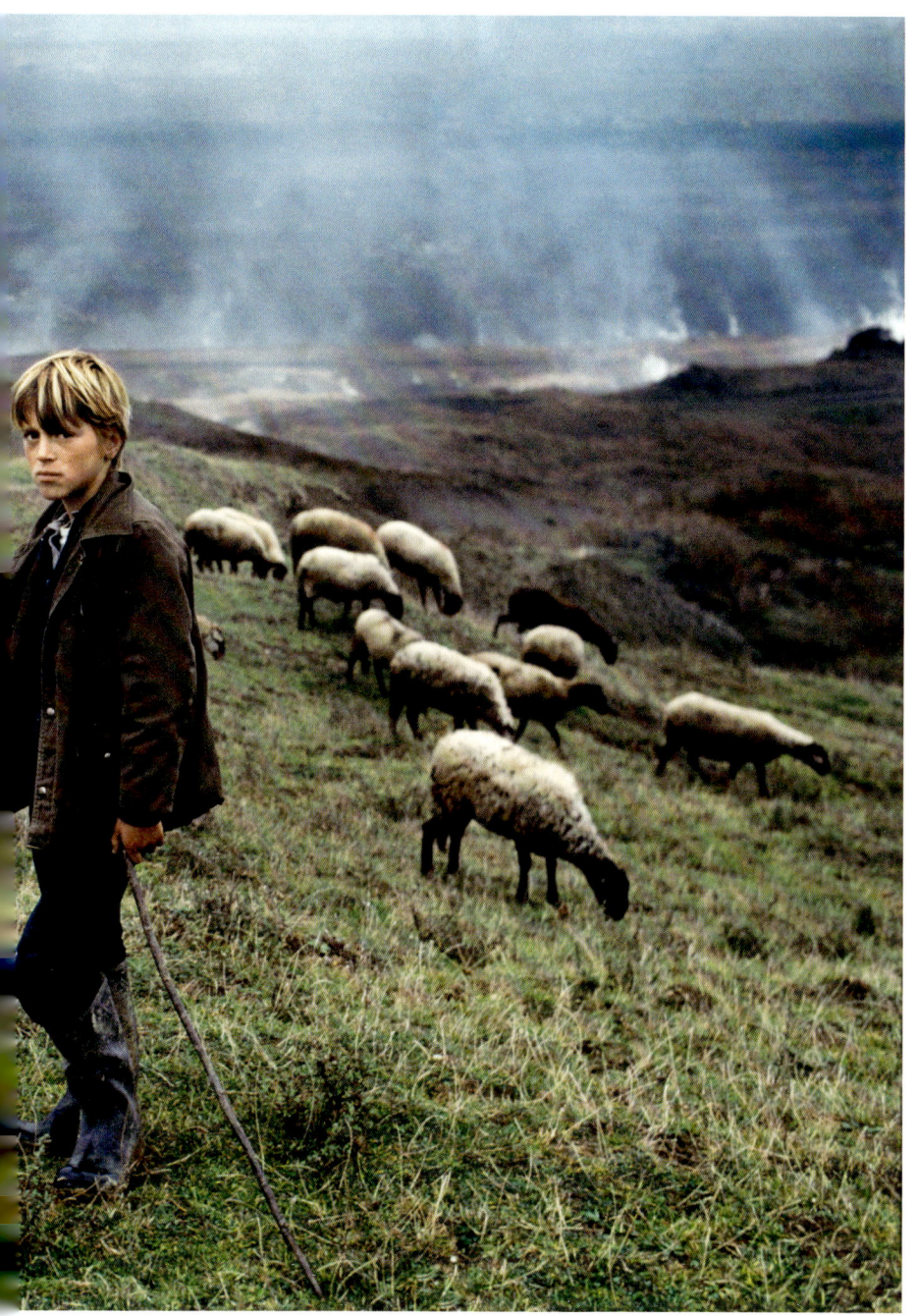

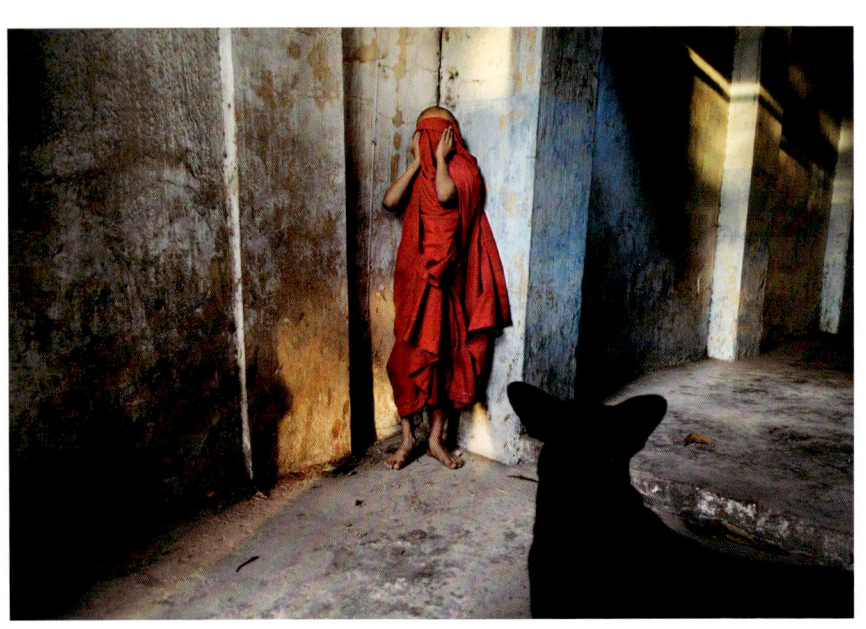

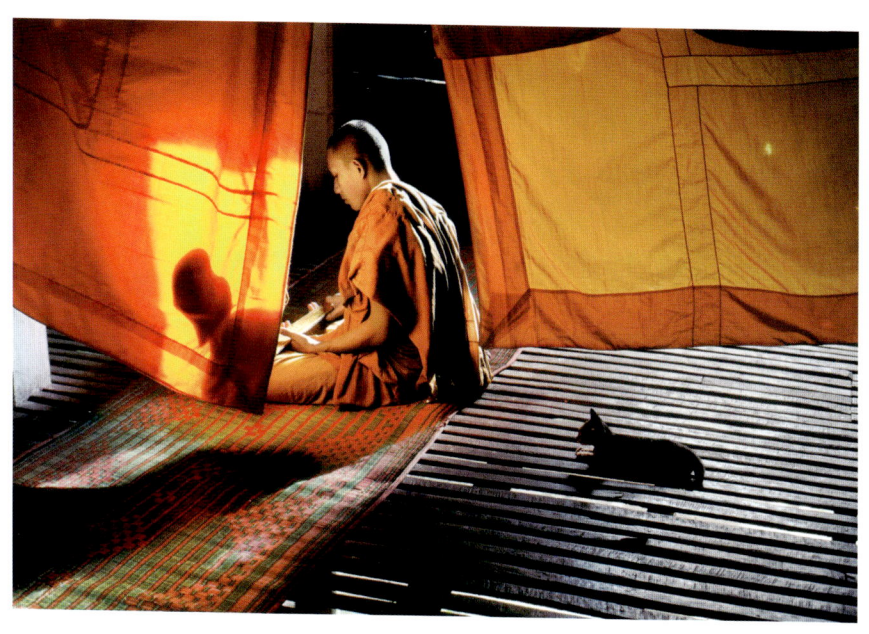

ARANYAPRATHET, THAILAND, 1998

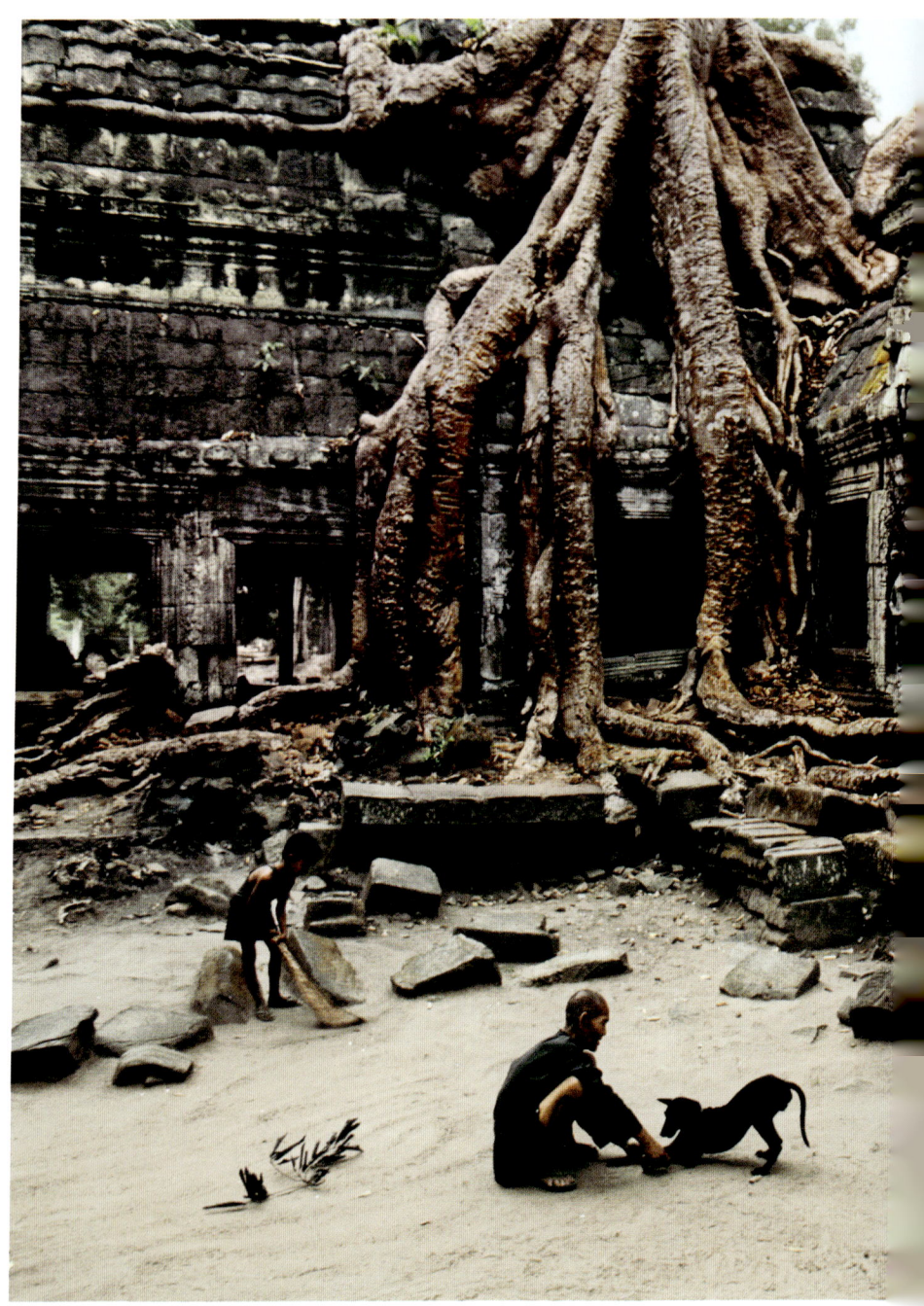

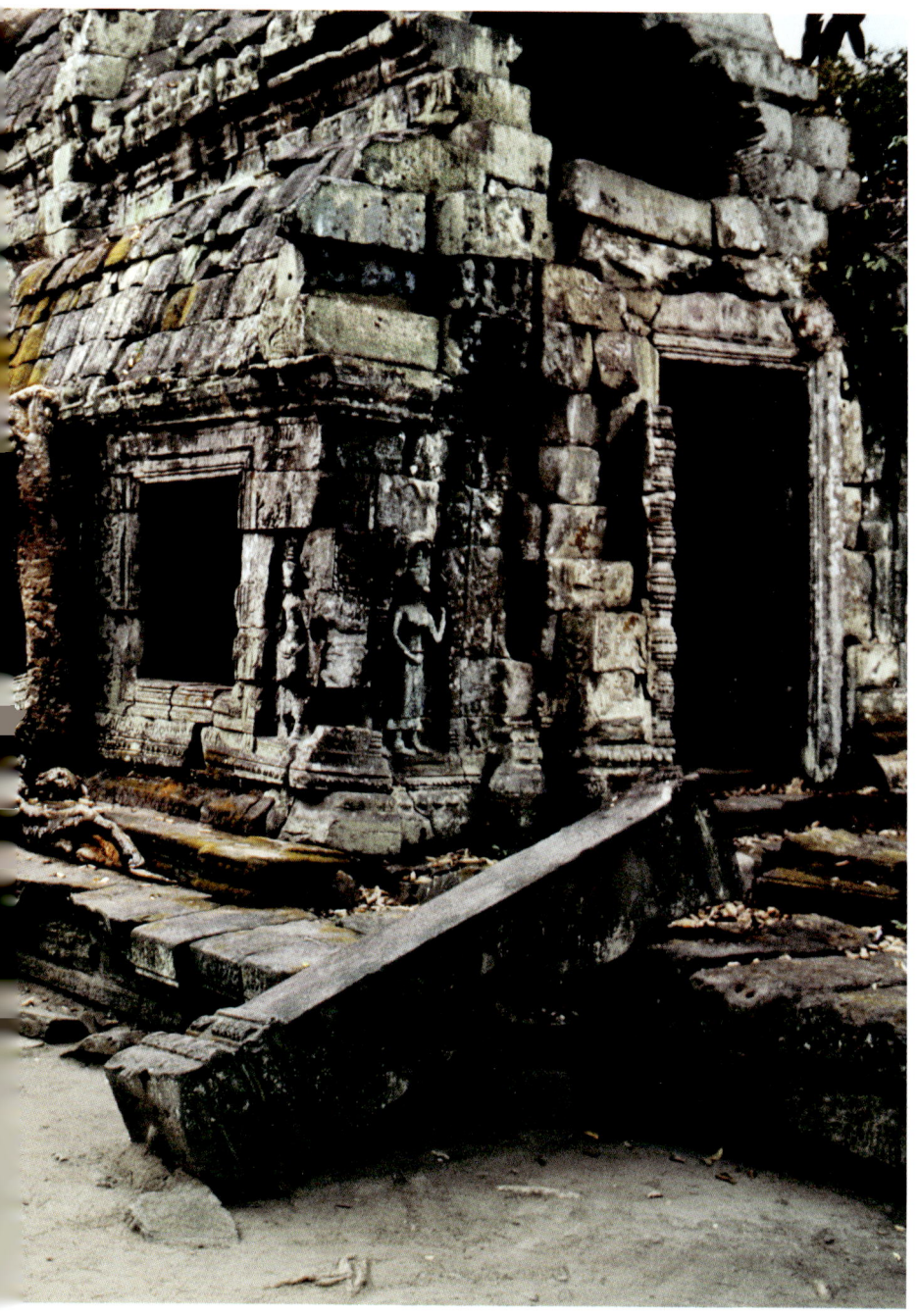

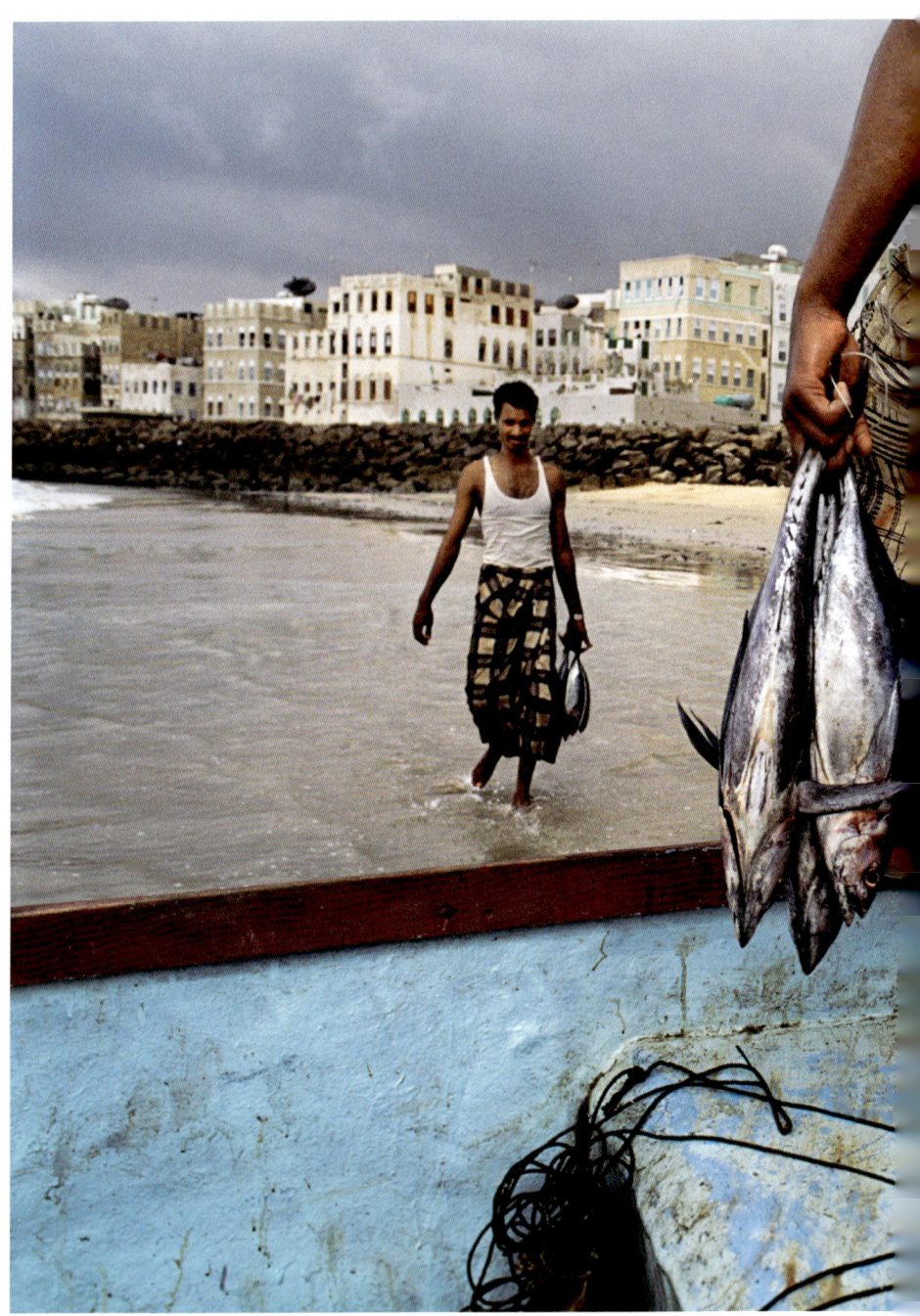

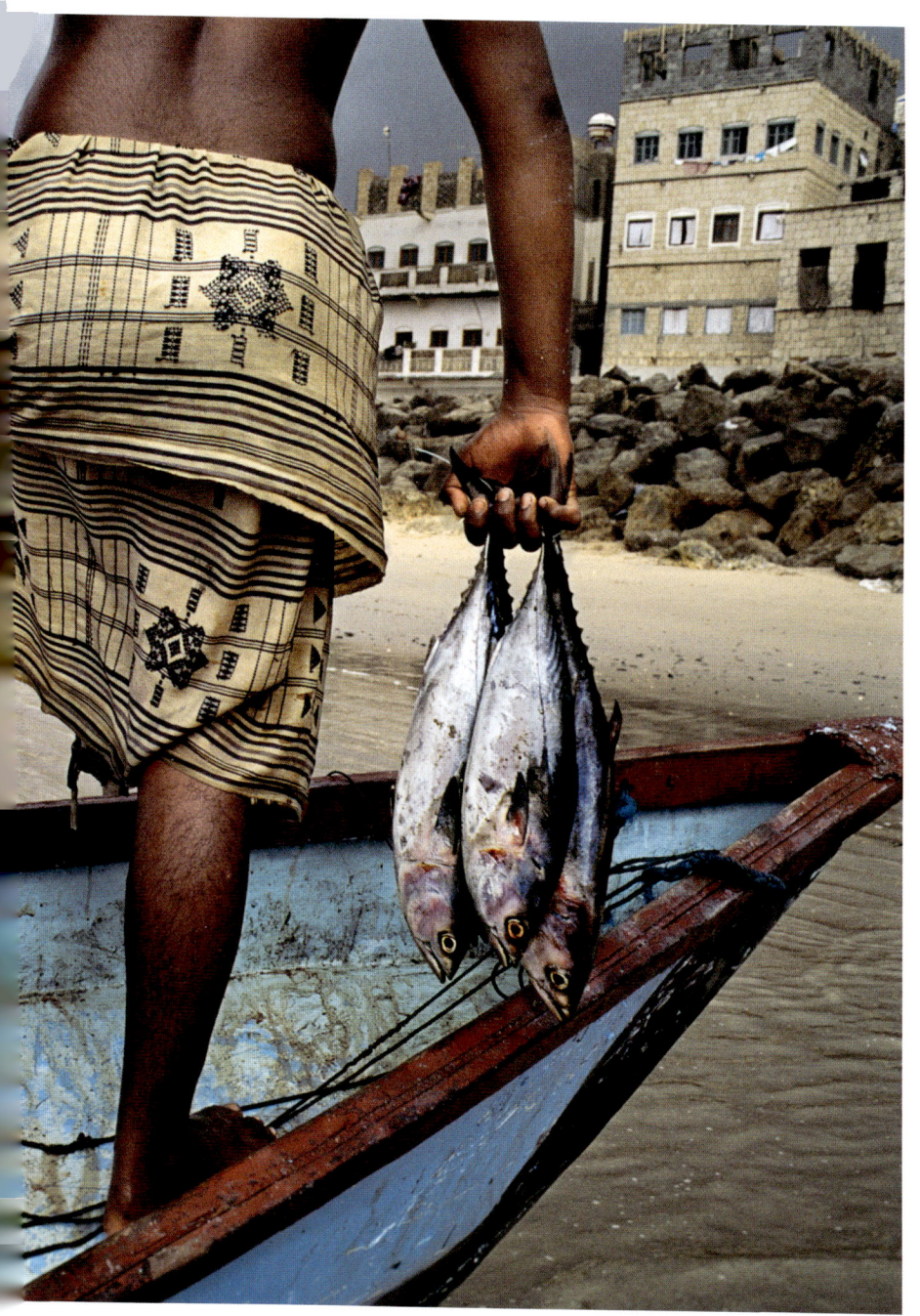

43

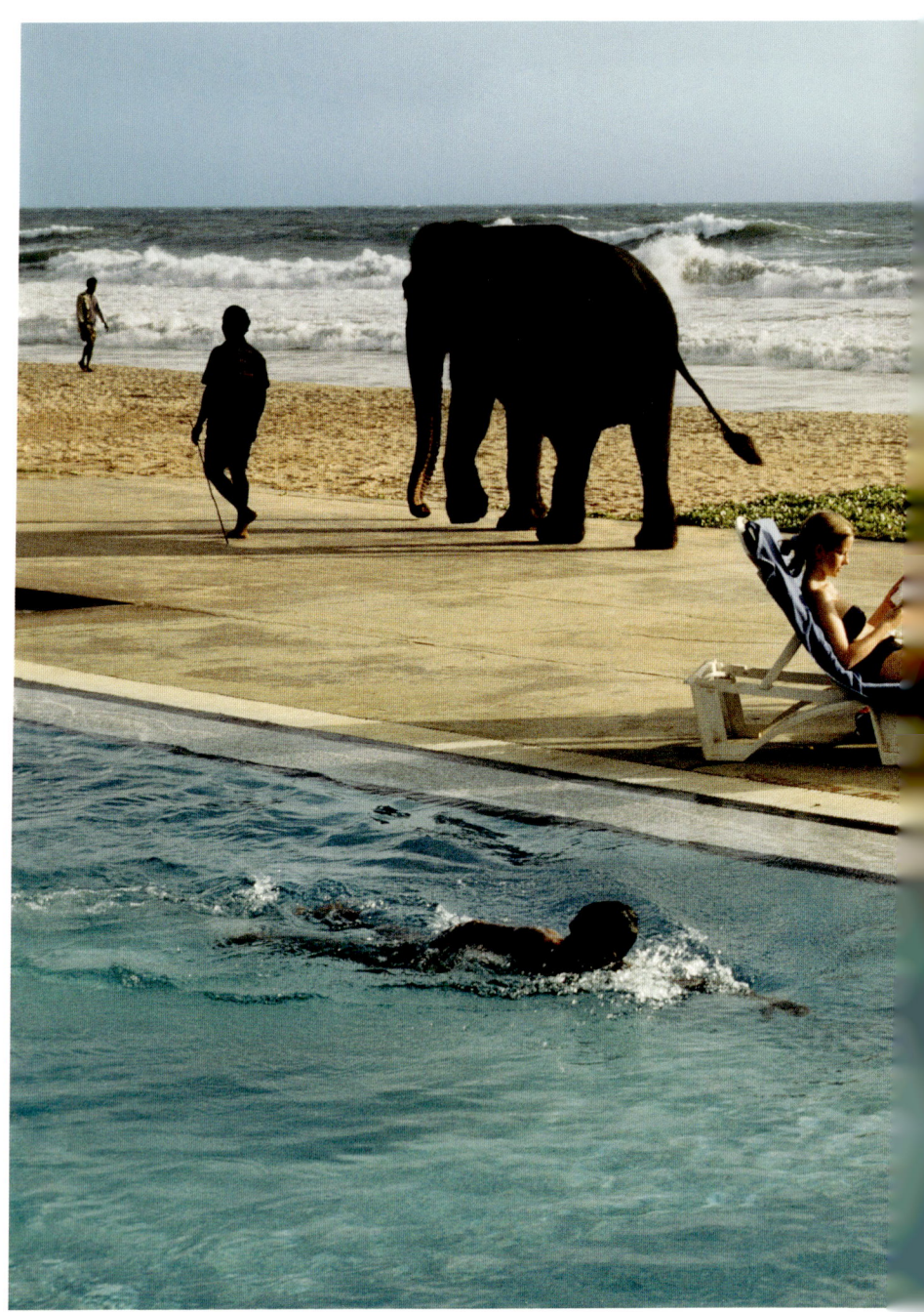

BENTOTA, SRI LANKA, 1995

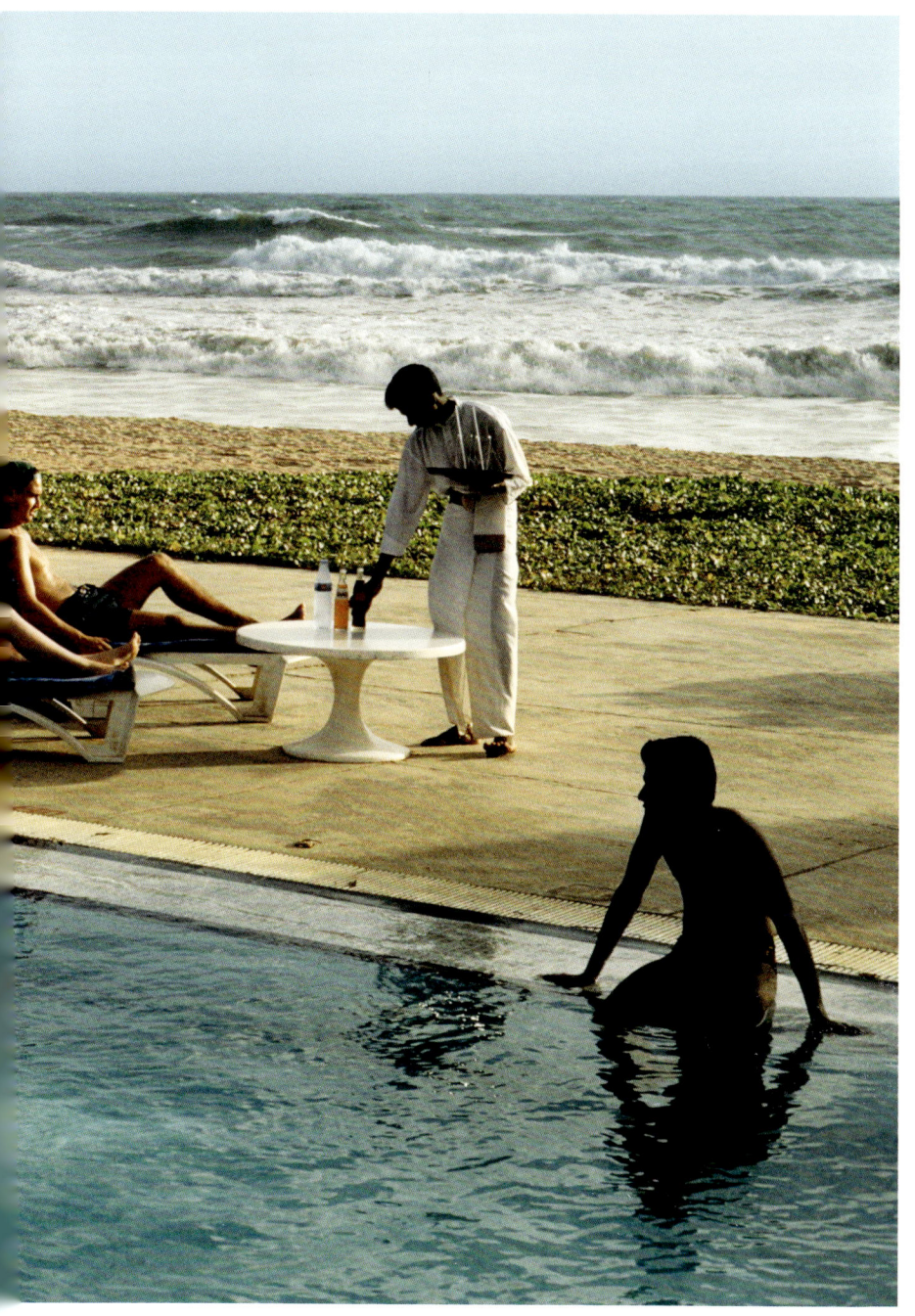

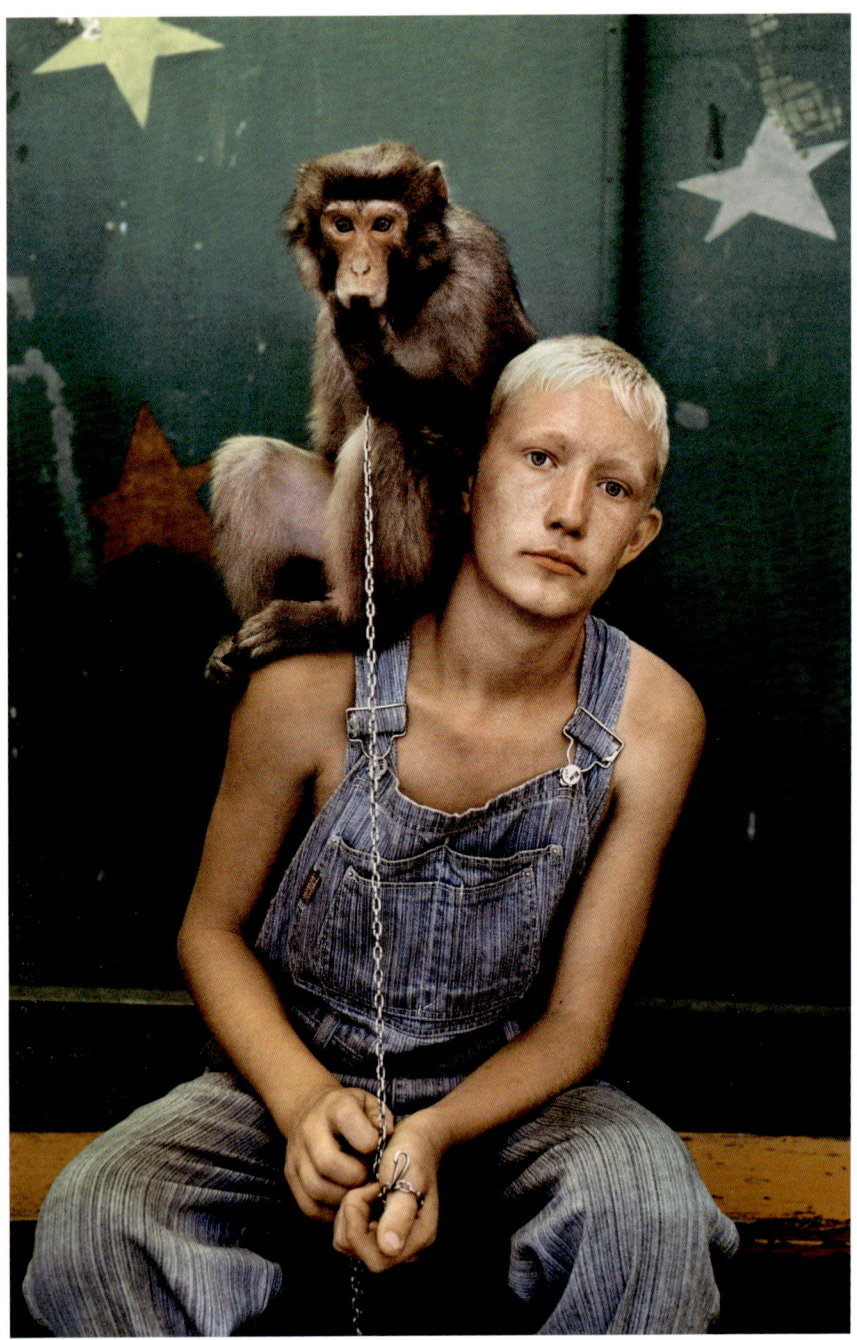

Uzbekistan has a centuries-long circus tradition. I photographed this boy in Tashkent, the location of the State Circus College, whose mission is to train performers and promote the centuries-old history and rich traditions of the Uzbek circus. Although animals have been trained for millennia for people's entertainment, today most people believe that animals should be free to live in their own environment.

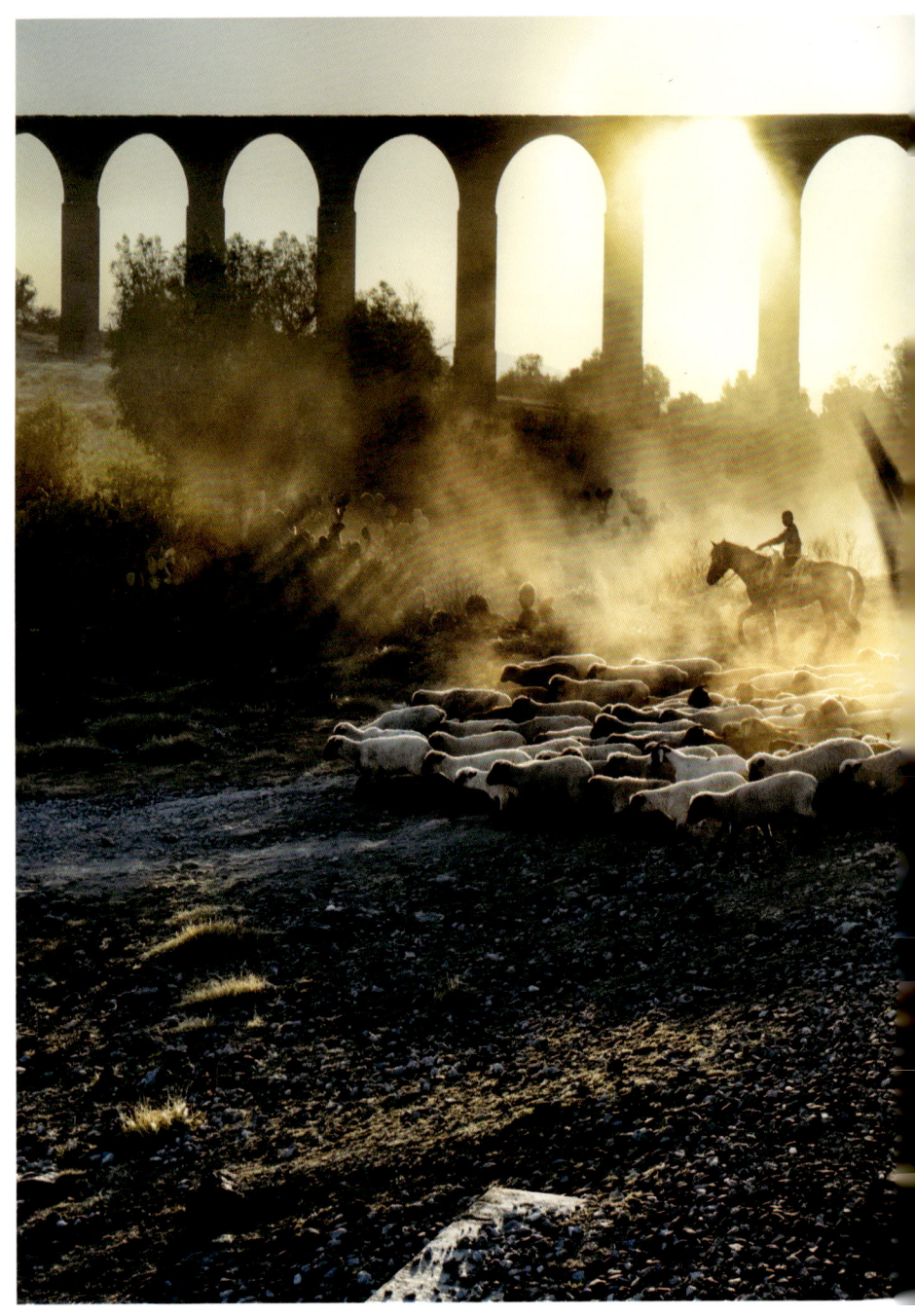

AQUEDUCT OF PADRE TEMBLEQUE, MEXICO, 2016

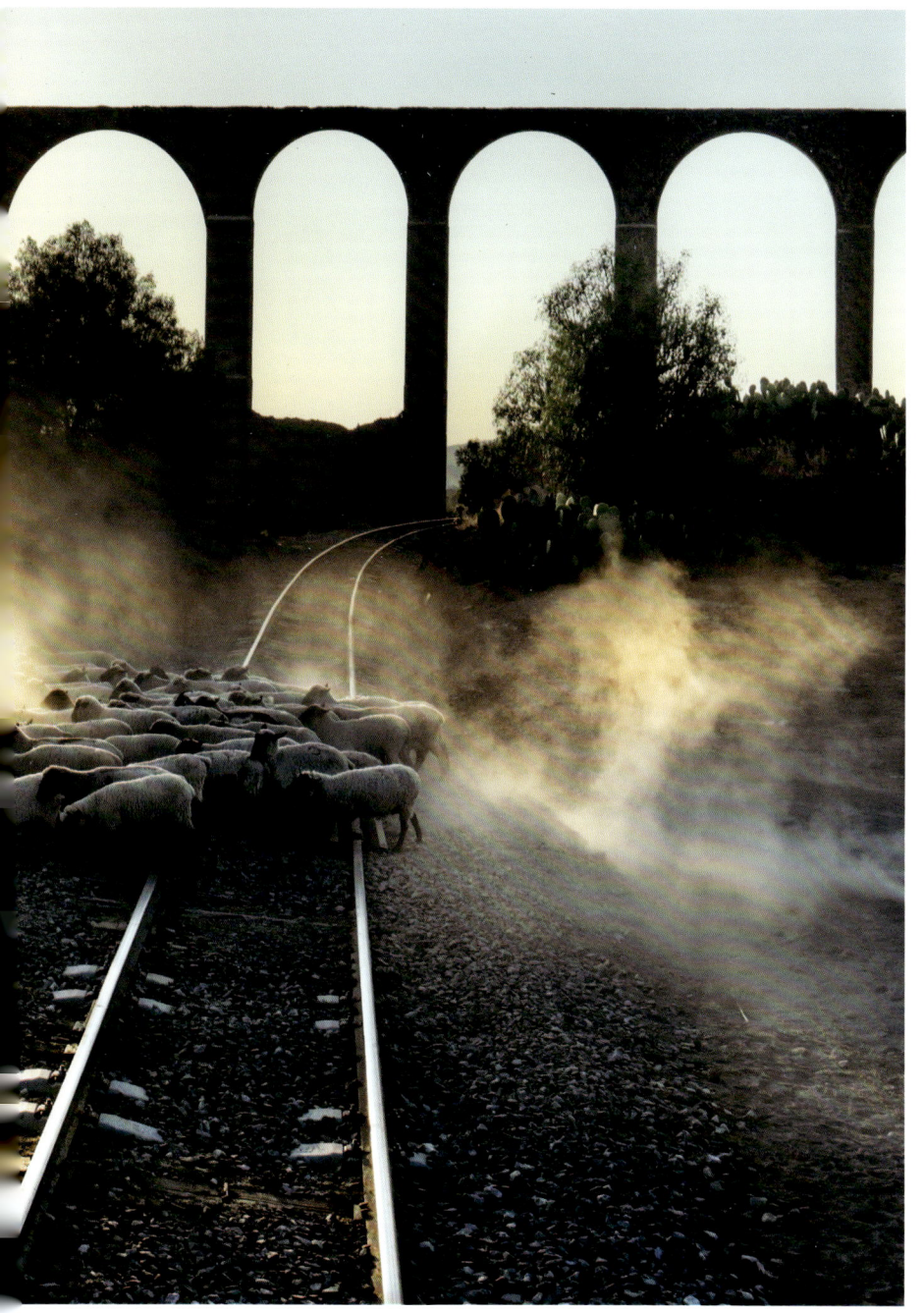

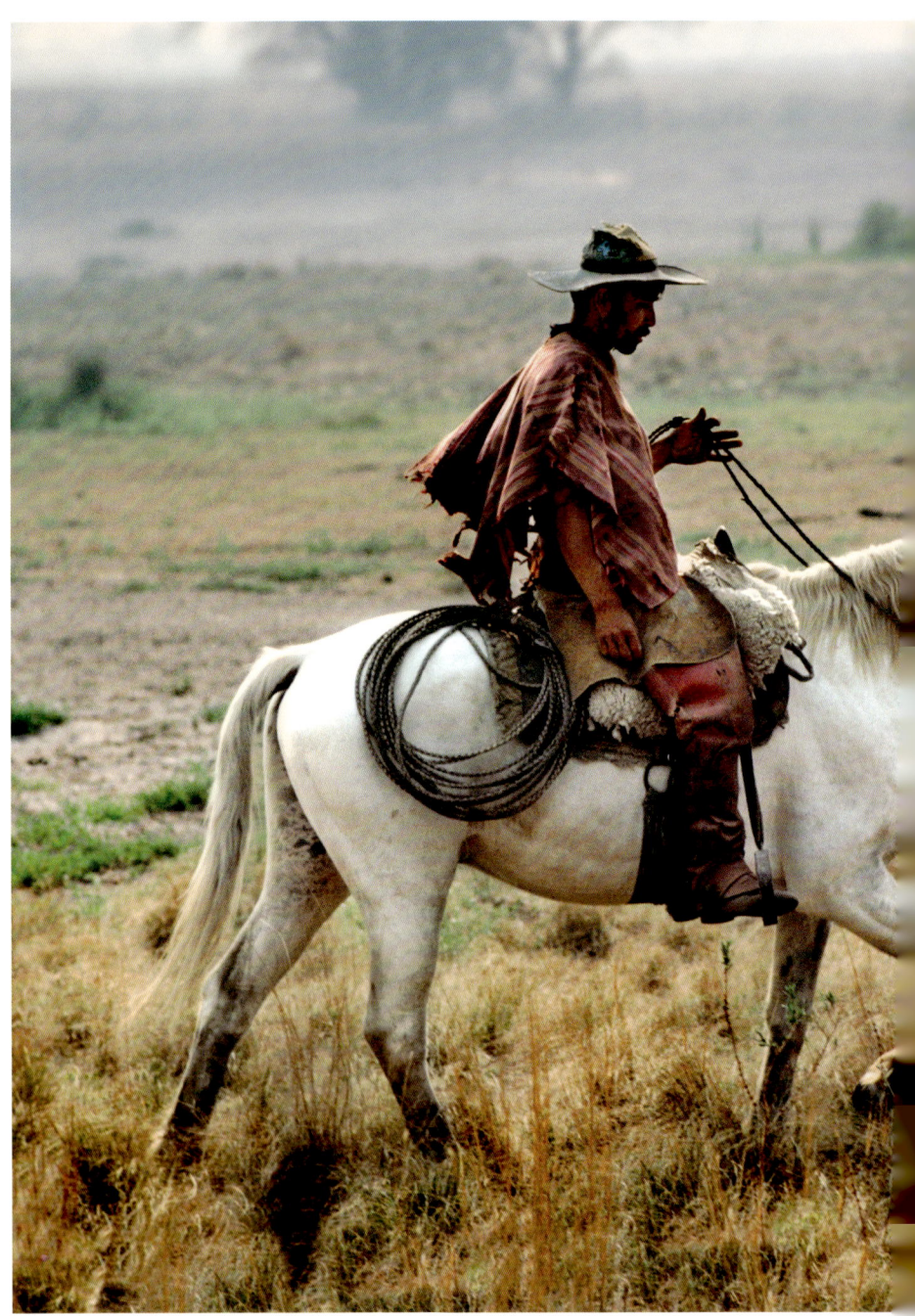

50   CHACO, PARAGUAY, 1988

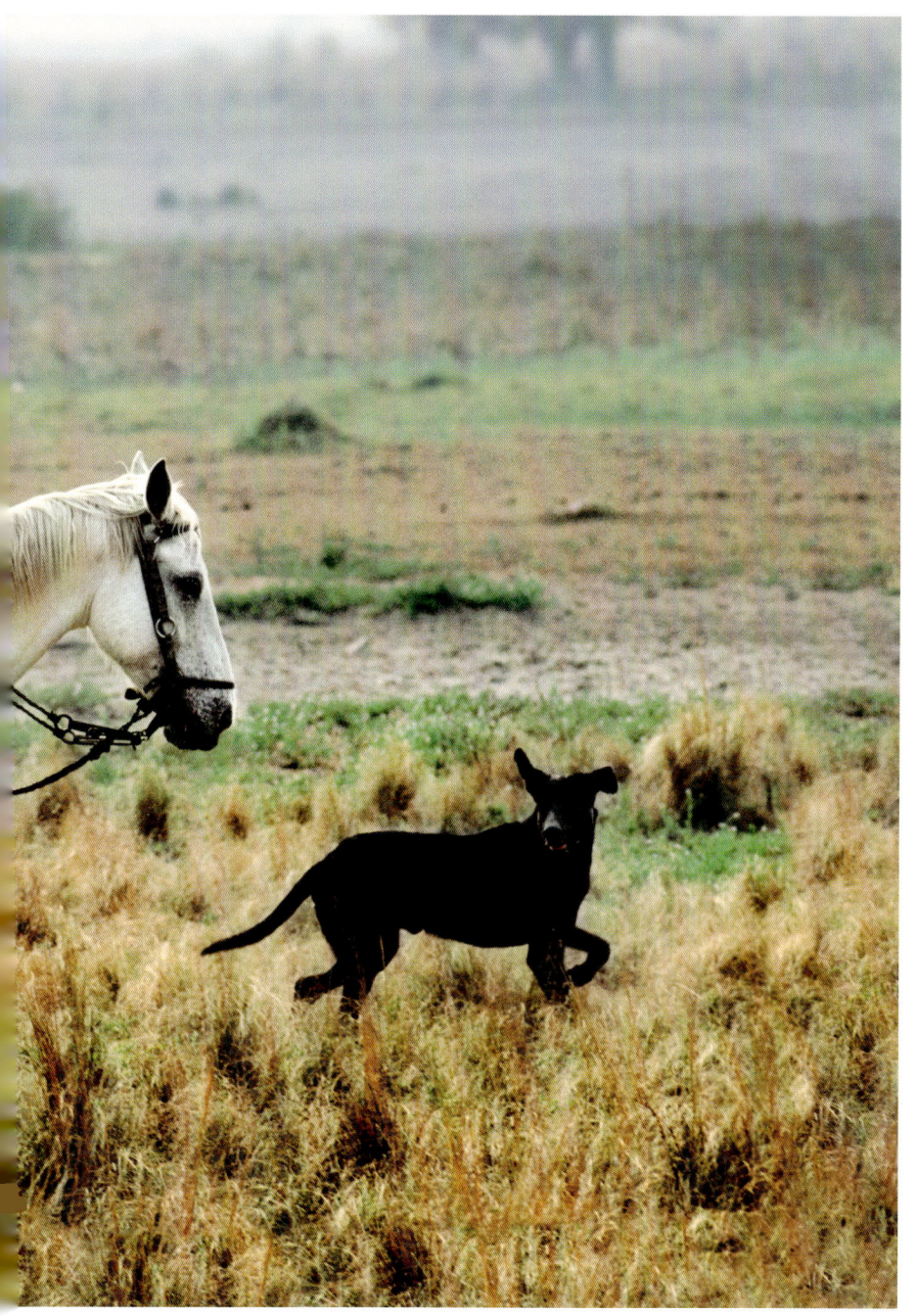

"All goats are mischievous thieves, gate-crashers and trespassers. Also, they possess individual character, intelligence and capacity for affection which can only be matched by the dog."

DAVID MACKENZIE

This Kalash shepherd feeds his goats in Northern Pakistan, deep in the Hindu Kush Mountains bordering Afghanistan, during their winter celebrations known as Caumus.

PAGES 54–55 Omo Valley, Ethiopia, 2016. This man is participating in a bull-jumping ceremony. The ceremony is a three-day-long rite of passage in the Omo Valley region in which a boy becomes a man. Once a young man completes the ceremony, he becomes Maza, an accomplished one.

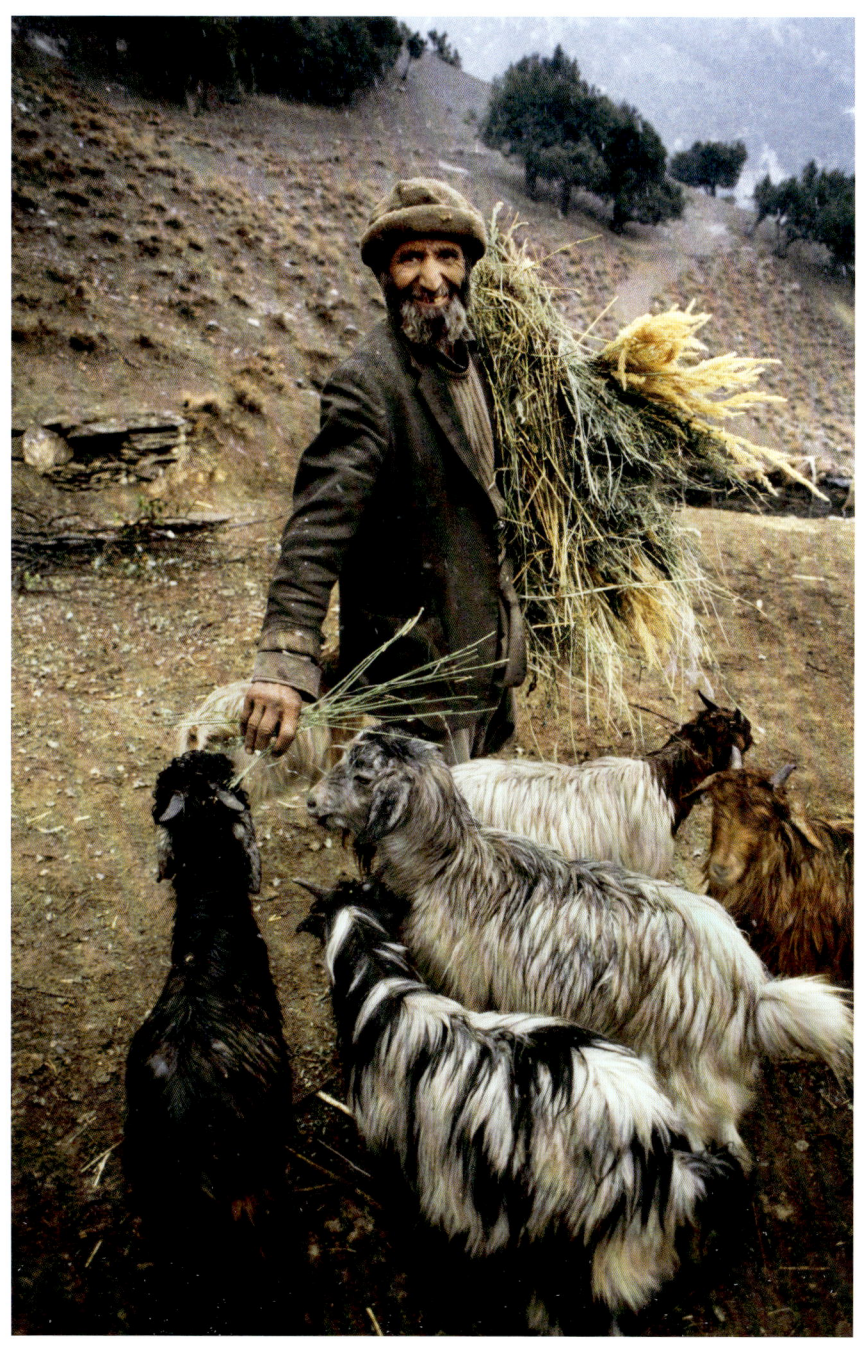

KALASH VALLEY, PAKISTAN, 1981

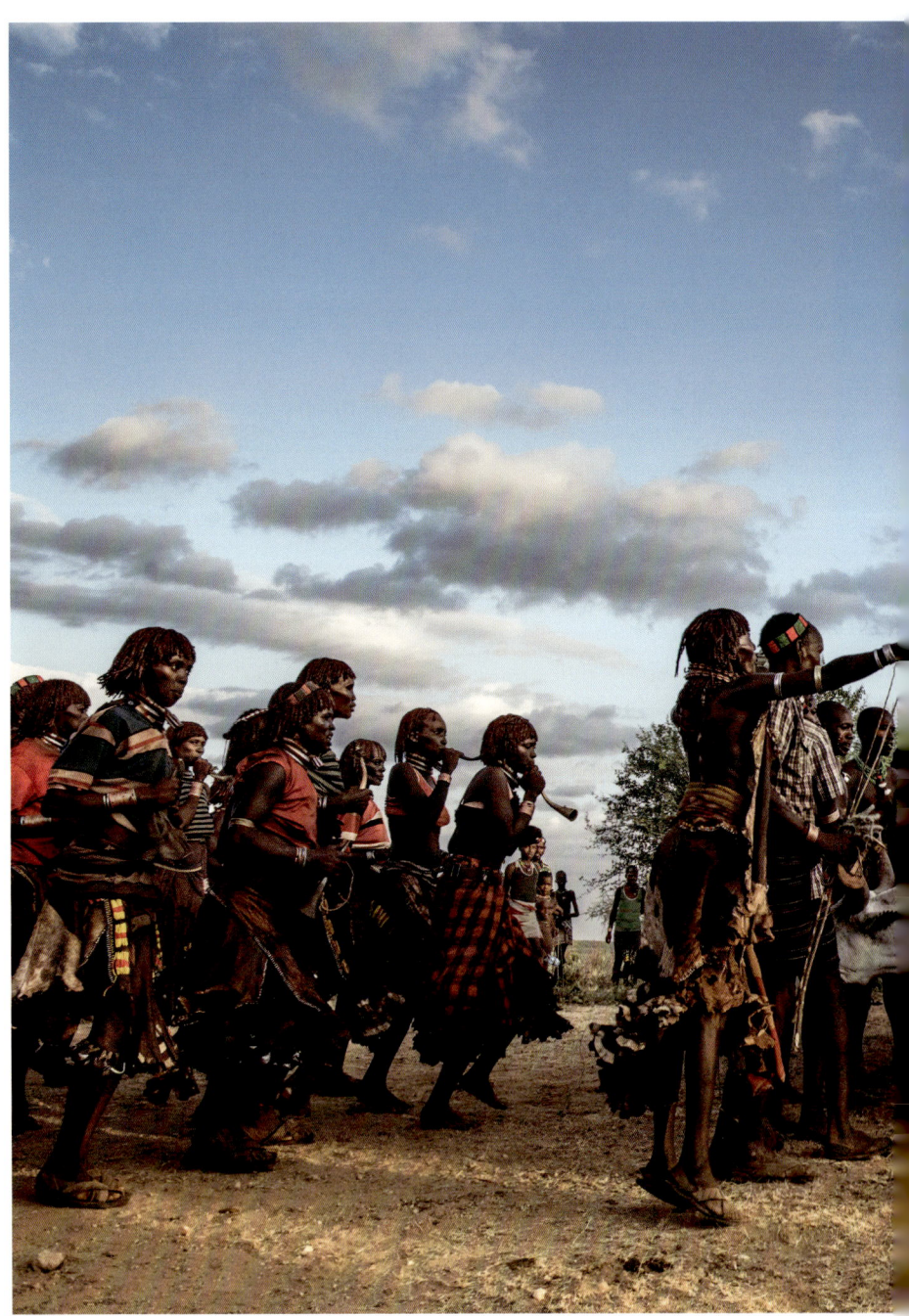

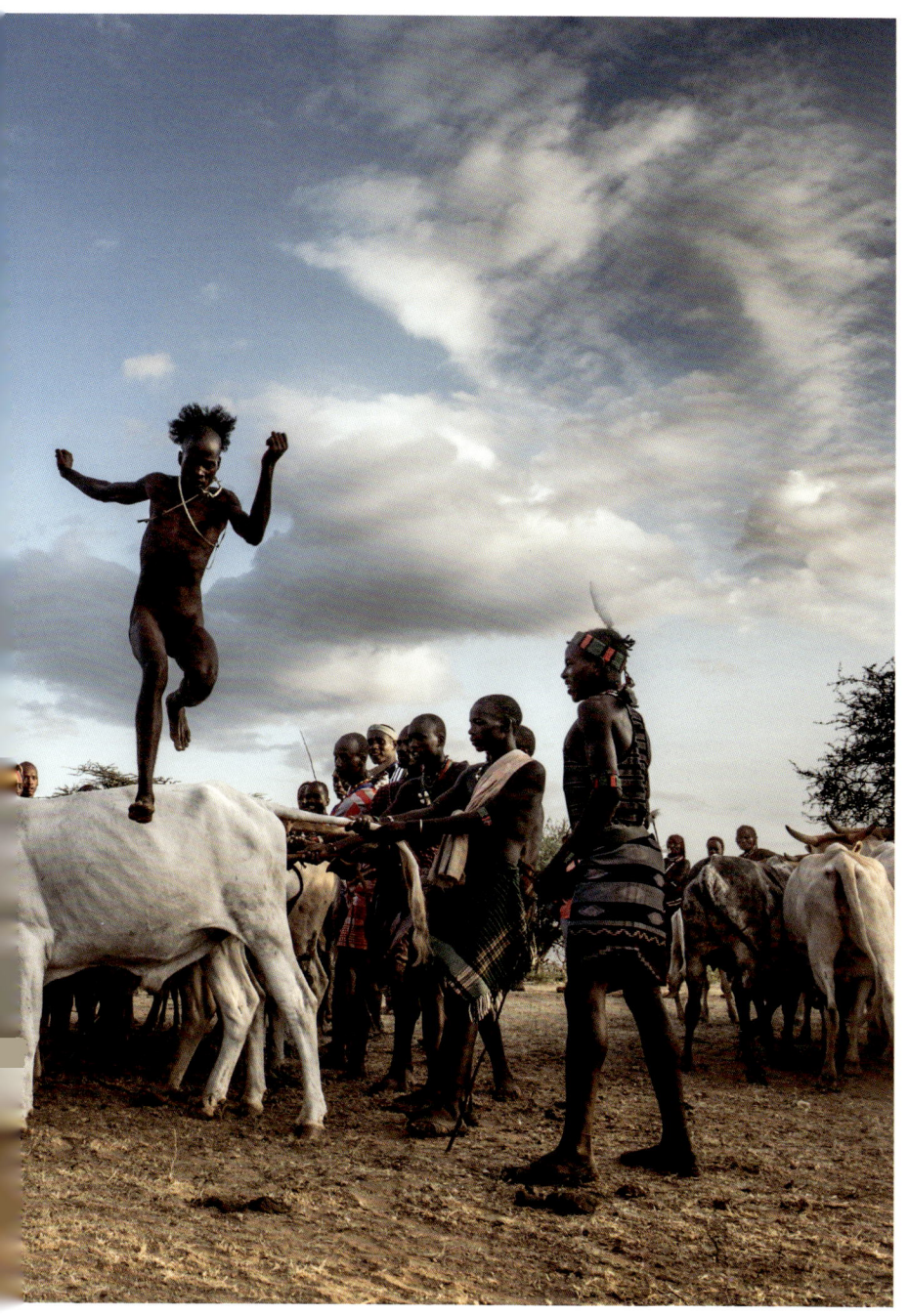

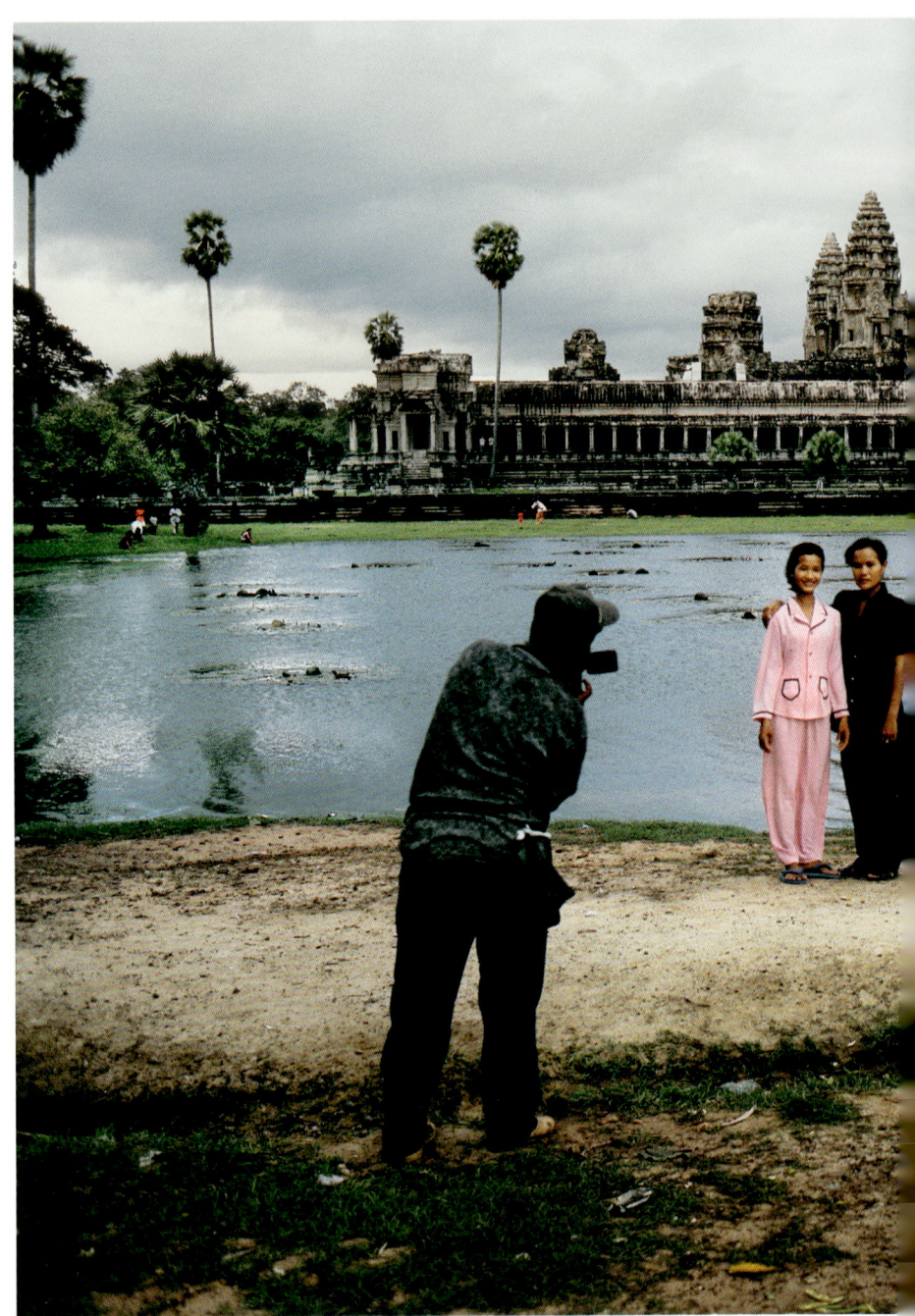

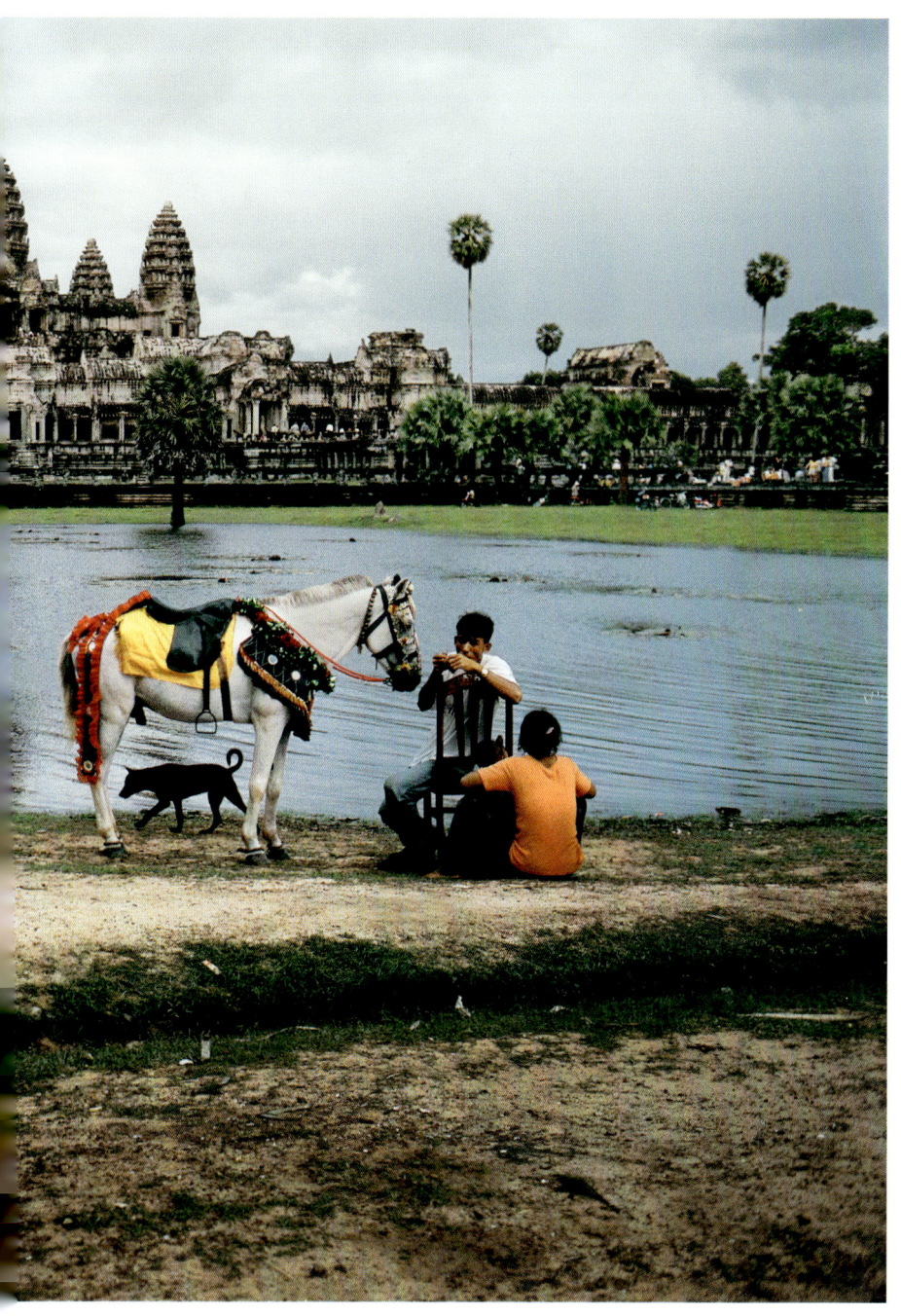

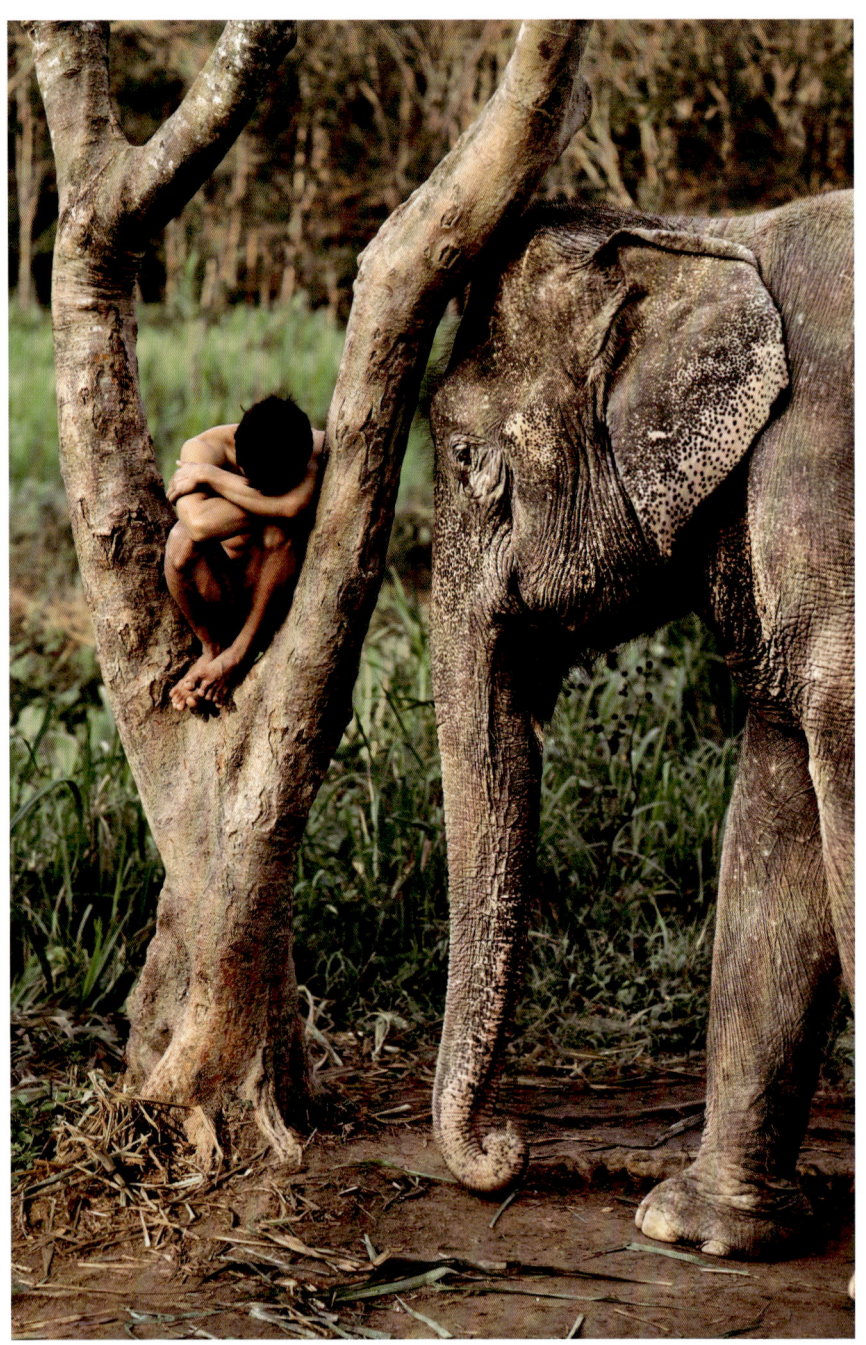

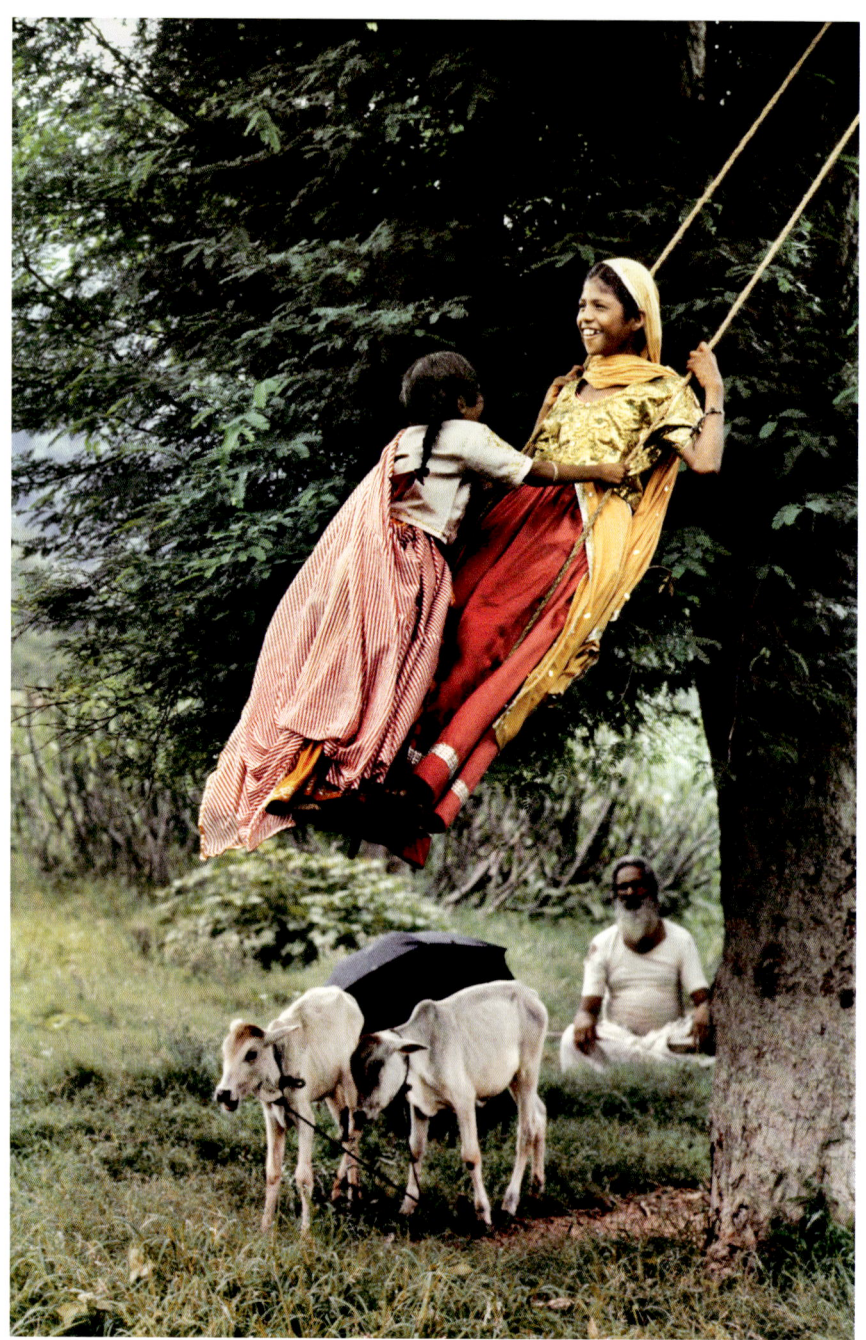

RAJASTHAN, INDIA, 1983

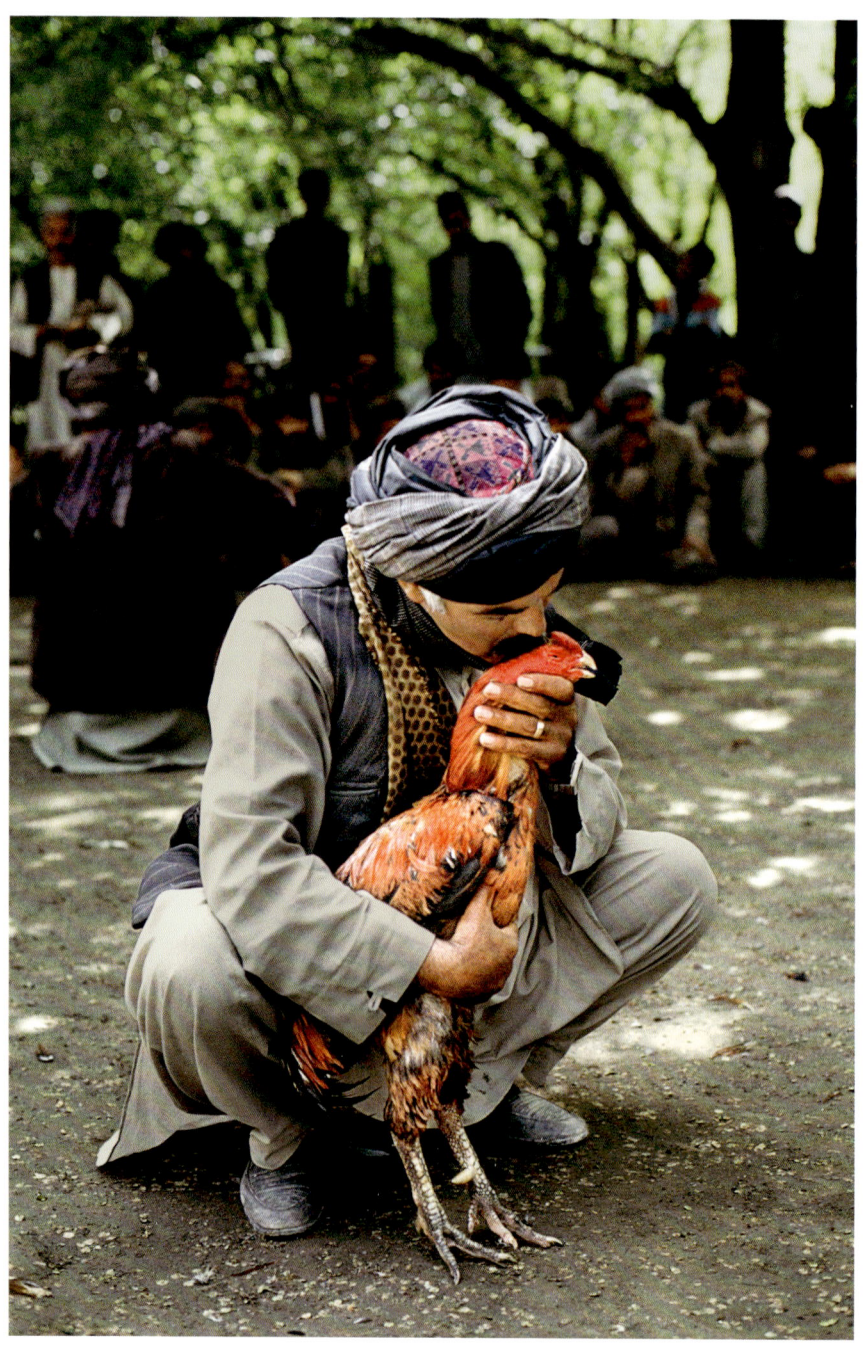

KABUL, AFGHANISTAN, 1992

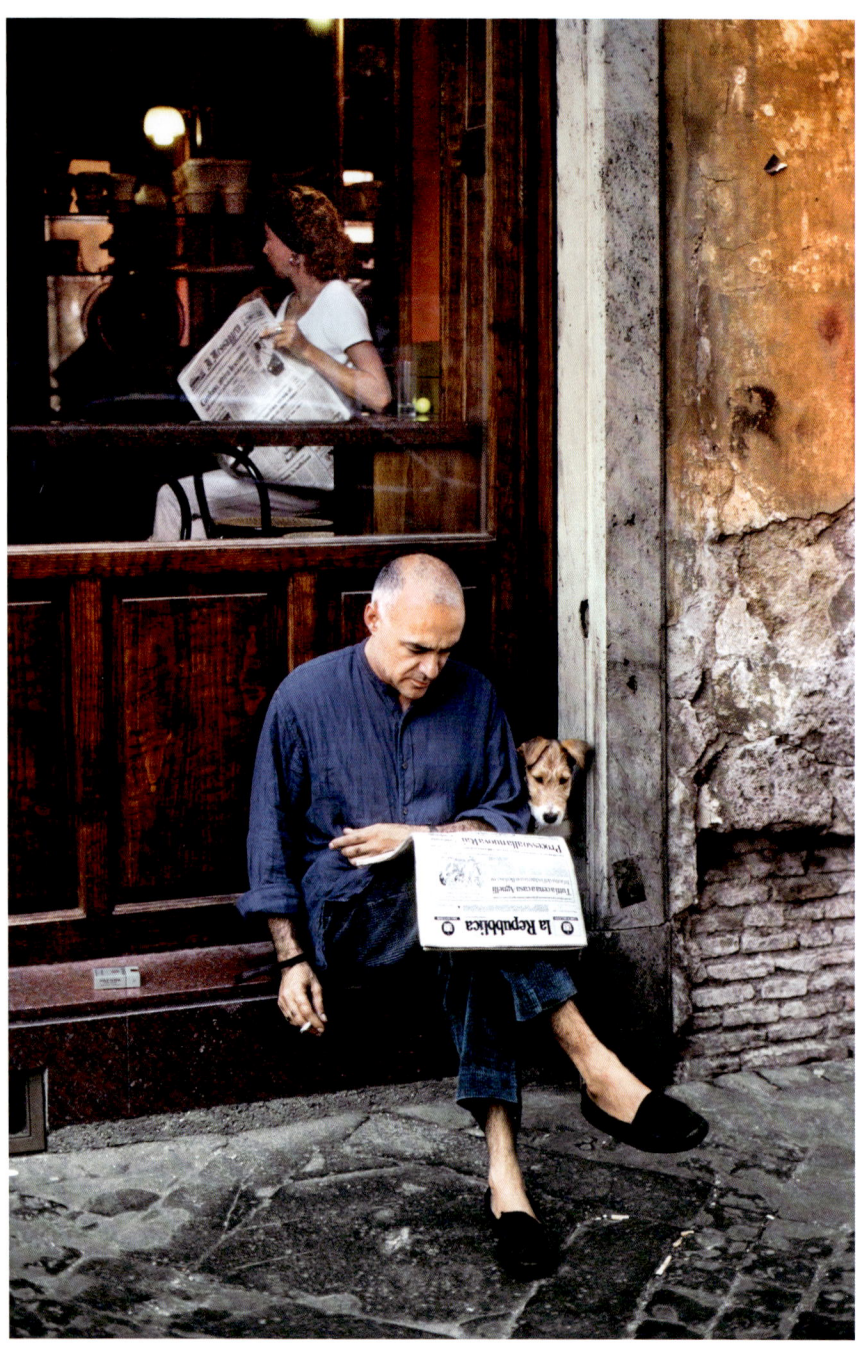

ROME, ITALY, 1994

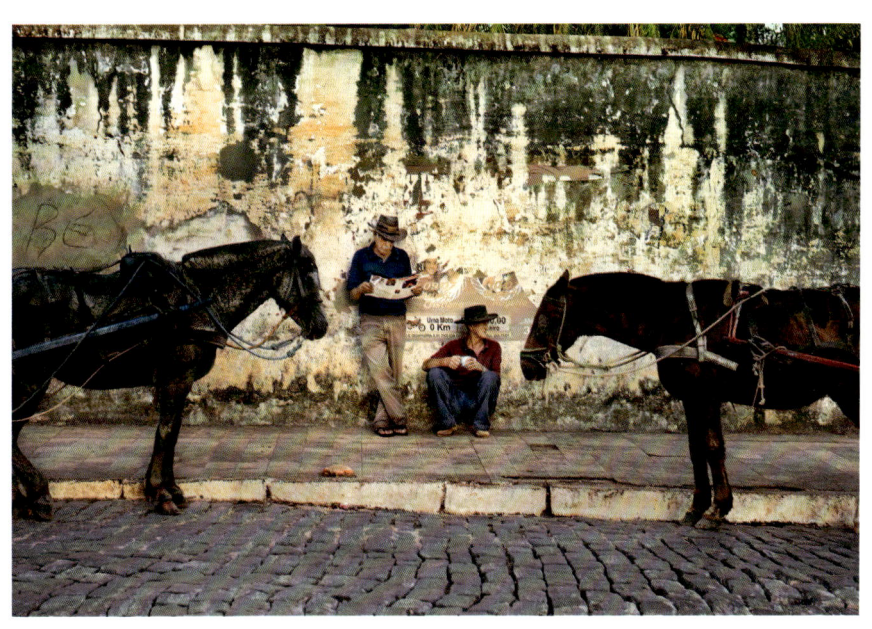

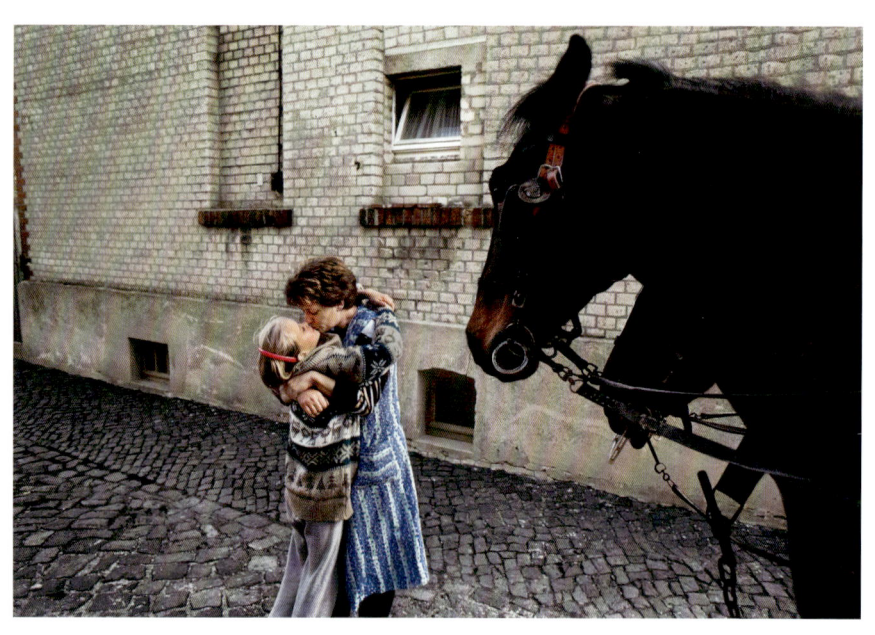

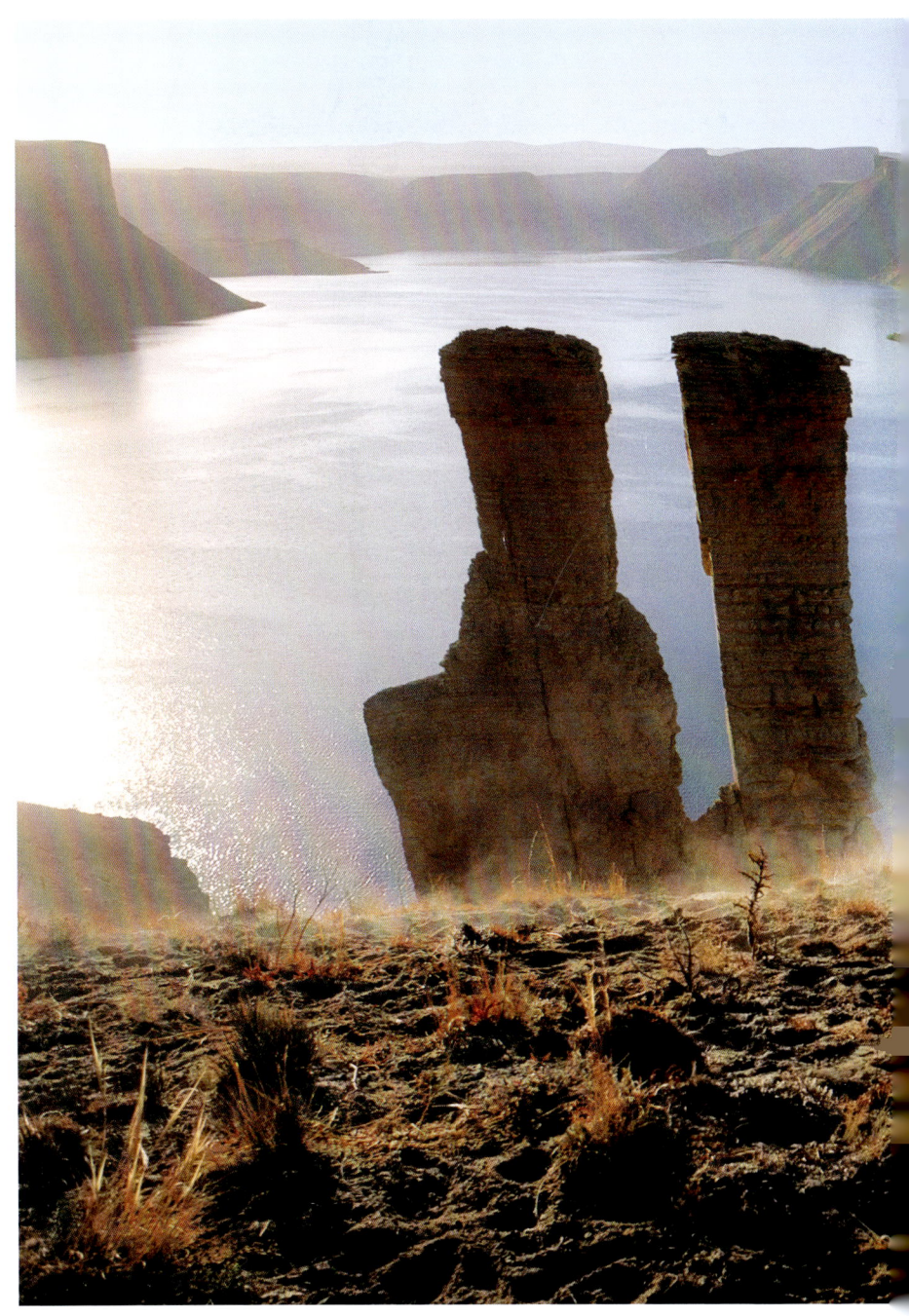

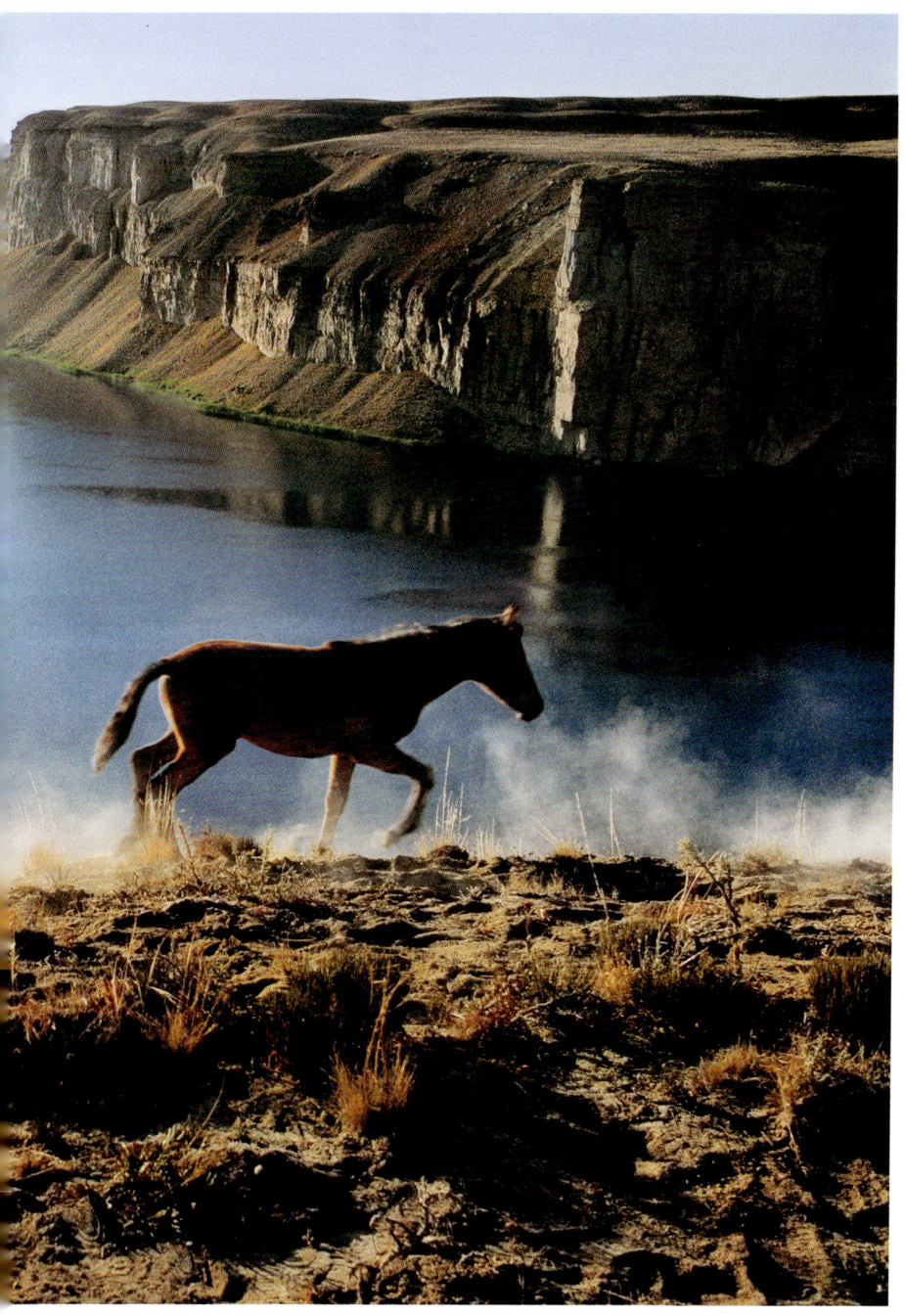

PAGES 66-67 Band-i-Amir, Afghanistan, 2002. A colt runs after its mother in Afghanistan's first national park, the lakes of Band-i-Amir. The tranquil lakes perfectly mirror the surrounding landscape and are believed to have healing properties.

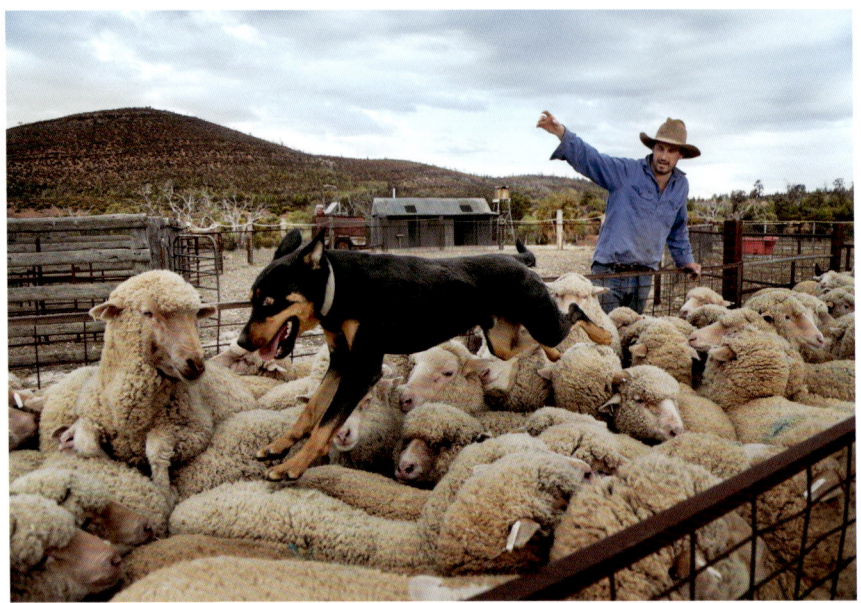

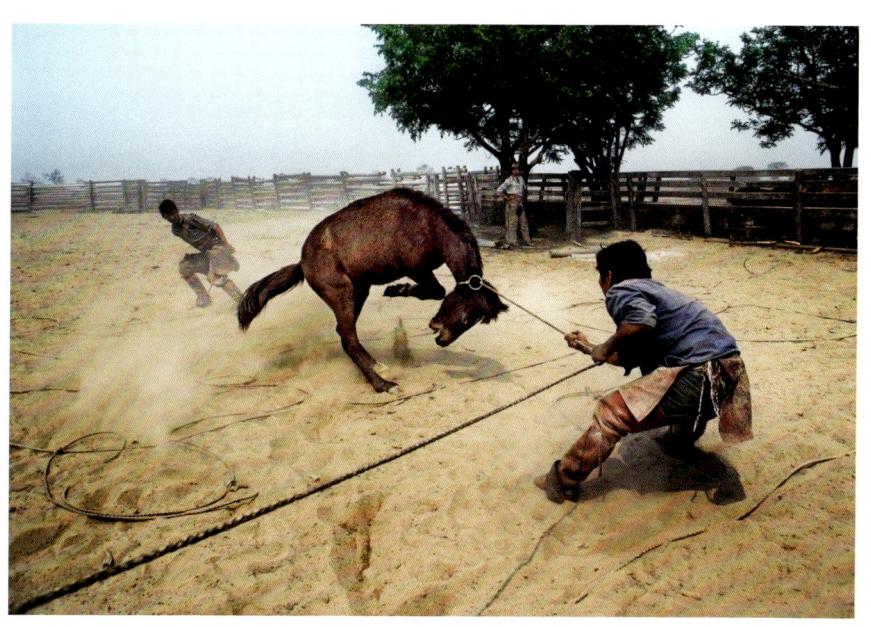

CHACO, PARAGUAY, 1988

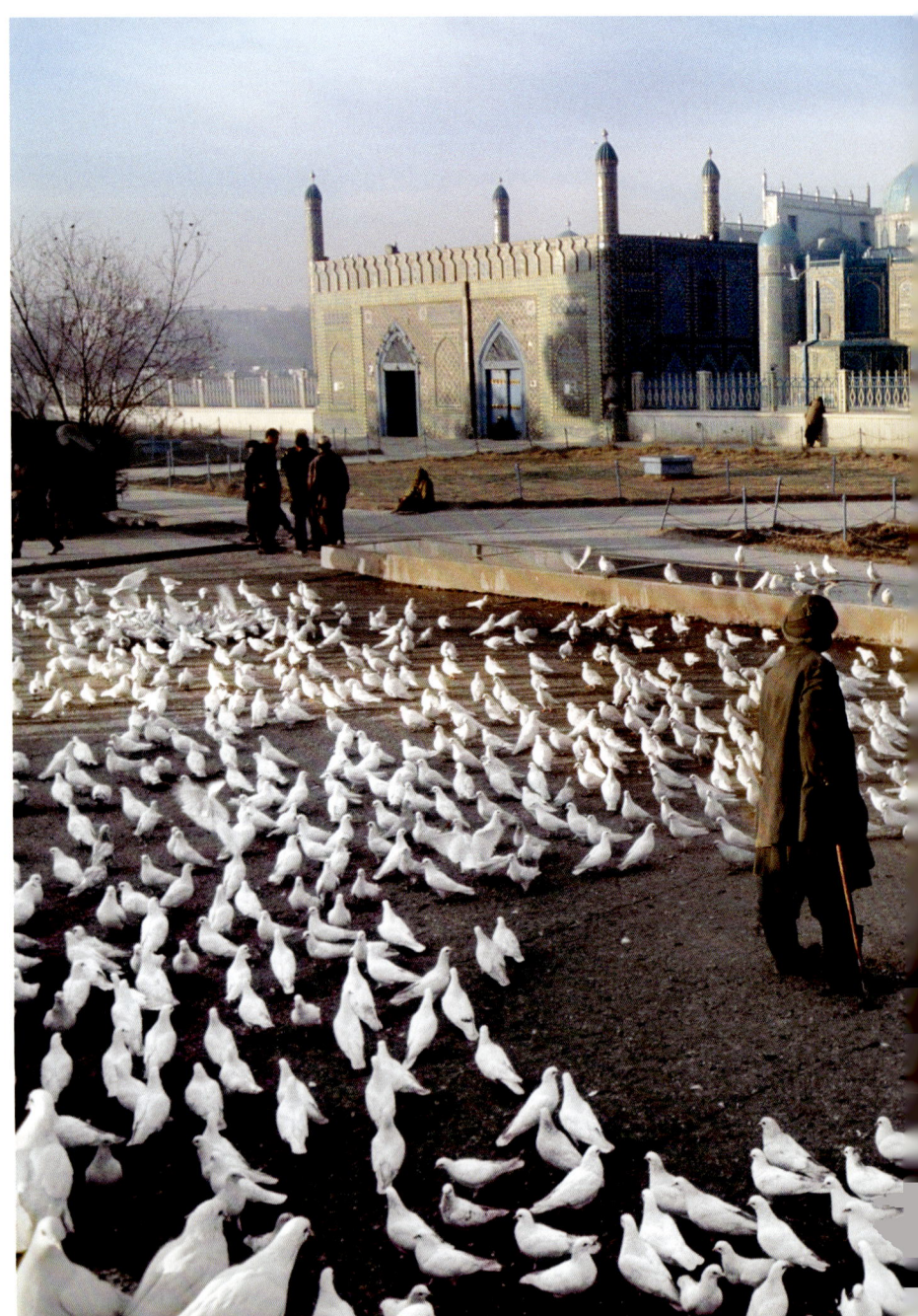

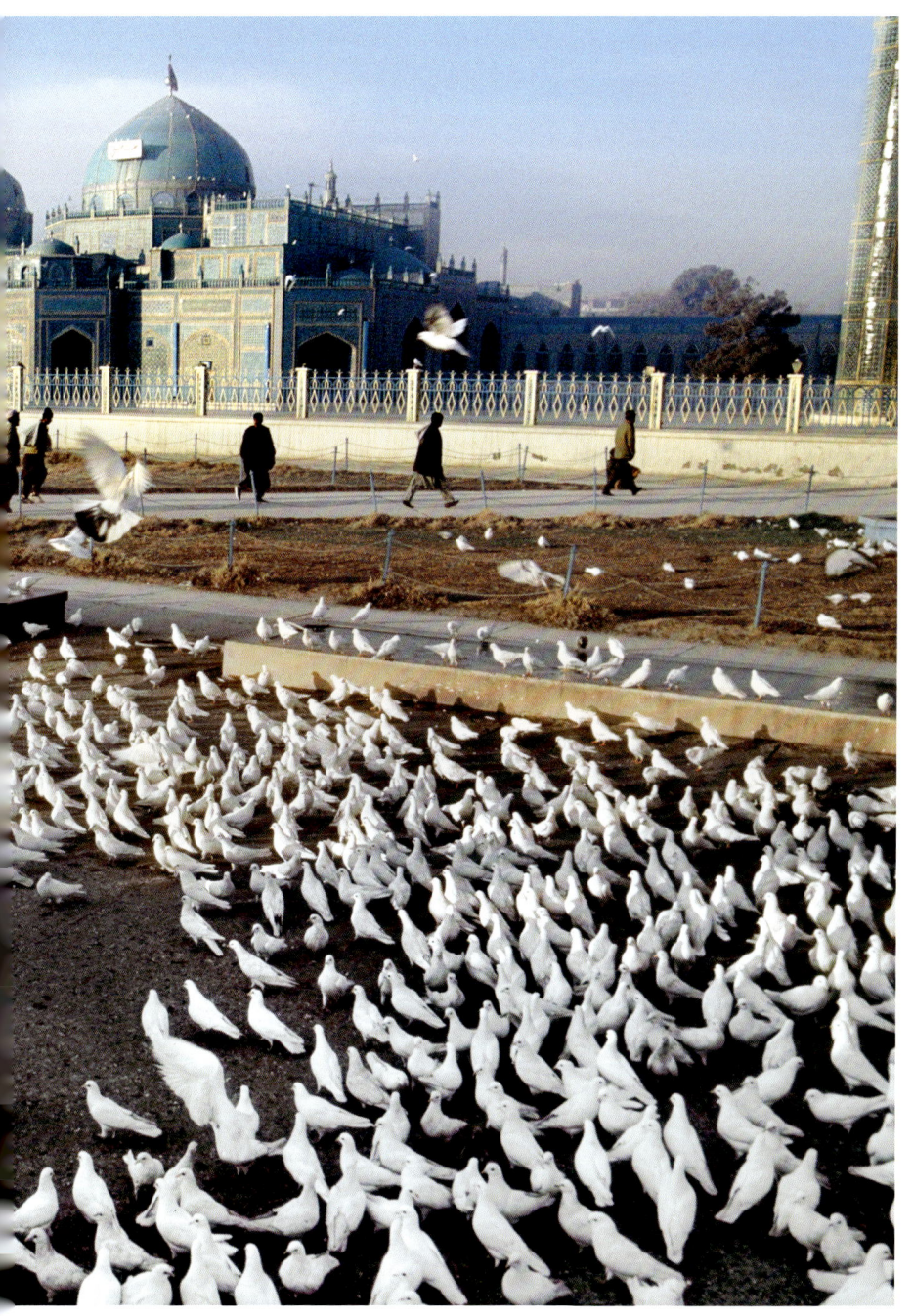

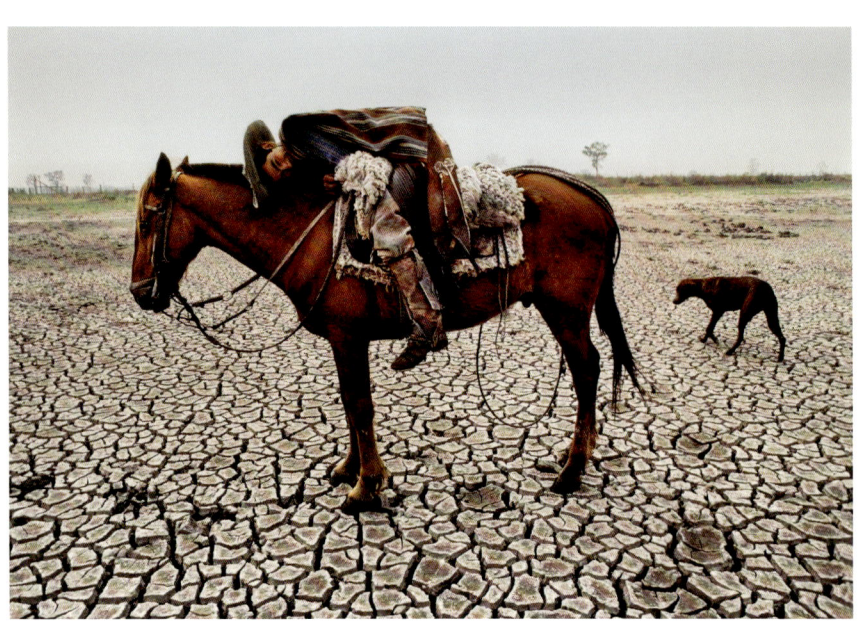

72   CHACO, PARAGUAY, 1988

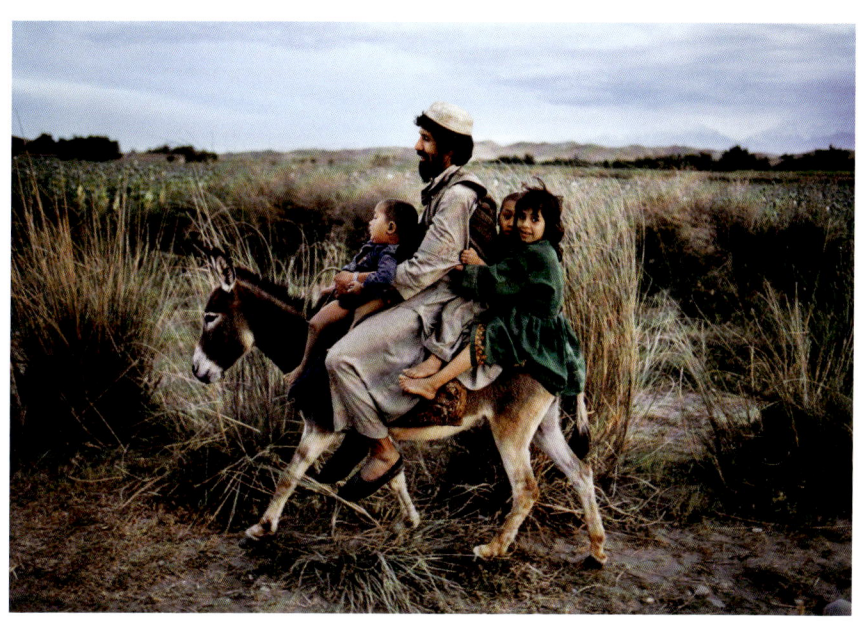

MAYMANA, AFGHANISTAN, 2003

"Do not free the camel of the burden of his hump; you may be freeing him from being a camel."

G. K. CHESTERTON

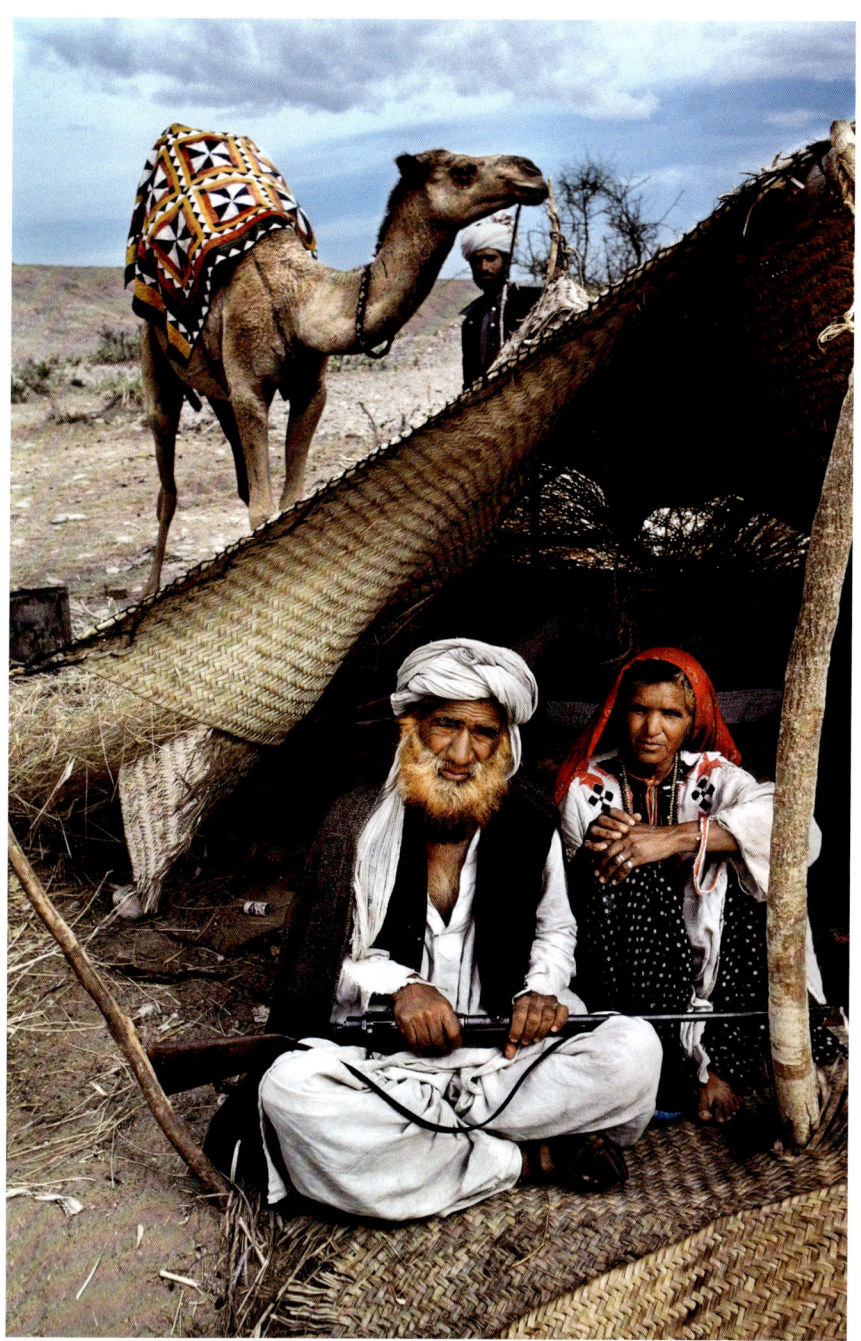

DERA BUGTI, BALOCHISTAN, PAKISTAN, 1981

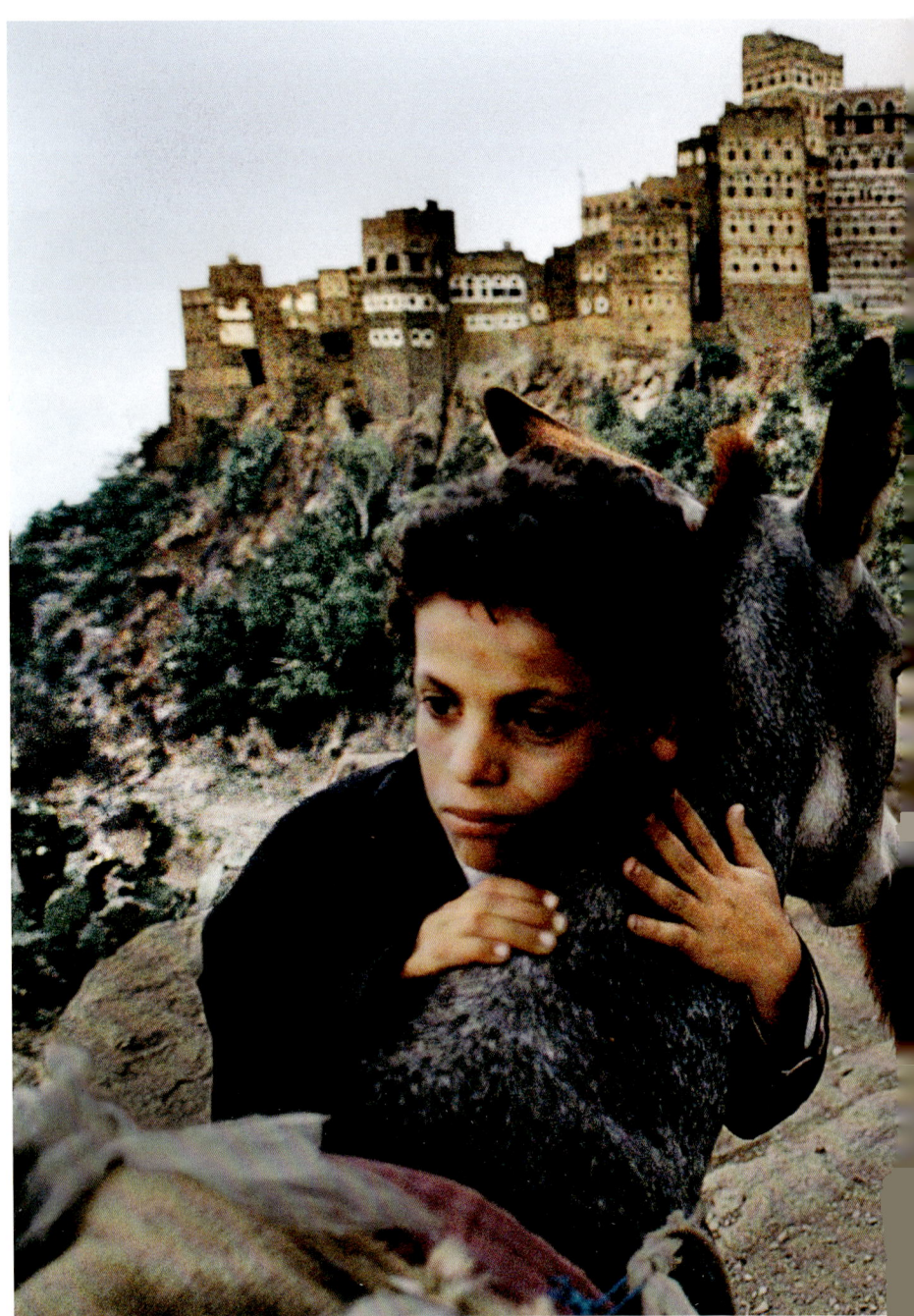

76   AL HAJJARAH, YEMEN, 1997

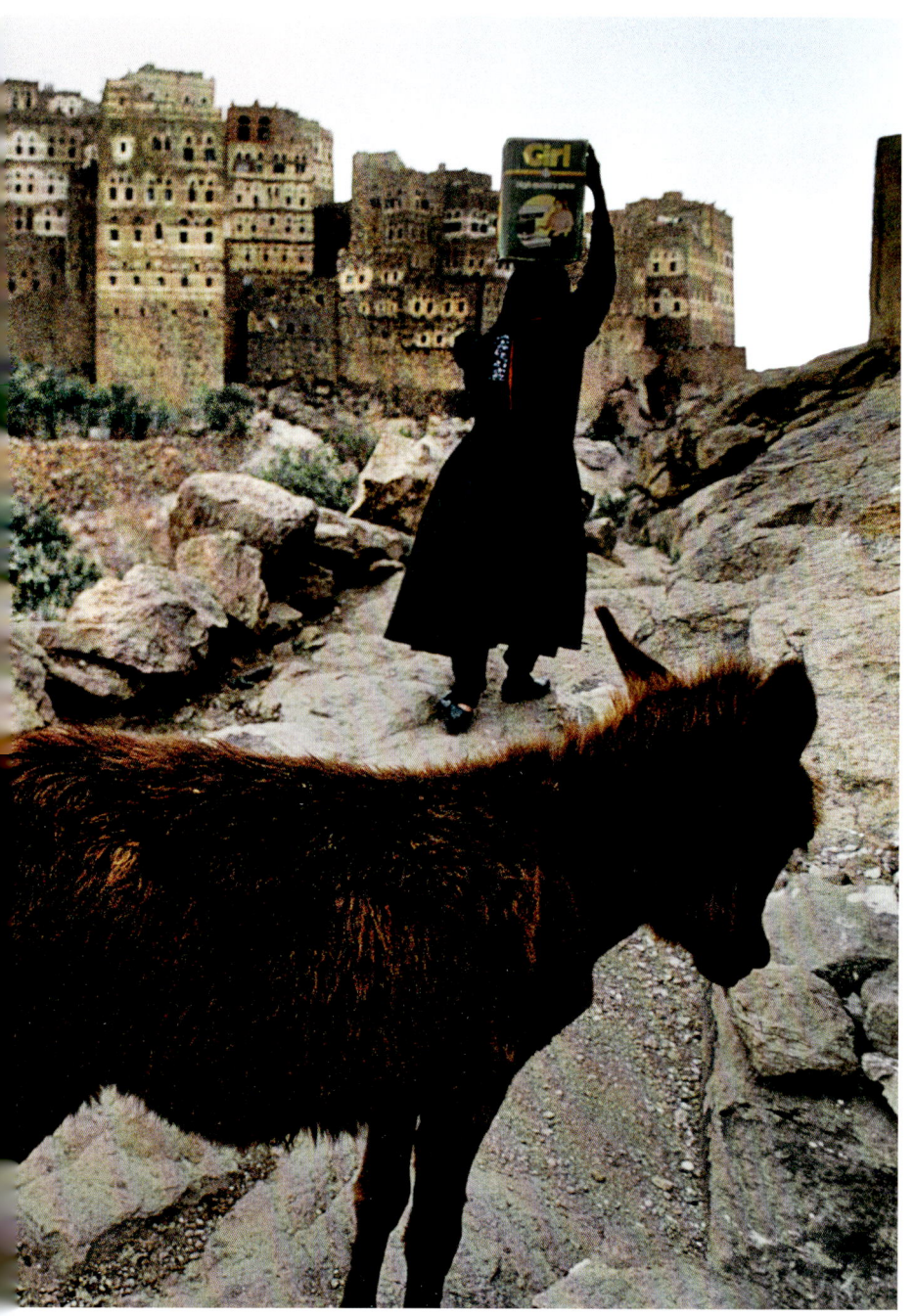

"There is no secret so close as that between a rider and his/her horse."

ROBERT SMITH SURTEES

PAGES 80-81 Yamanouchi, Japan, 2018. In Nagano, northern Japan, there are hot springs and man-made ponds that the monkeys use to keep warm. Japanese snow monkeys get their name because they live in areas where snow covers the ground for months each year – they are one of the only species who live in the cold climate which can be as low -10°C / 14°F.

PAGE 85 Litang, Tibet, 2001. This young nomad boy is with his family's goat near Litang, a major center of Tibetan culture. With an elevation of nearly 4,000 meters, it has a subarctic climate. These goats produce fine cashmere wool.

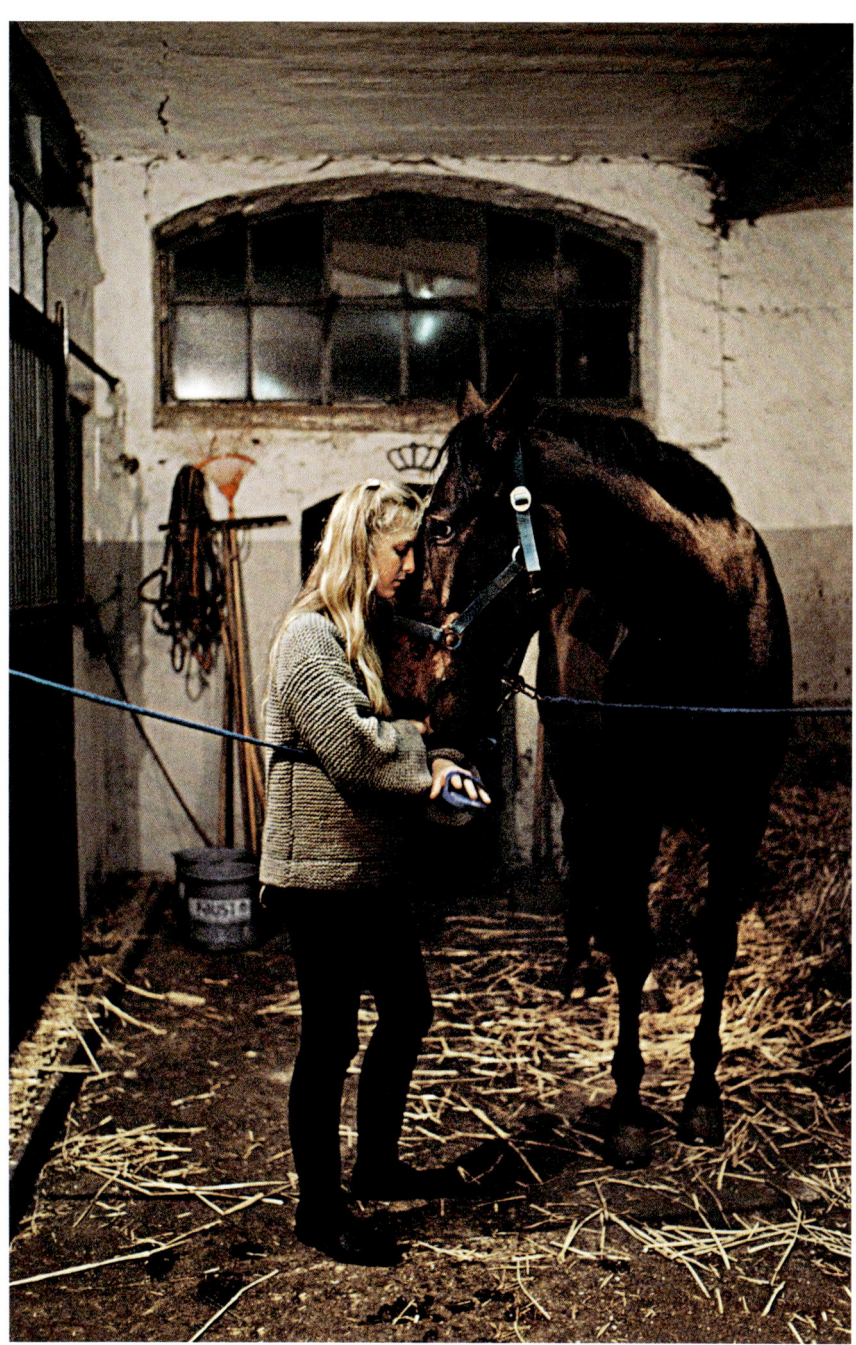

KÖNIGSLUTTER, GERMANY, 1991

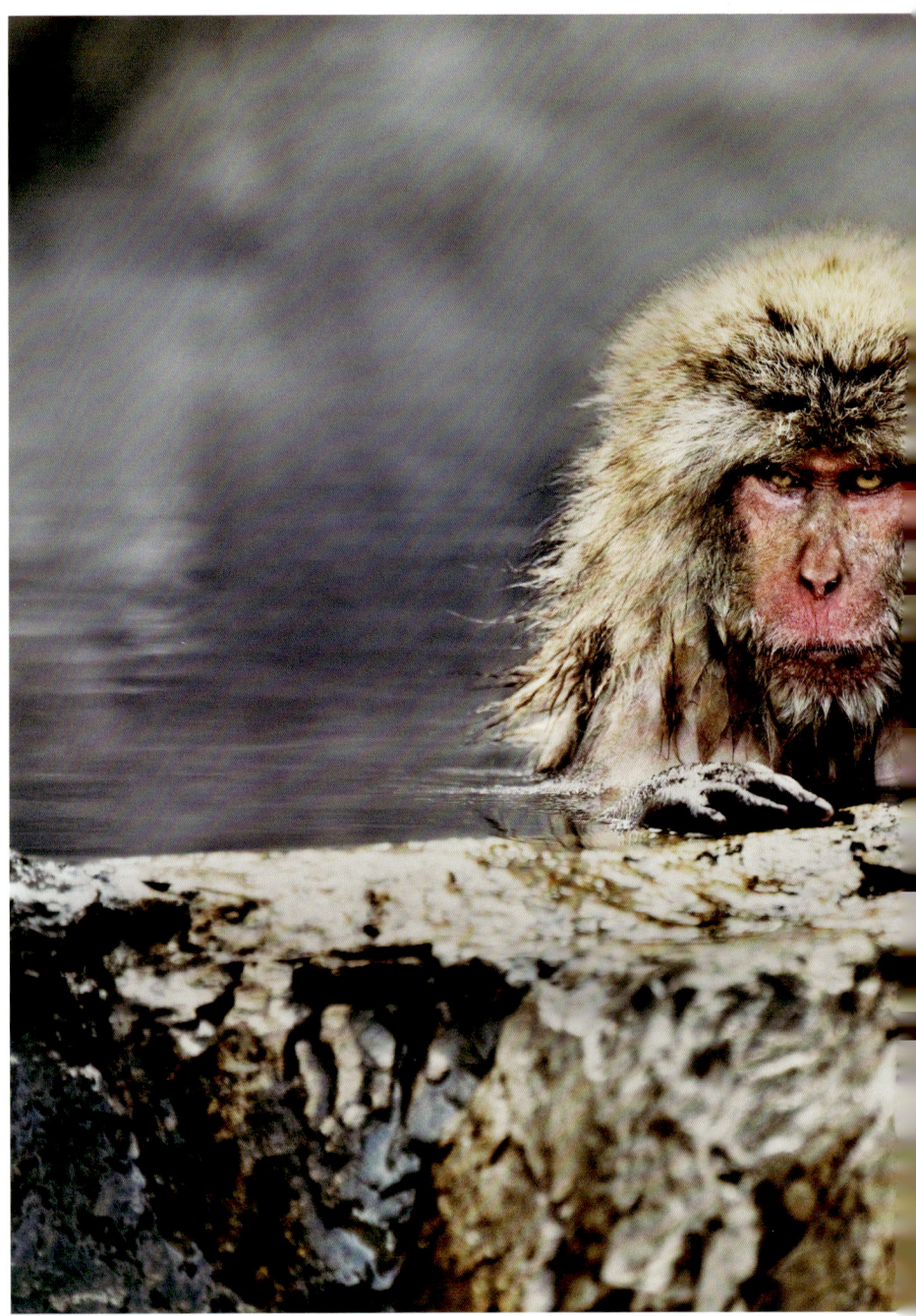

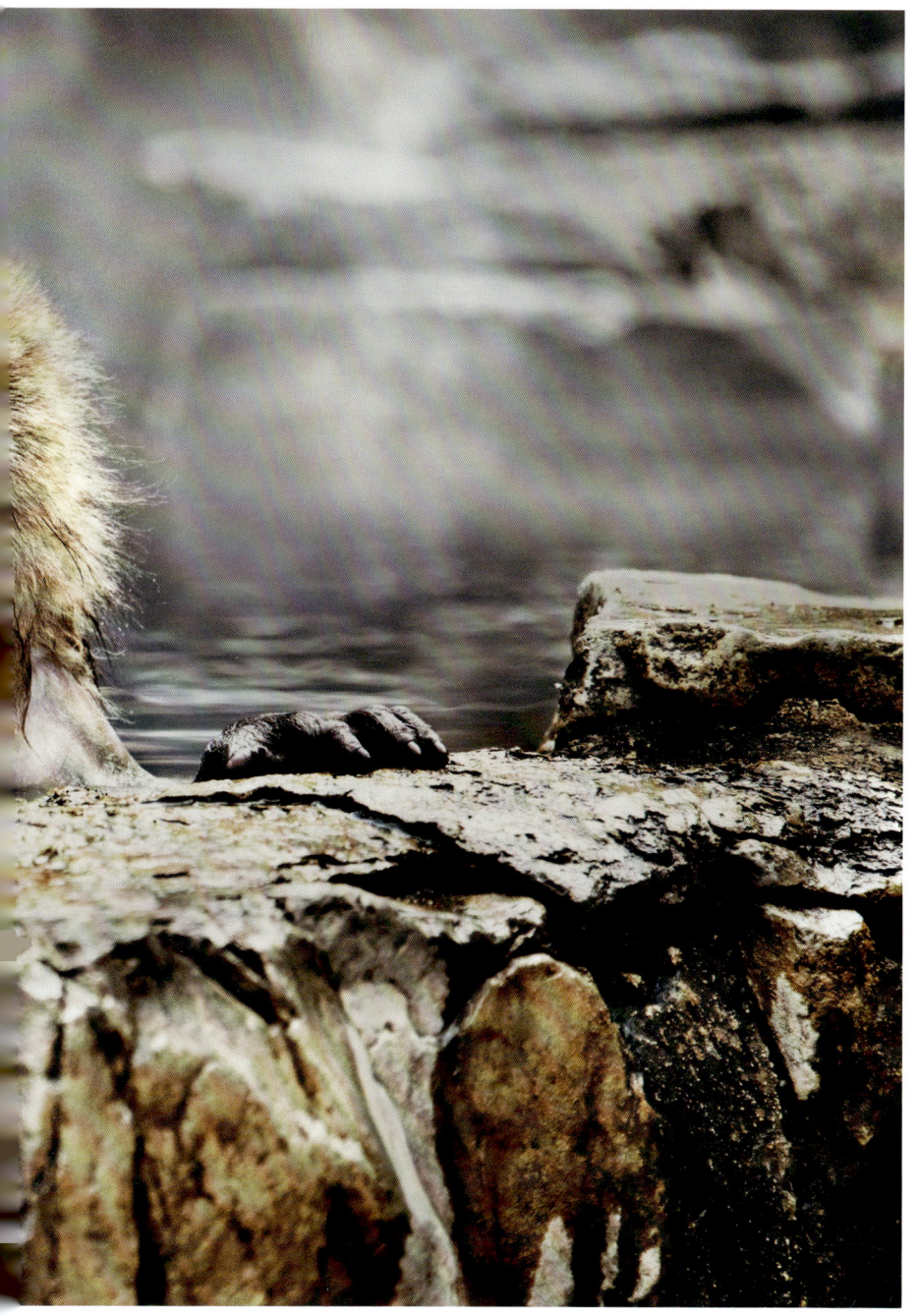

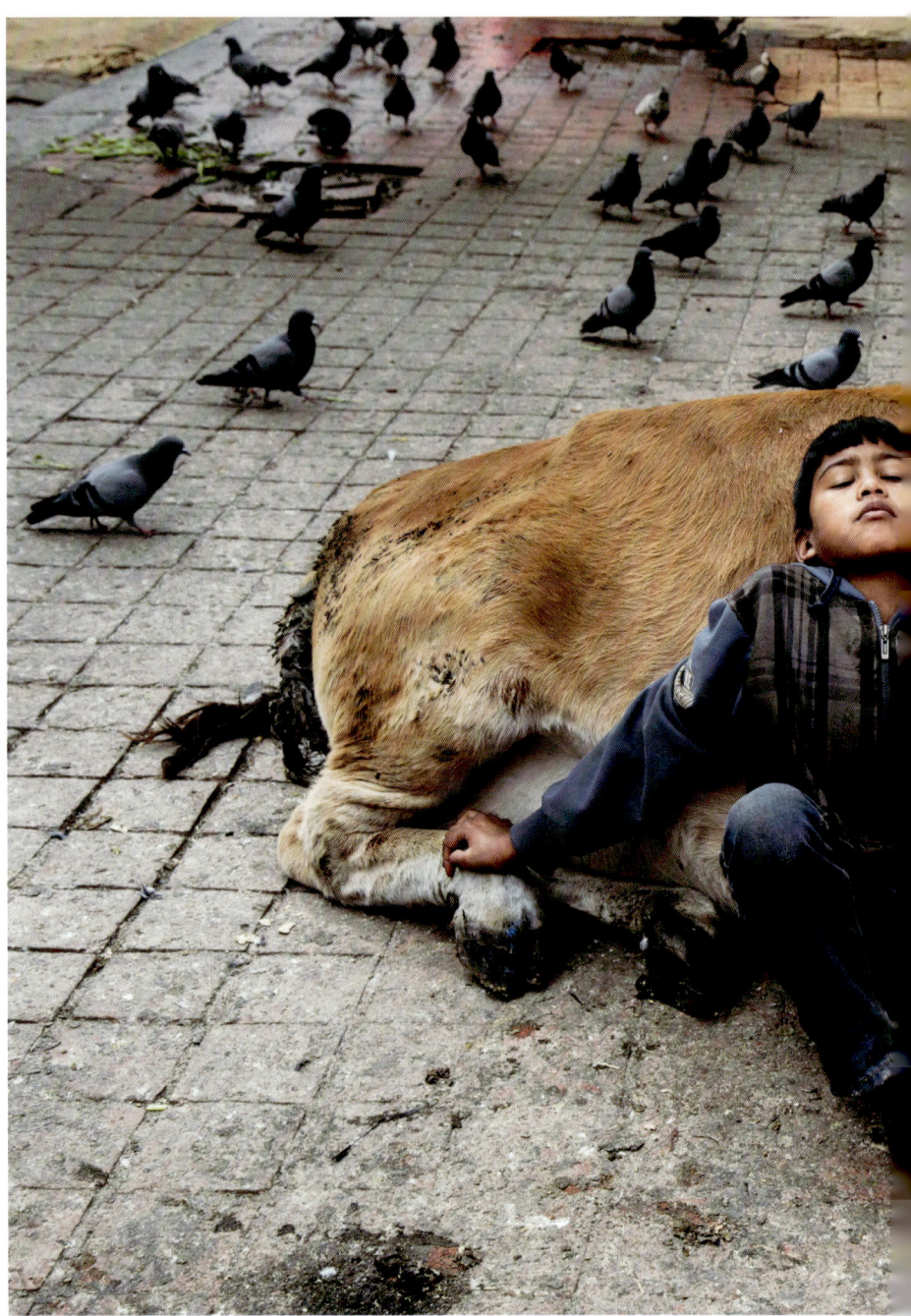

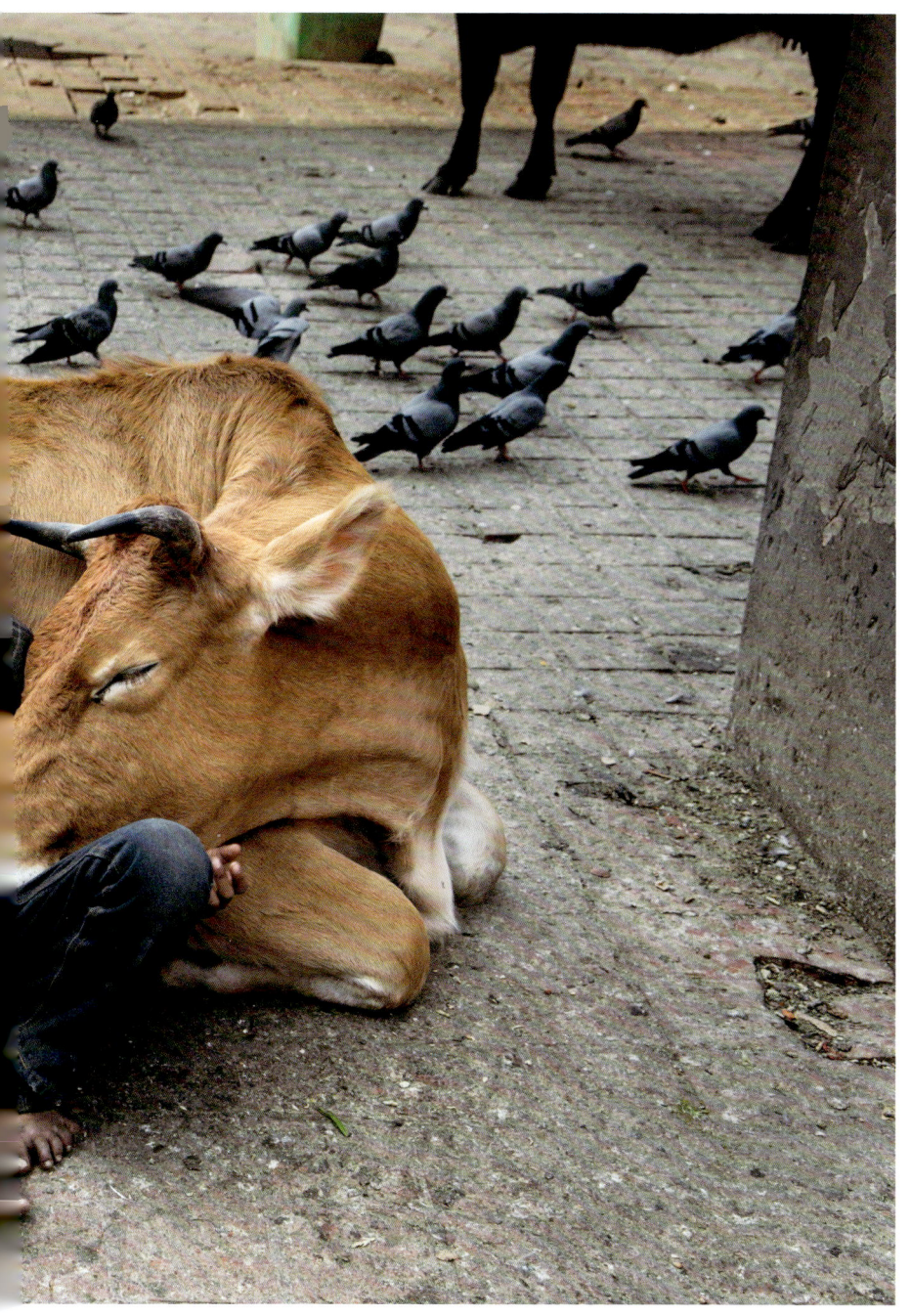

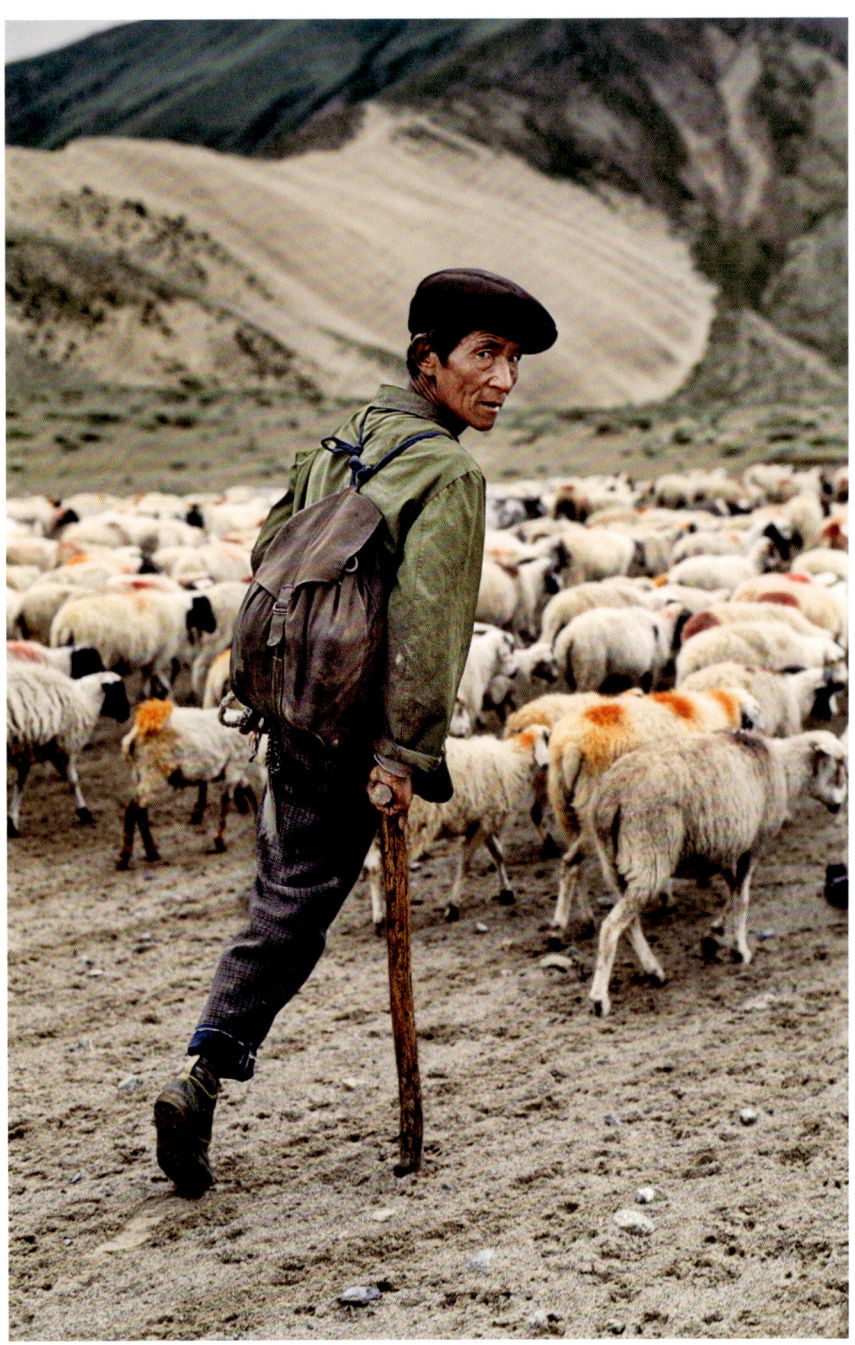

84   NEAR SAMYE, TIBET, 2002

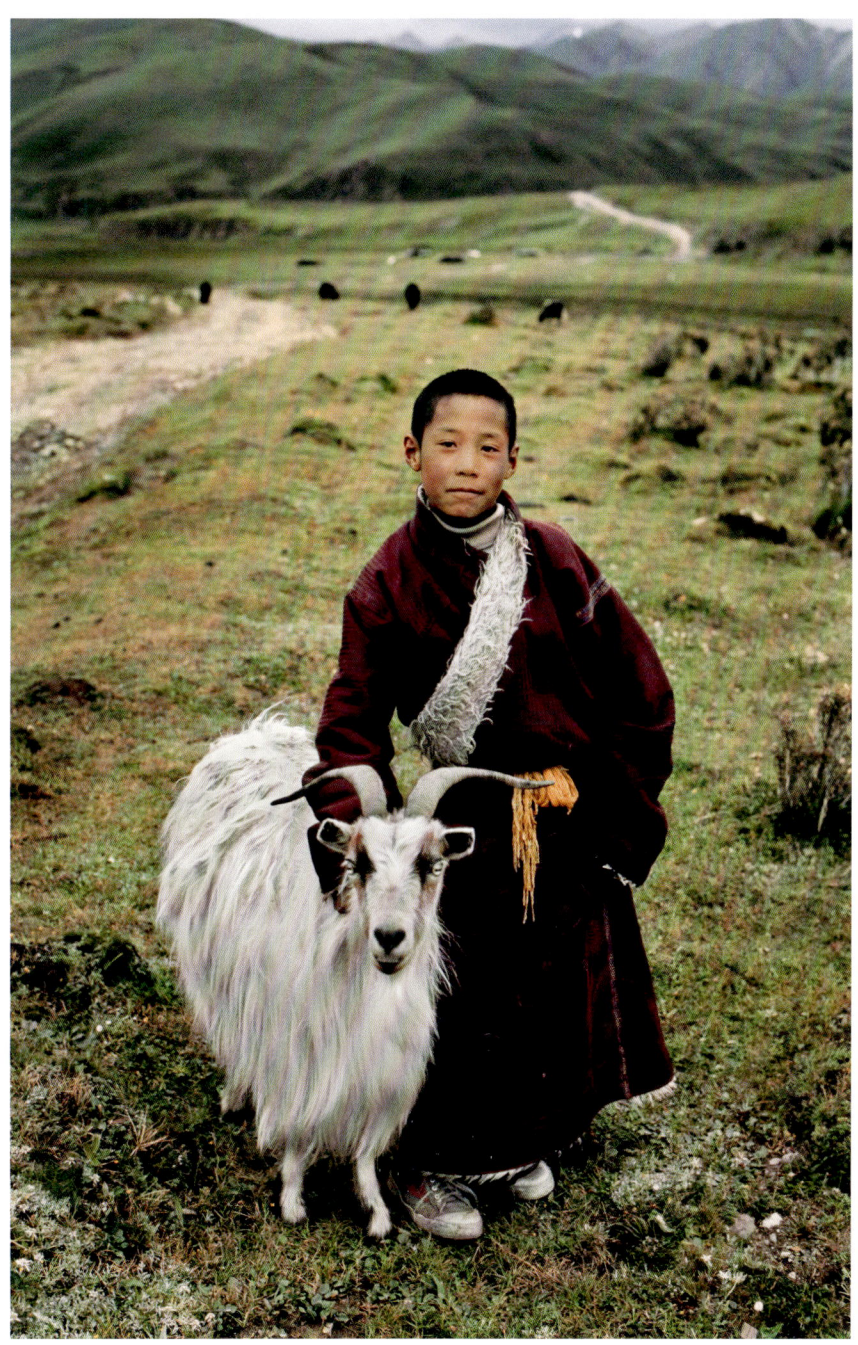

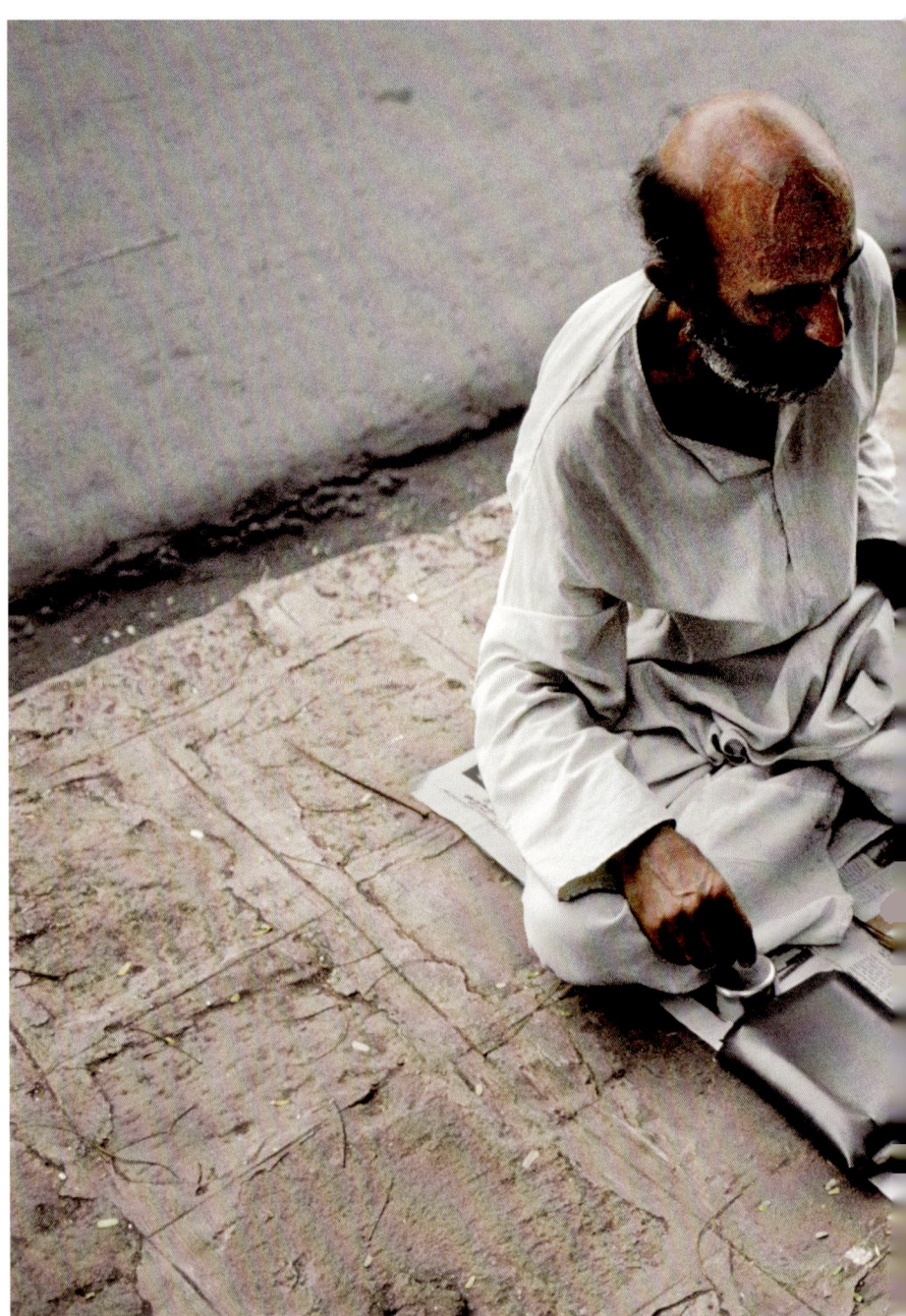

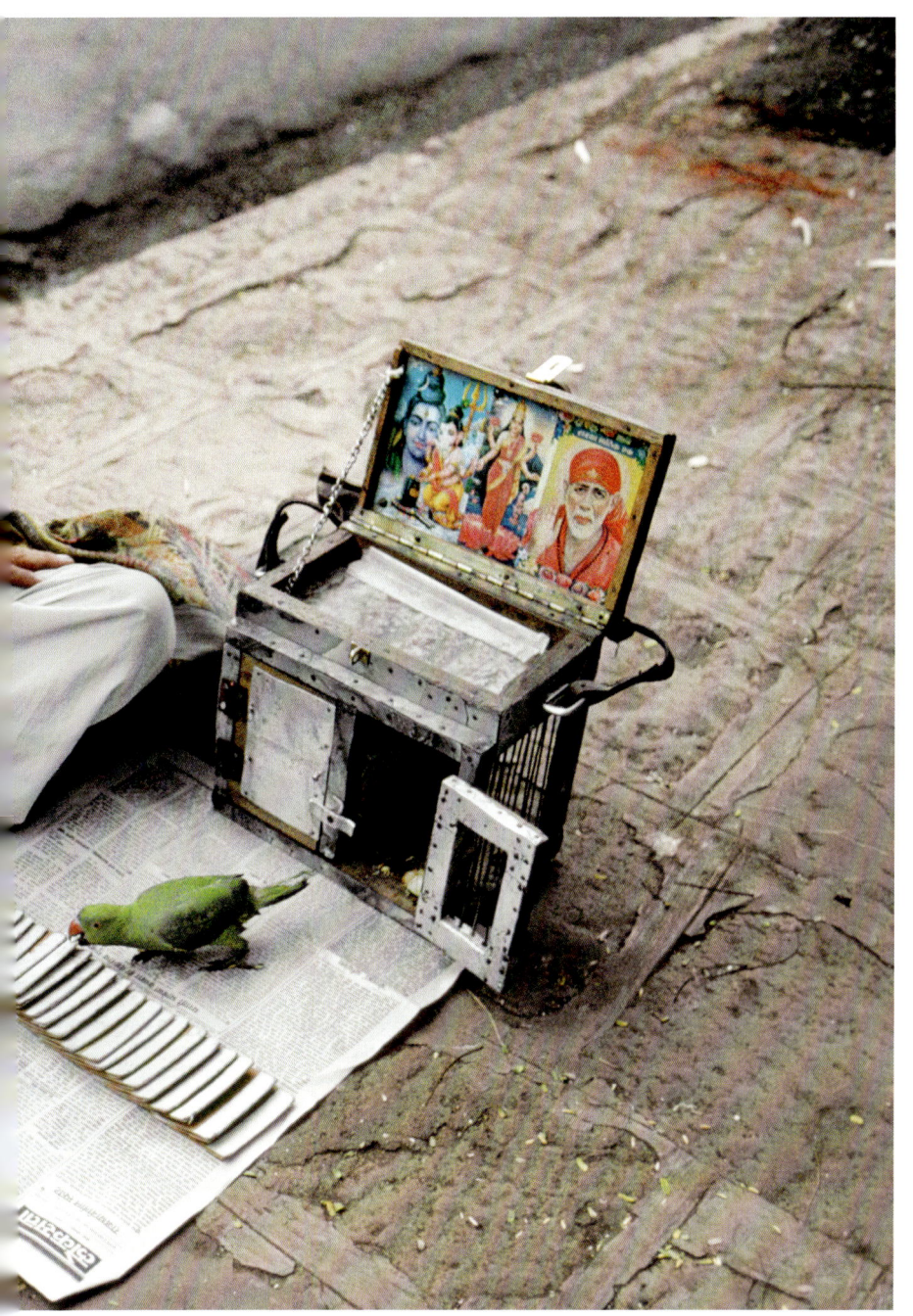

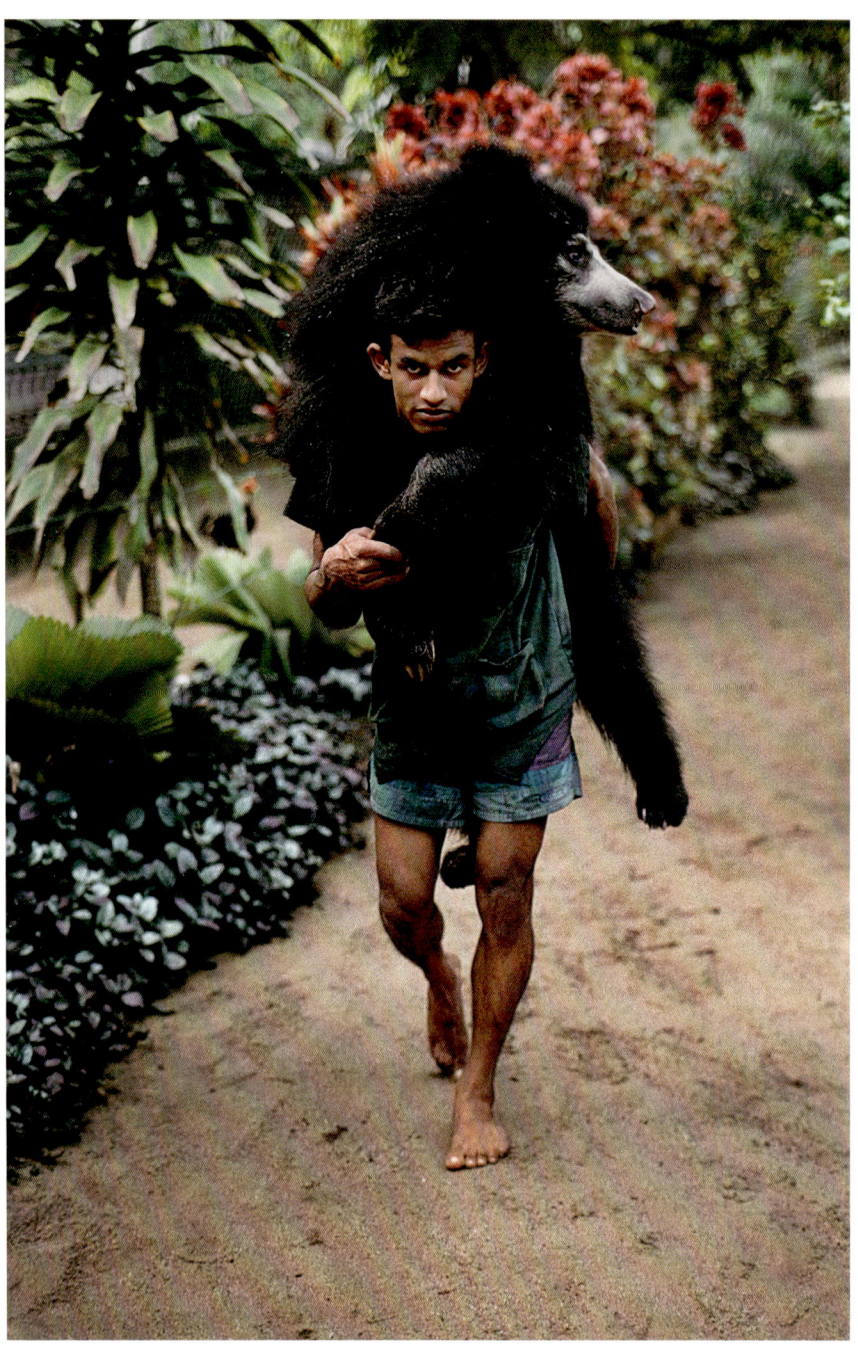

88   NEAR GALLE, SRI LANKA, 1995

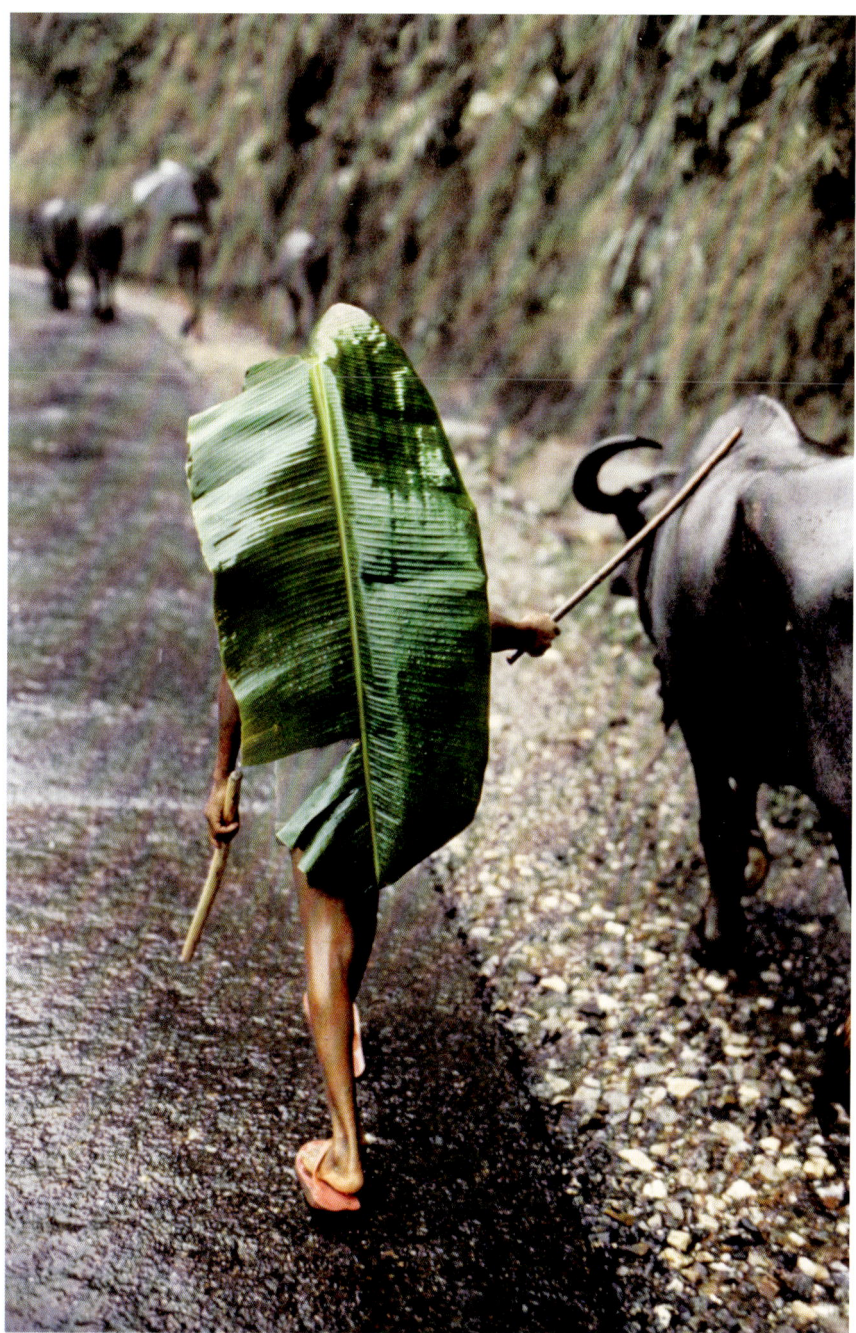

KATHMANDU, NEPAL, 1984

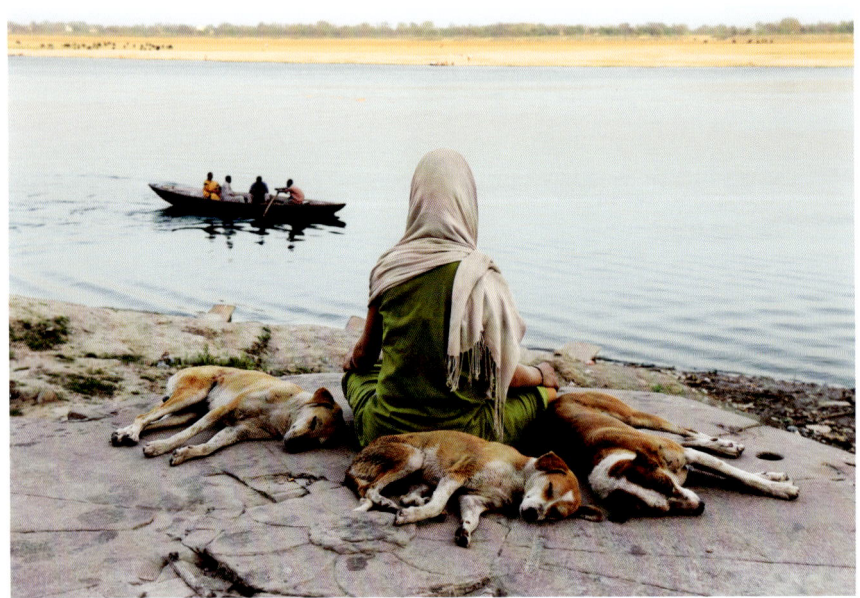

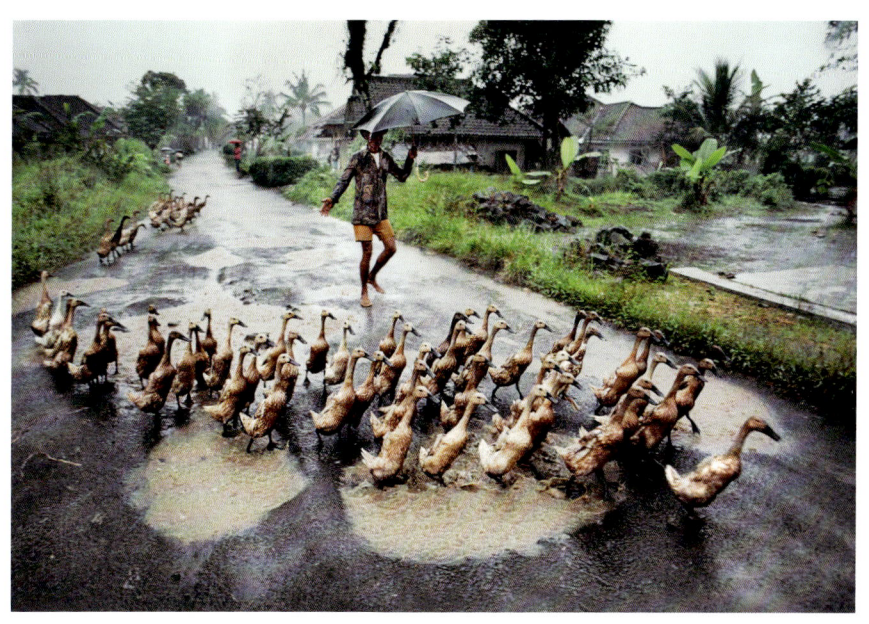

JAVA, INDONESIA, 1984

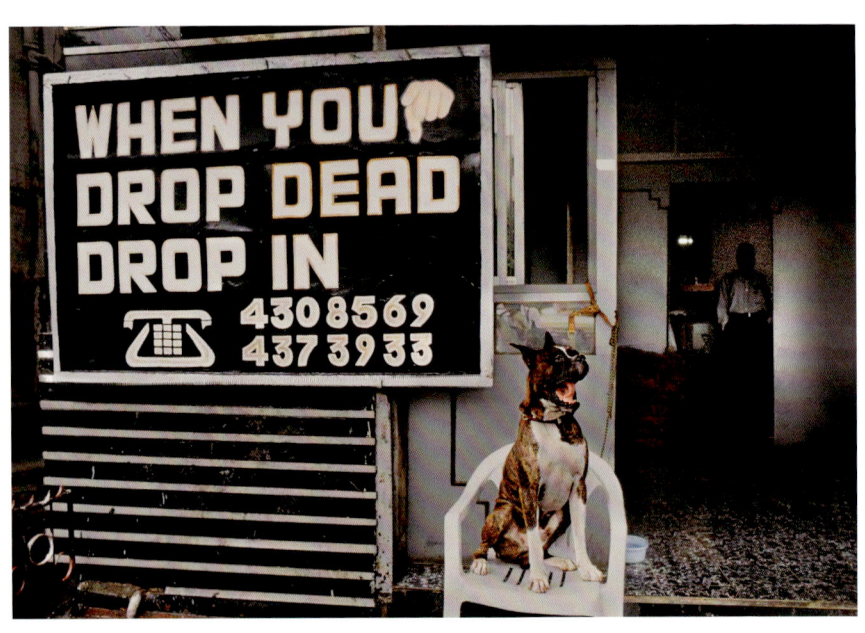

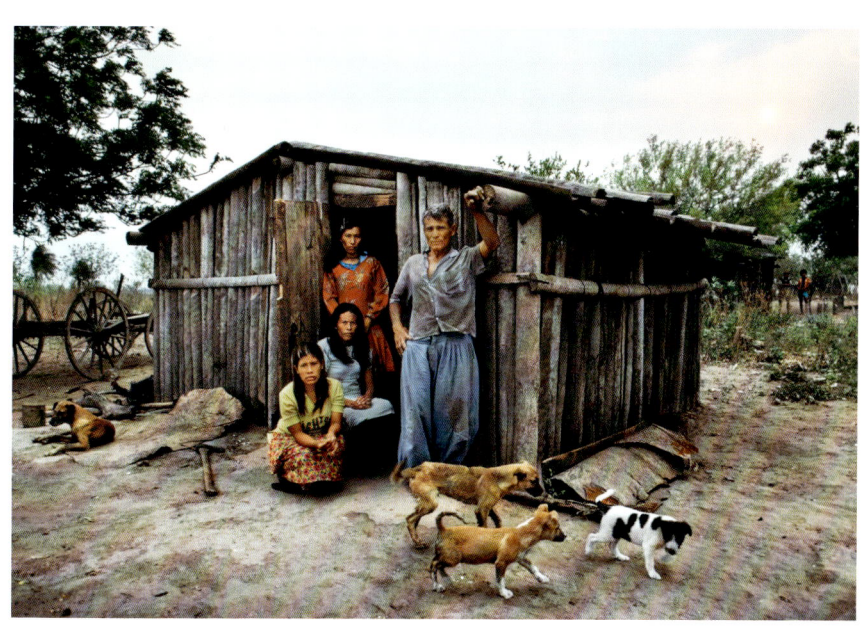

CHACO, PARAGUAY, 1988

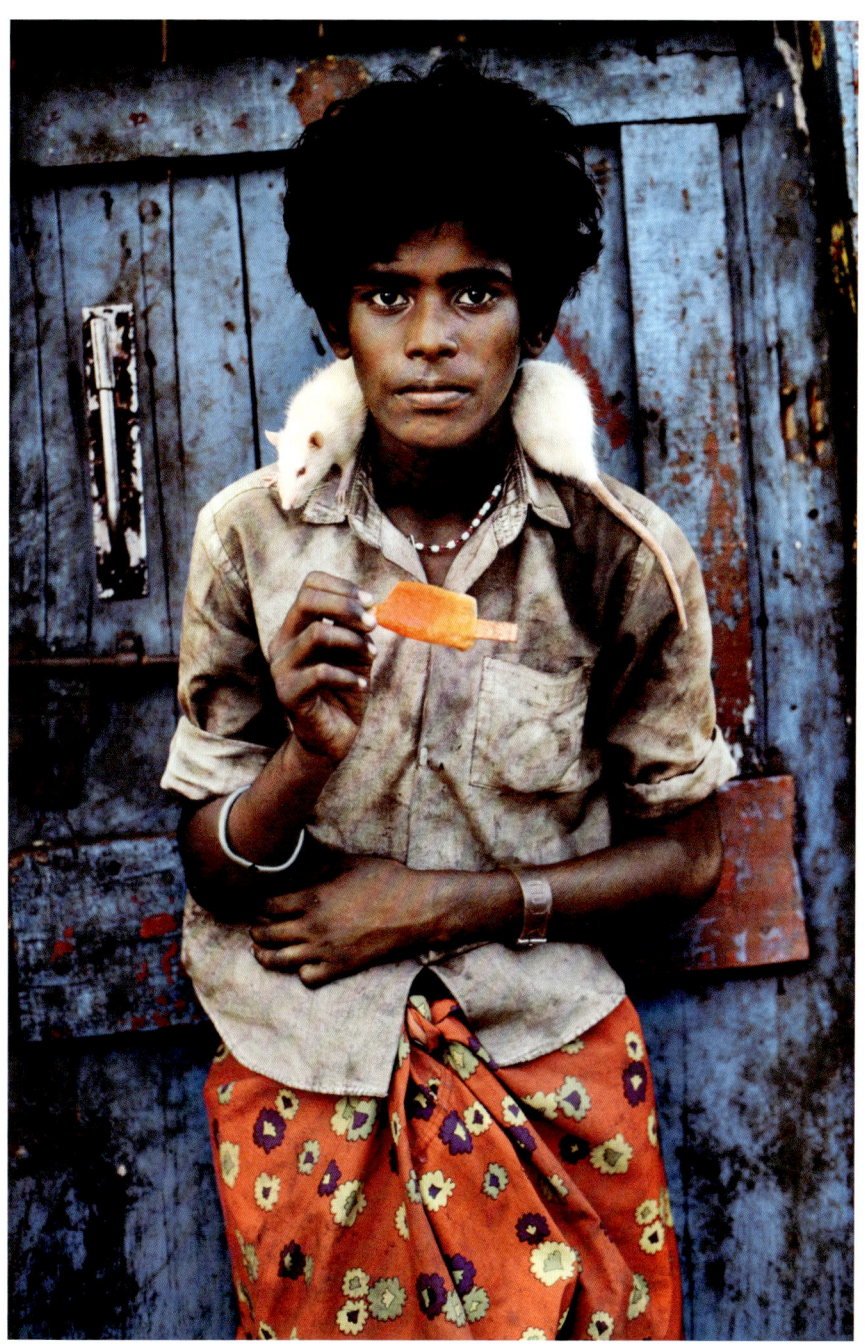

CHENNAI, INDIA, 1996

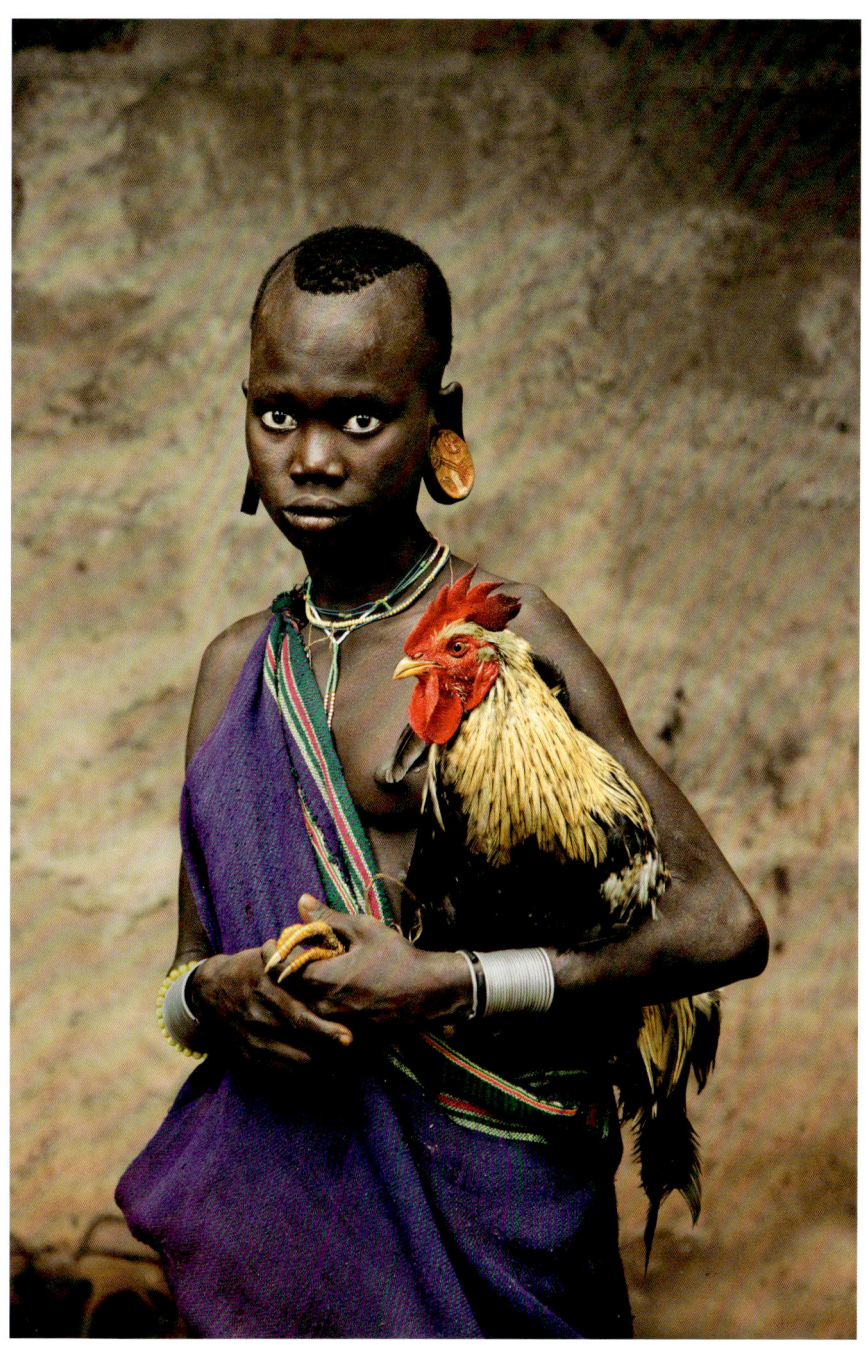

OMO VALLEY, ETHIOPIA, 2013

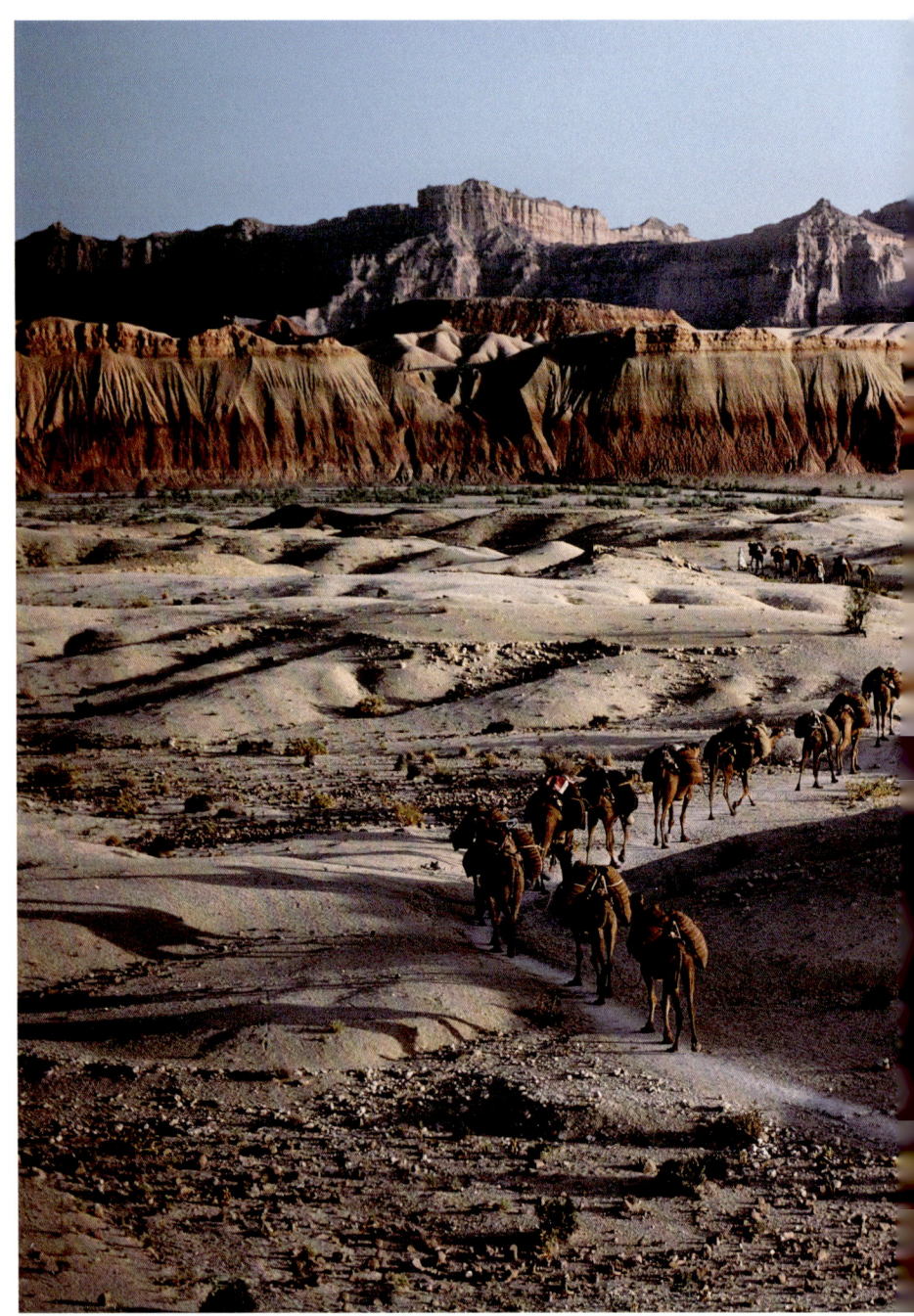

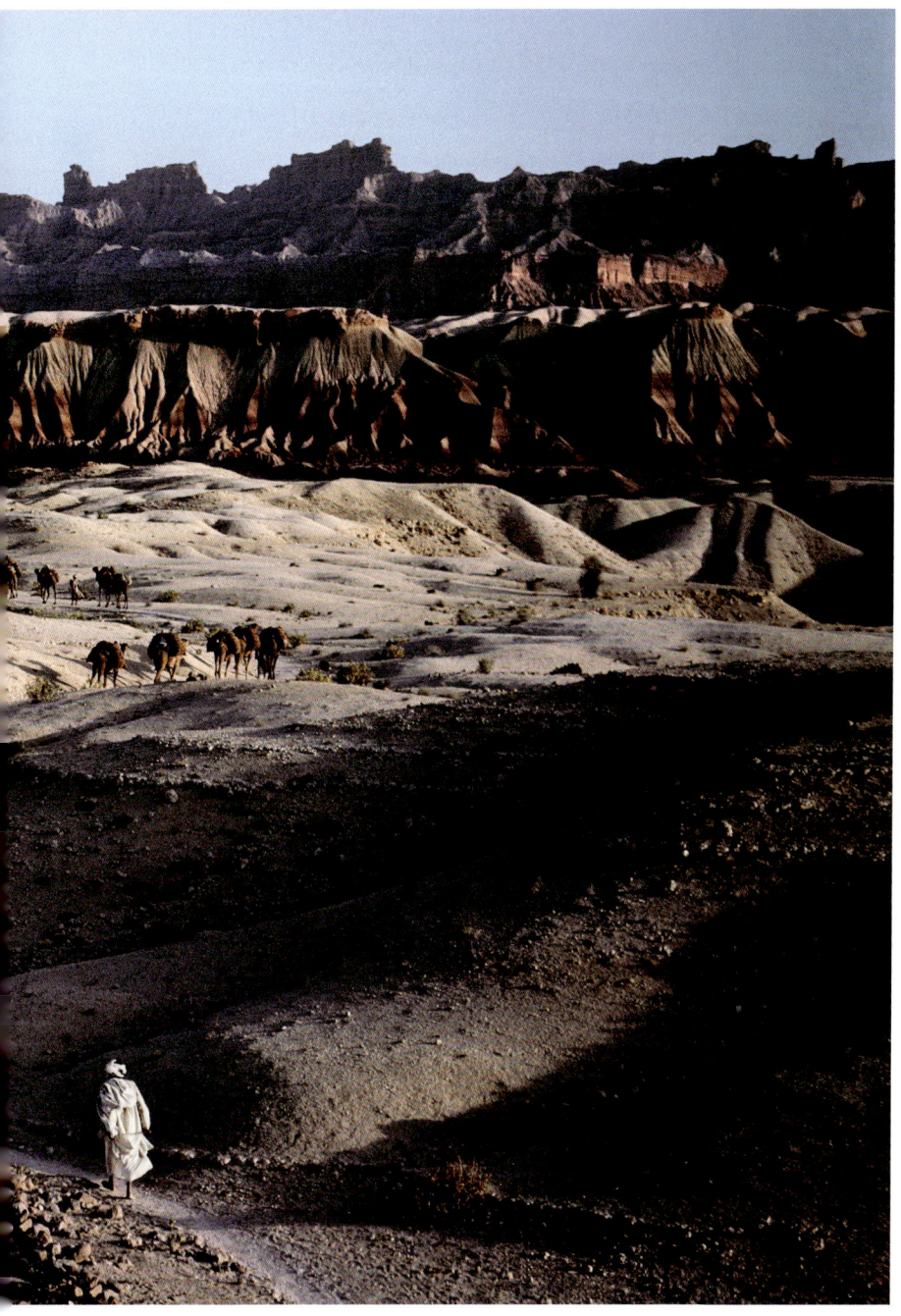

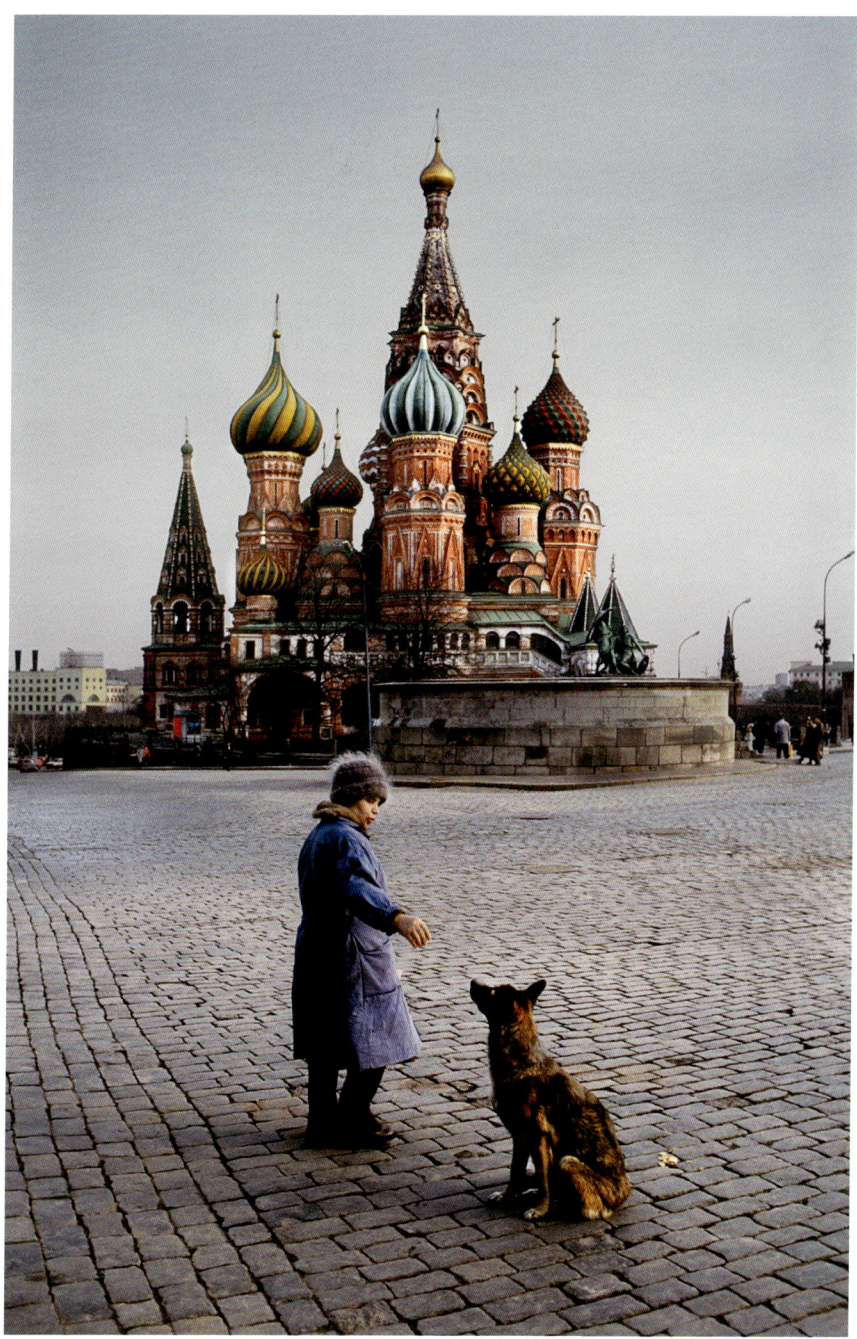

MOSCOW, RUSSIA, 1993

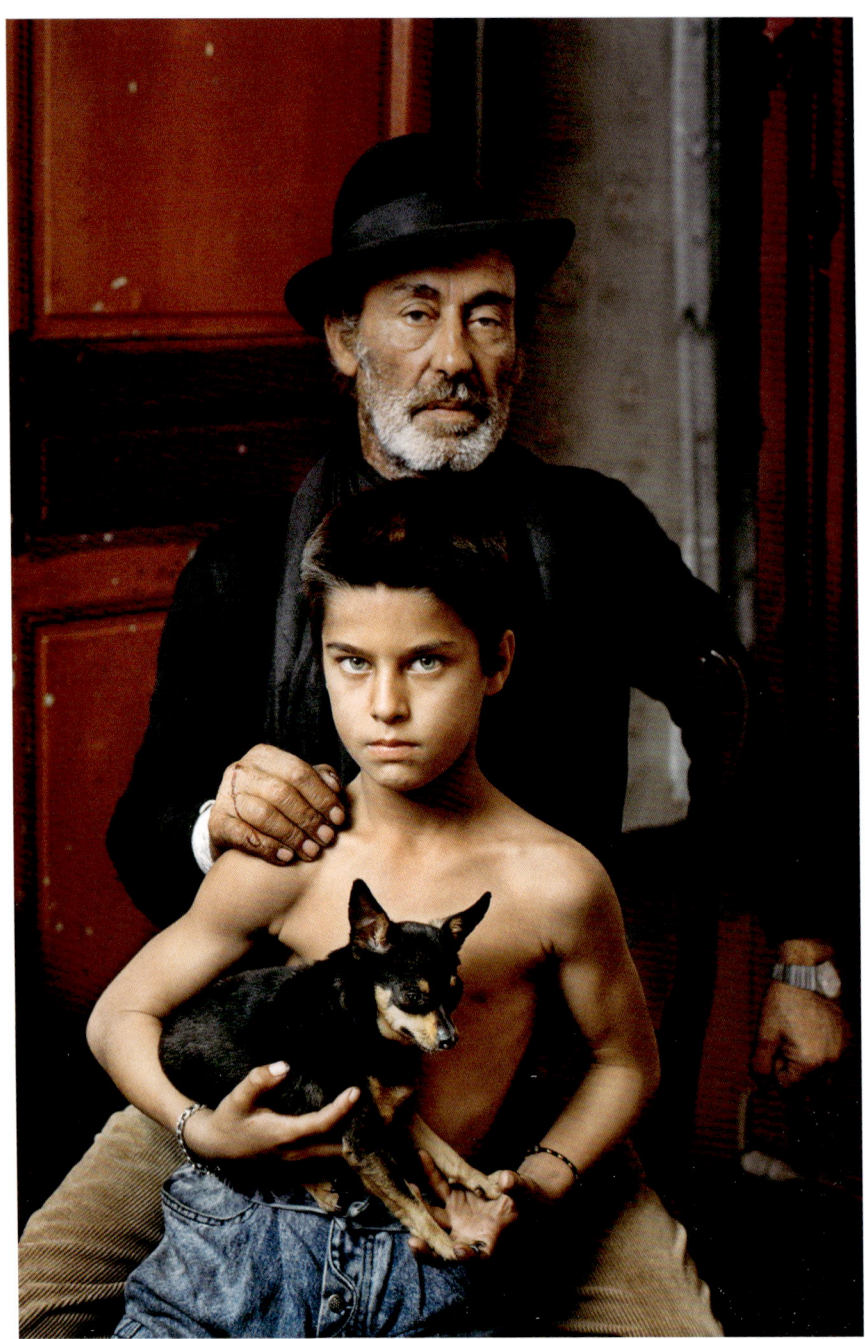

102   MARSEILLE, FRANCE, 1989

"We can judge the heart of a man by his treatment of animals."

IMMANUEL KANT

PAGES 106-107 Porbandar, India, 1983. This pet dog was trying to escape the monsoon floodwaters after his owner let him outside. After realizing he had nowhere to go, a bark signaled the homeowner to let him back inside.

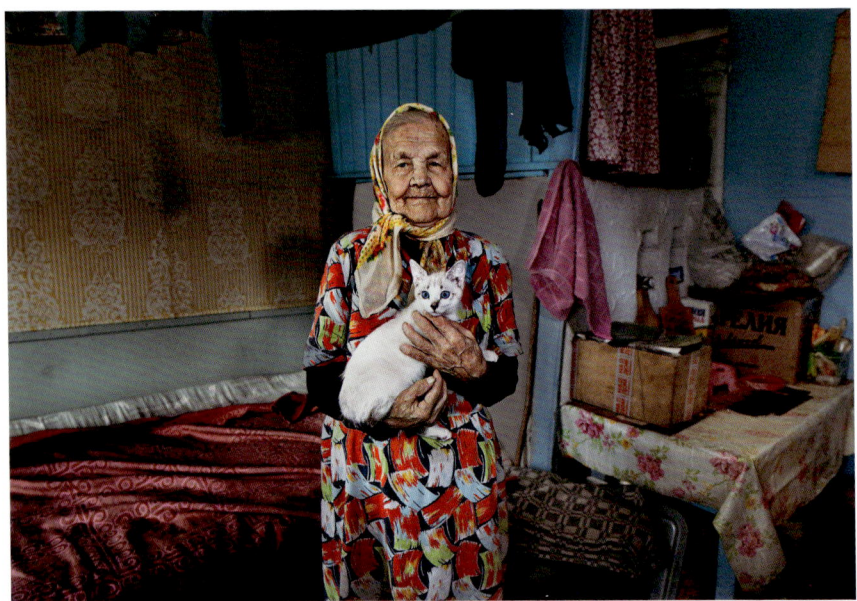

PAGES 110-111 Kabul, Afghanistan, 1995. Lying between two hills next to the Kabul River, the Kabul zoo was often on the front lines during the civil war in the 1990s. Many animals were killed during the shelling or starved to death when there was little interest in preserving the unique animals and plants native to Afghanistan. This fighter sits on a preserved tiger.

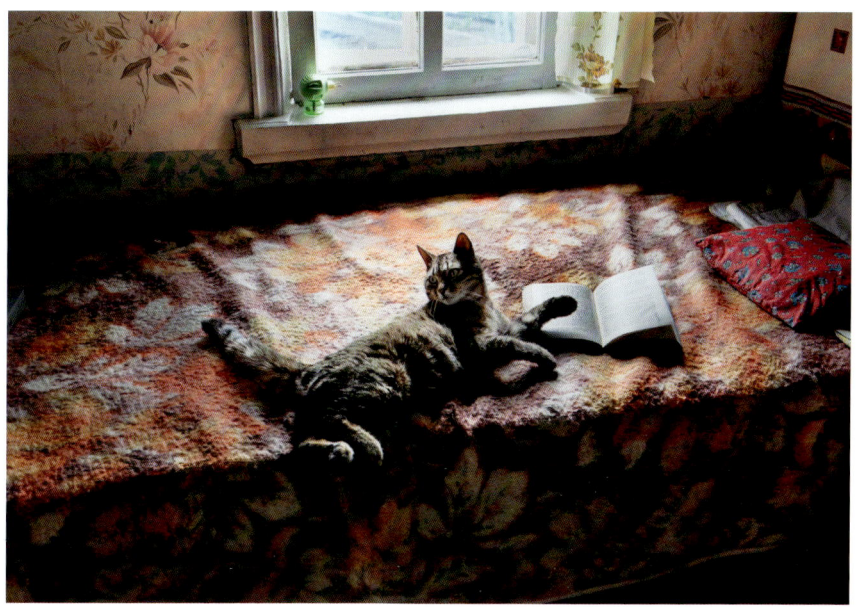

KARELIA, RUSSIA, 2012

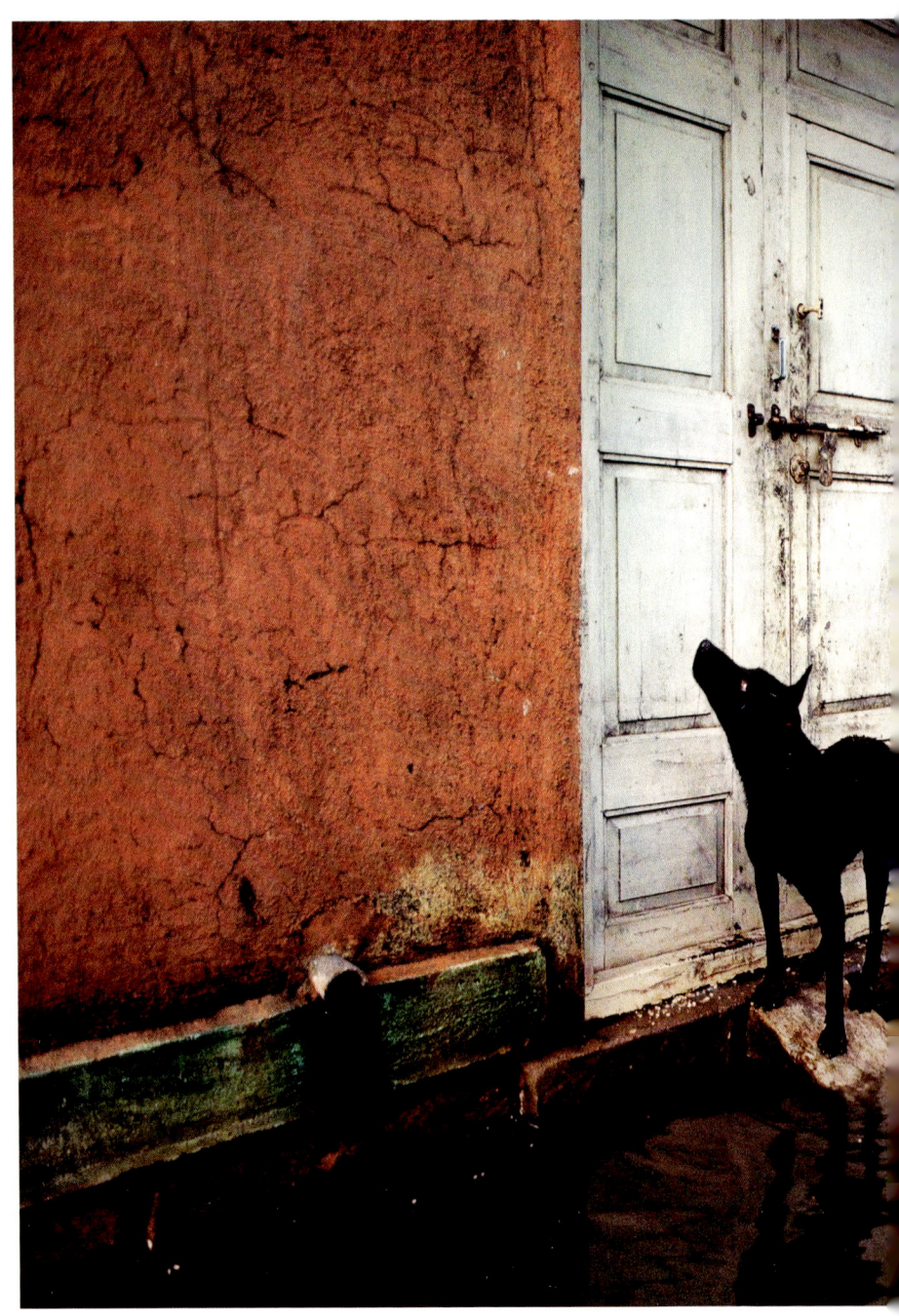

106   PORBANDAR, INDIA, 1983

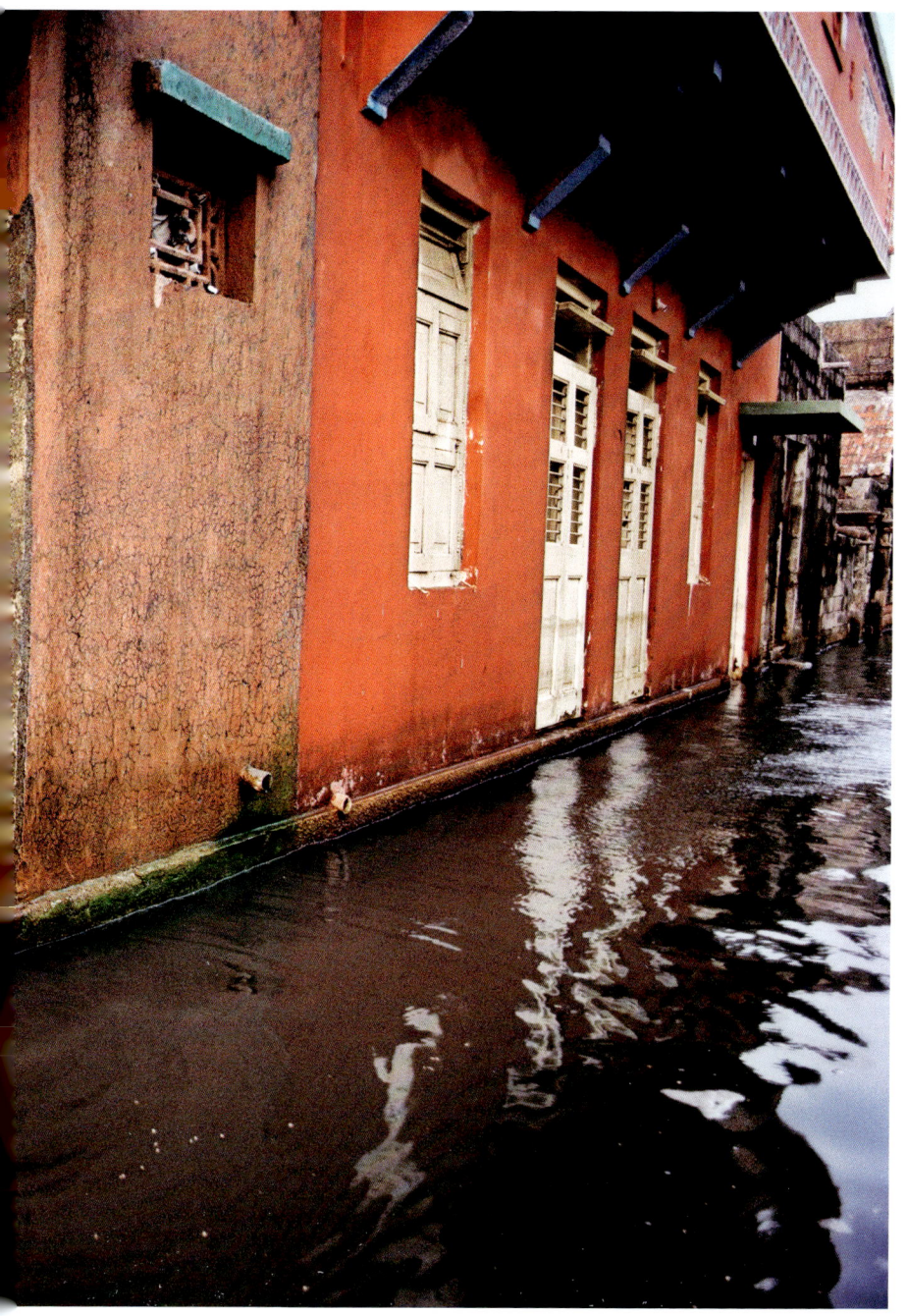

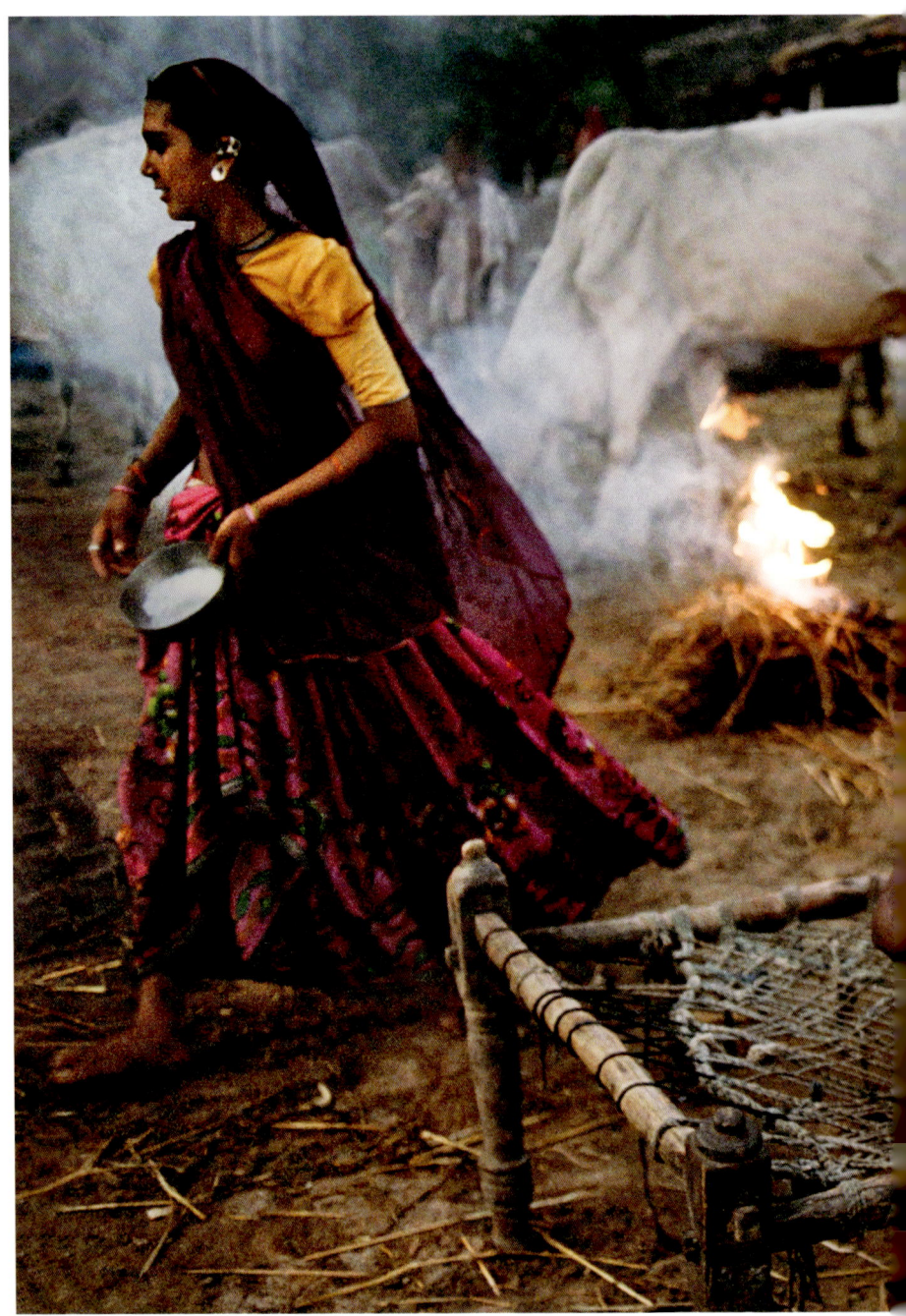

108   GUJARAT, INDIA, 1996

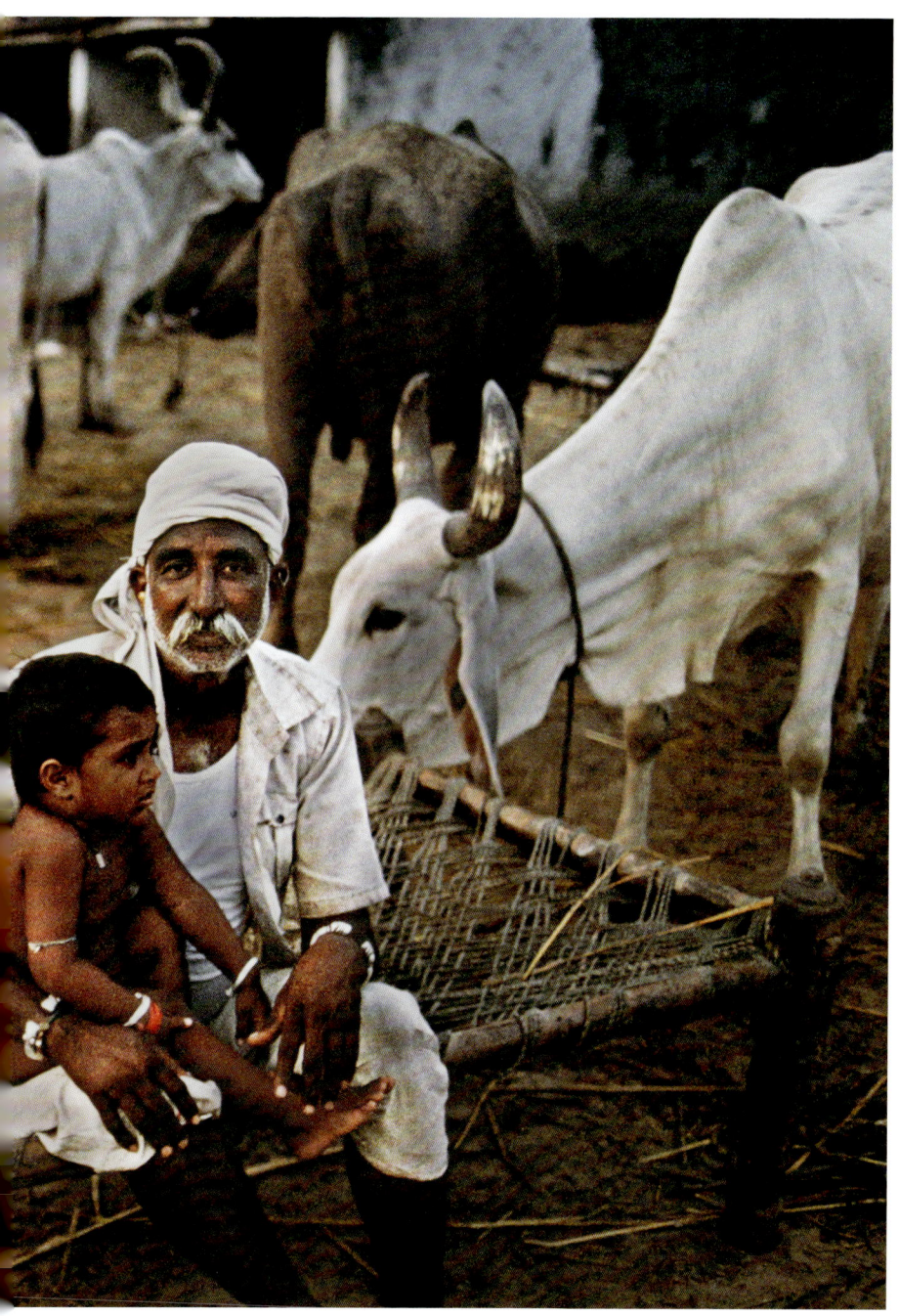

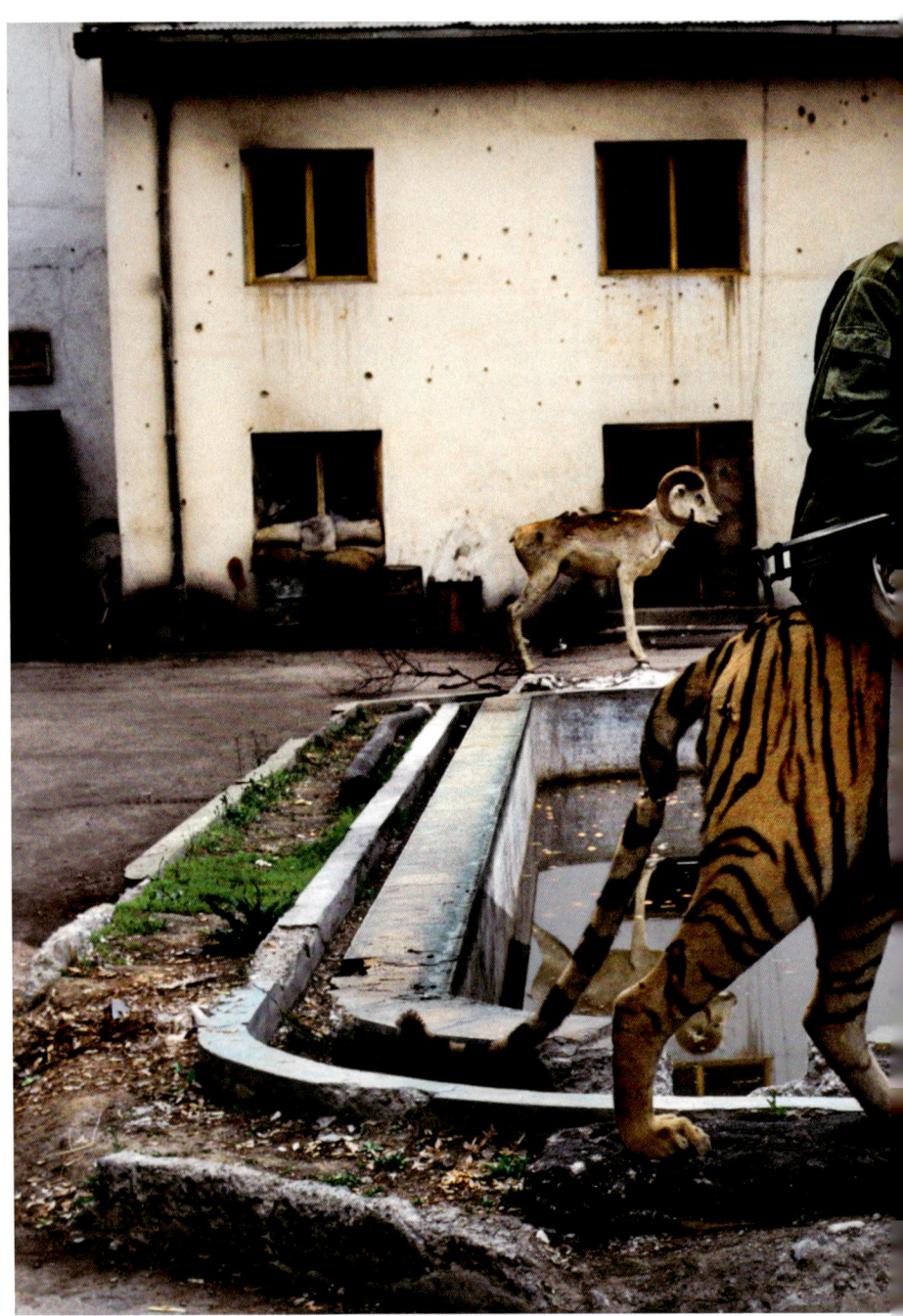

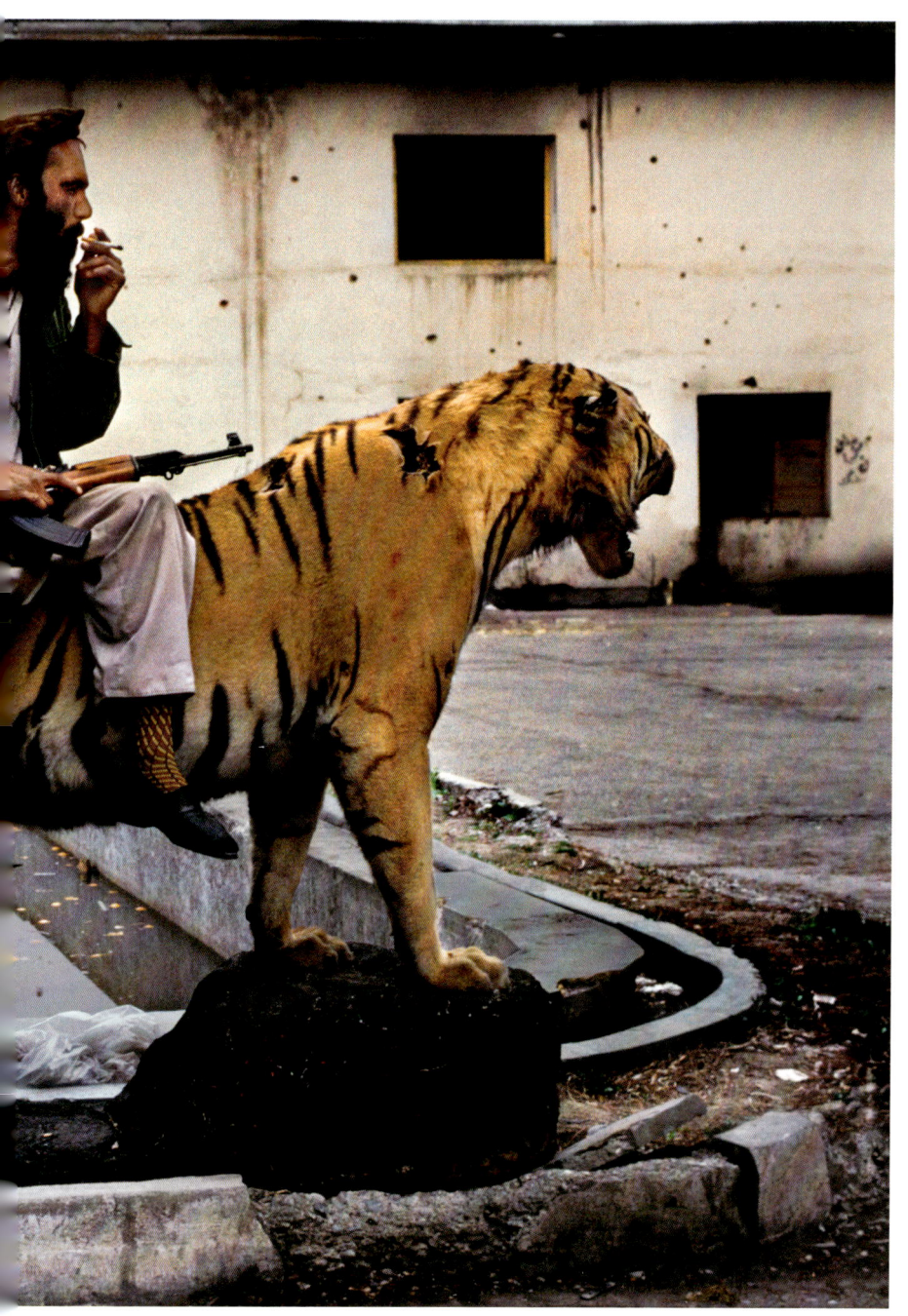

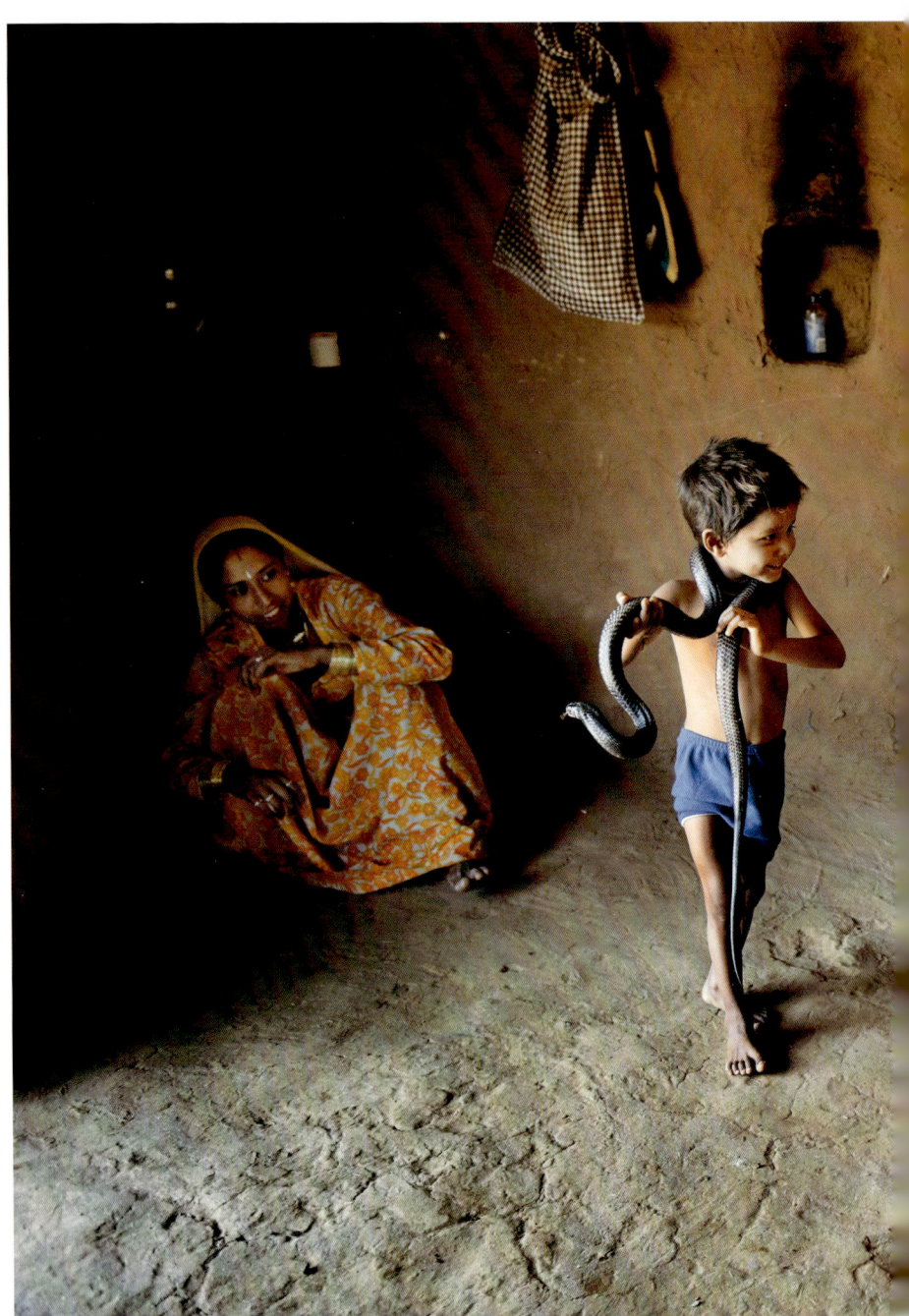

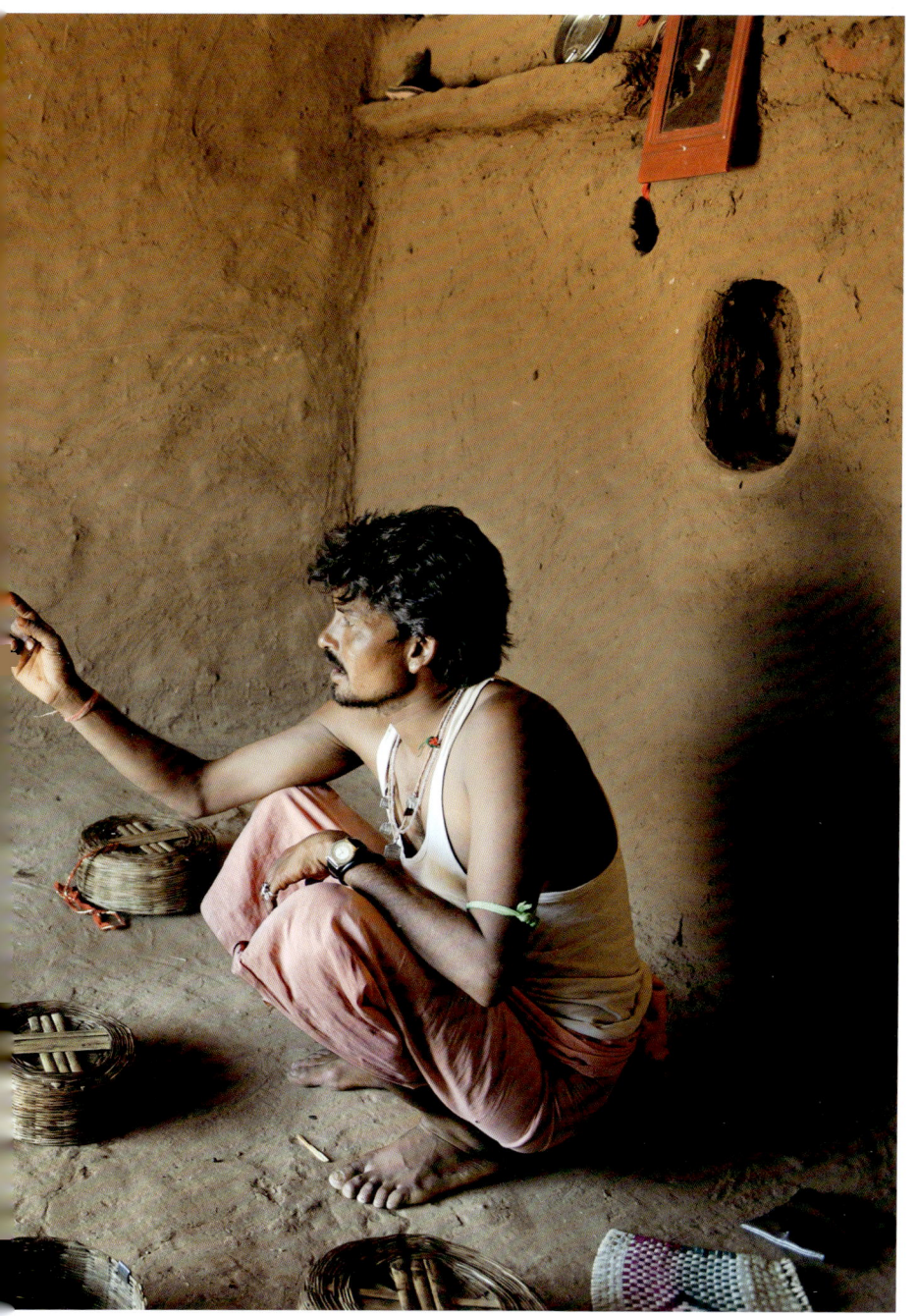

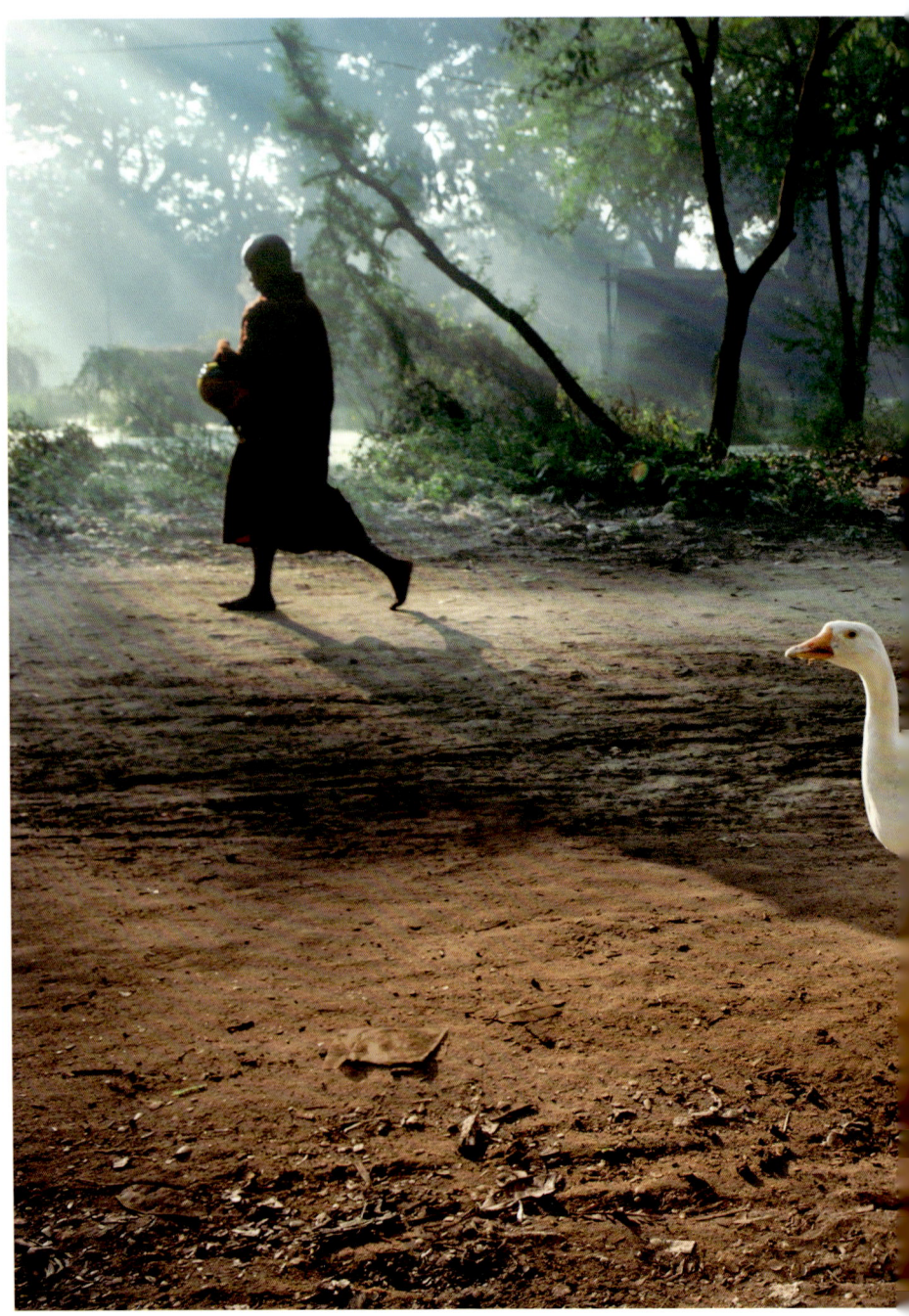

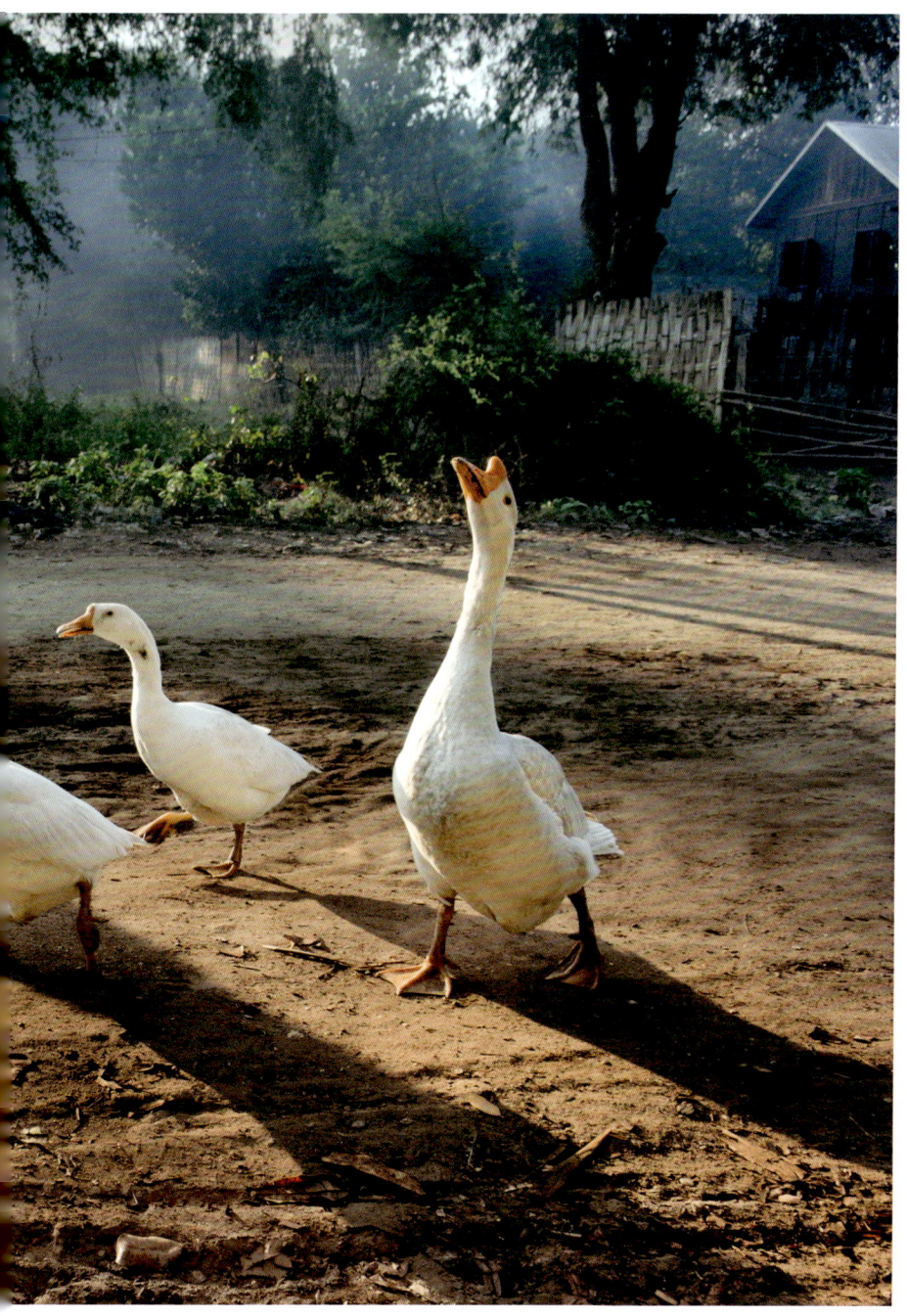

PAGES 112-113 Rajasthan, India, 2009. This family is part of a nomadic caste called the Vadi, which has a long tradition of snake handling. They use techniques that have been passed down through generations. Children begin training at a young age to handle many different kinds of snakes, some harmless, others venomous.

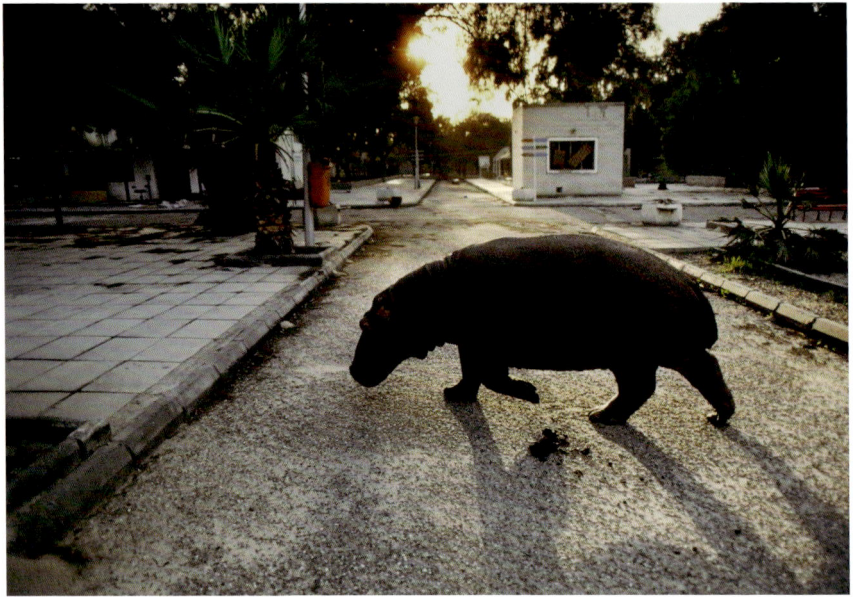

This baby hippo suffering from a skin infection from a stagnant pool was wandering around looking for food.

PAGES 118-119 Al Ahmadi, Kuwait, 1991. I was sitting on the hood of my car, about 30 feet from the fire as we were driving through the desert. I saw the camels come into view and immediately visualized the image. The smoke was black, and there was a little space where you could see the fire; I followed the camels until they walked past and were silhouetted.

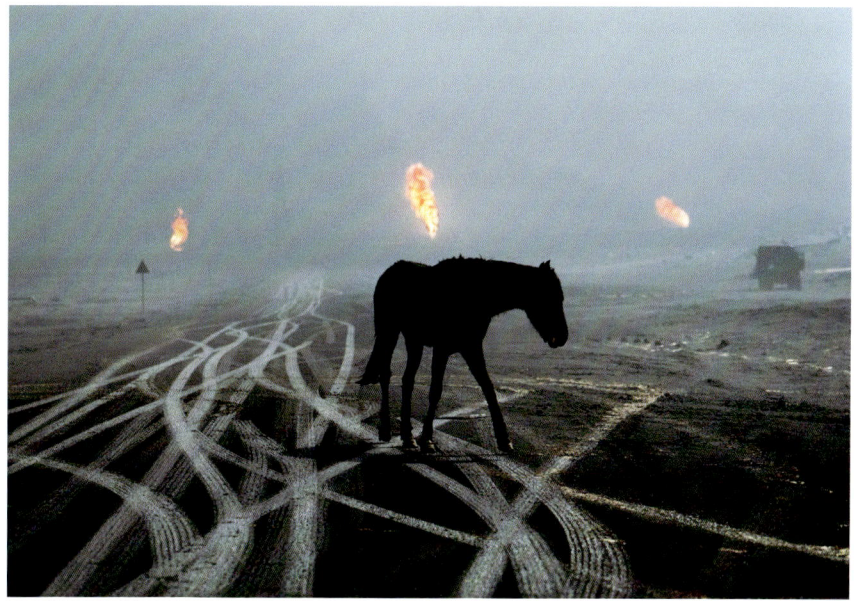

As we drove into the burning oil fields, it was as dark as night. The ground was completely blackened with oil. This horse was one of the many animals abandoned during the fighting.

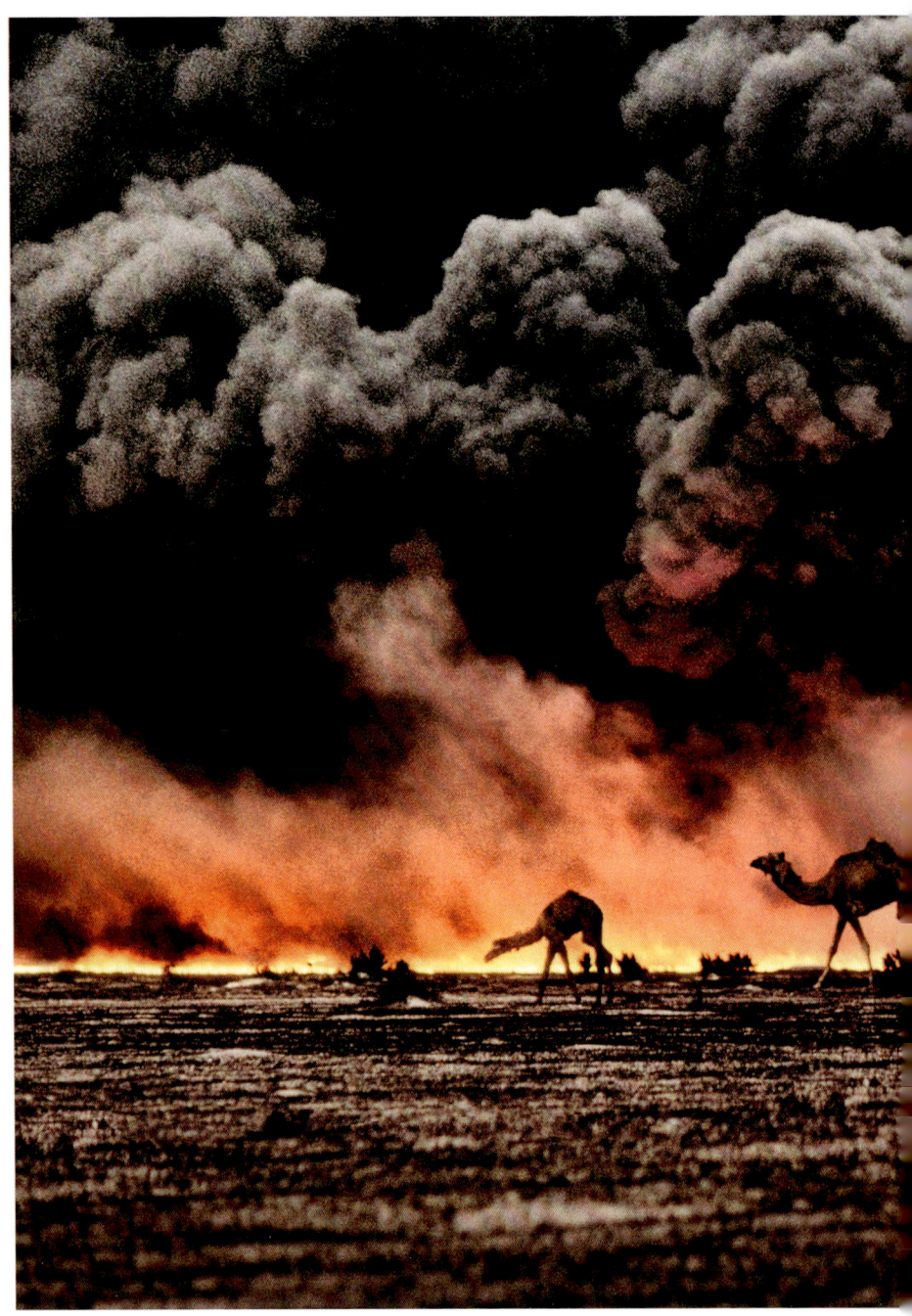

118   AL AHMADI, KUWAIT, 1991

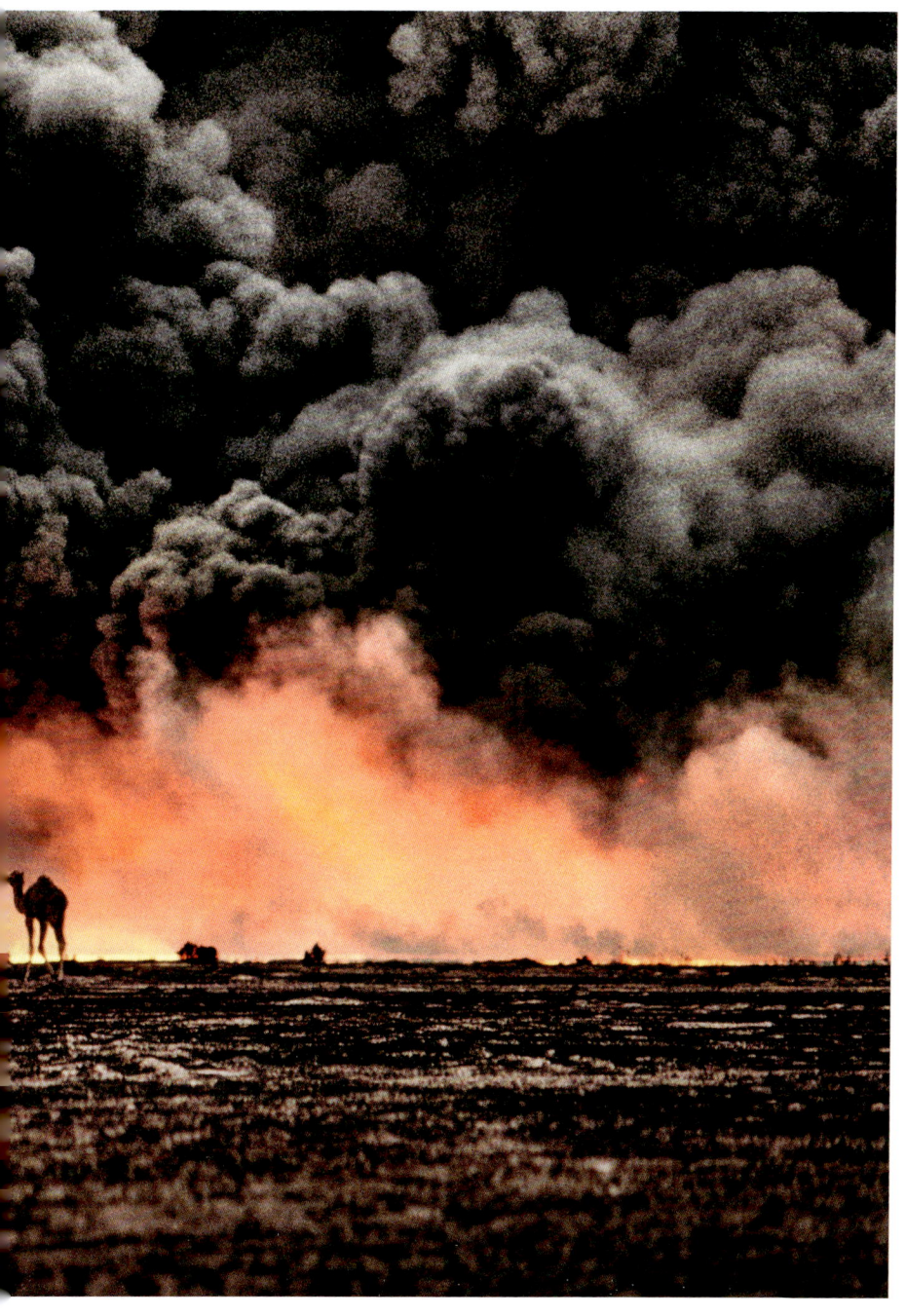

119

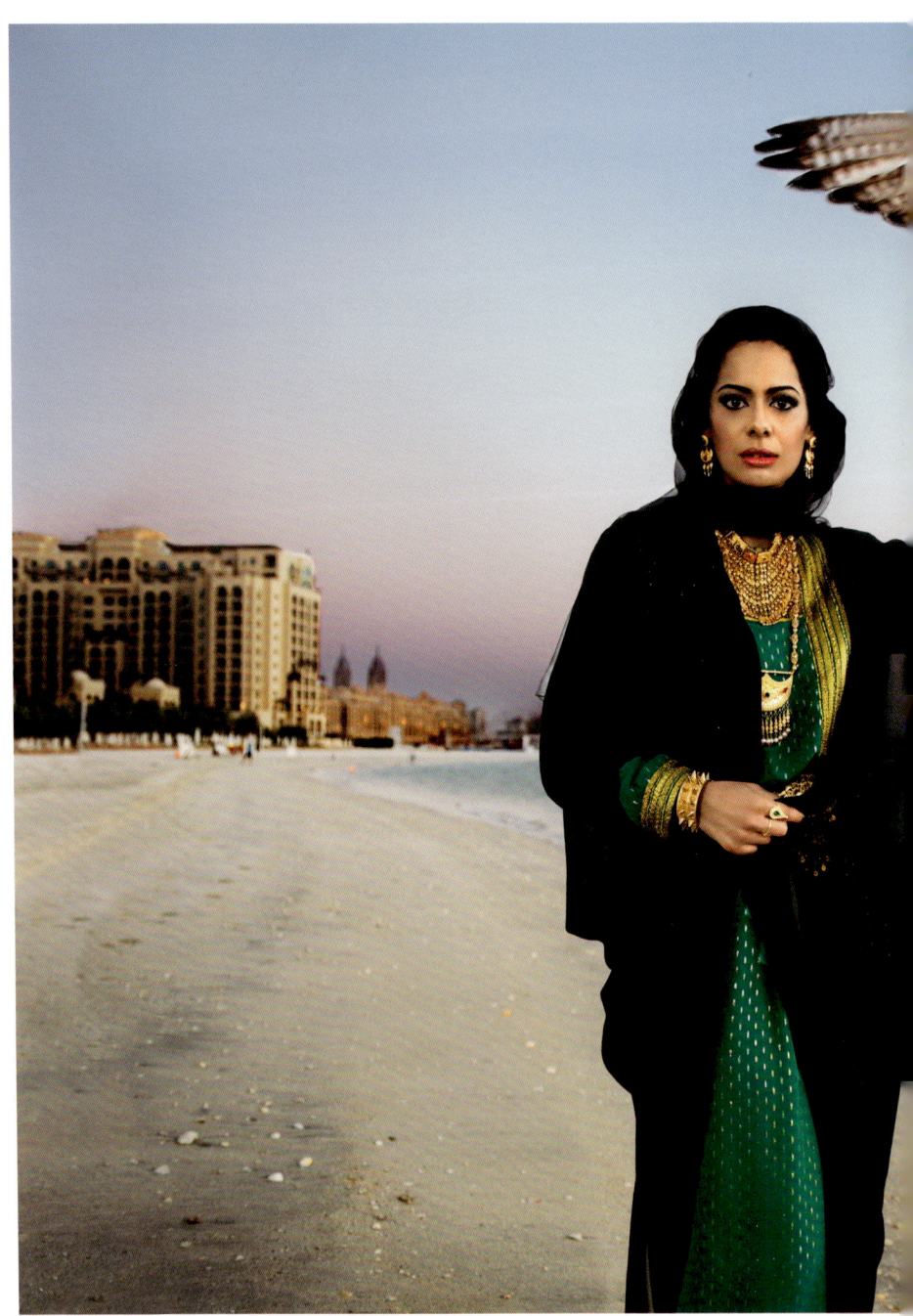

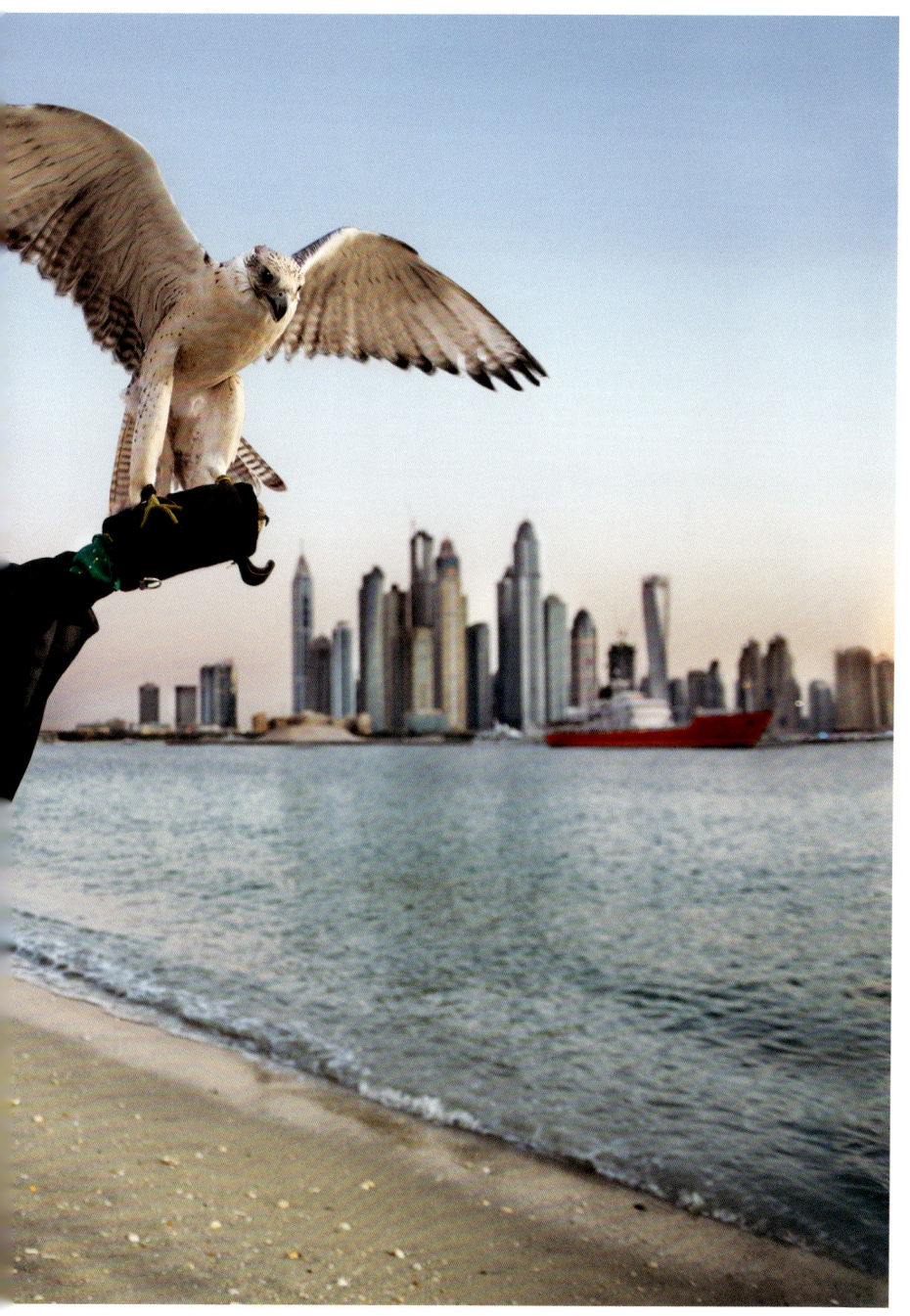

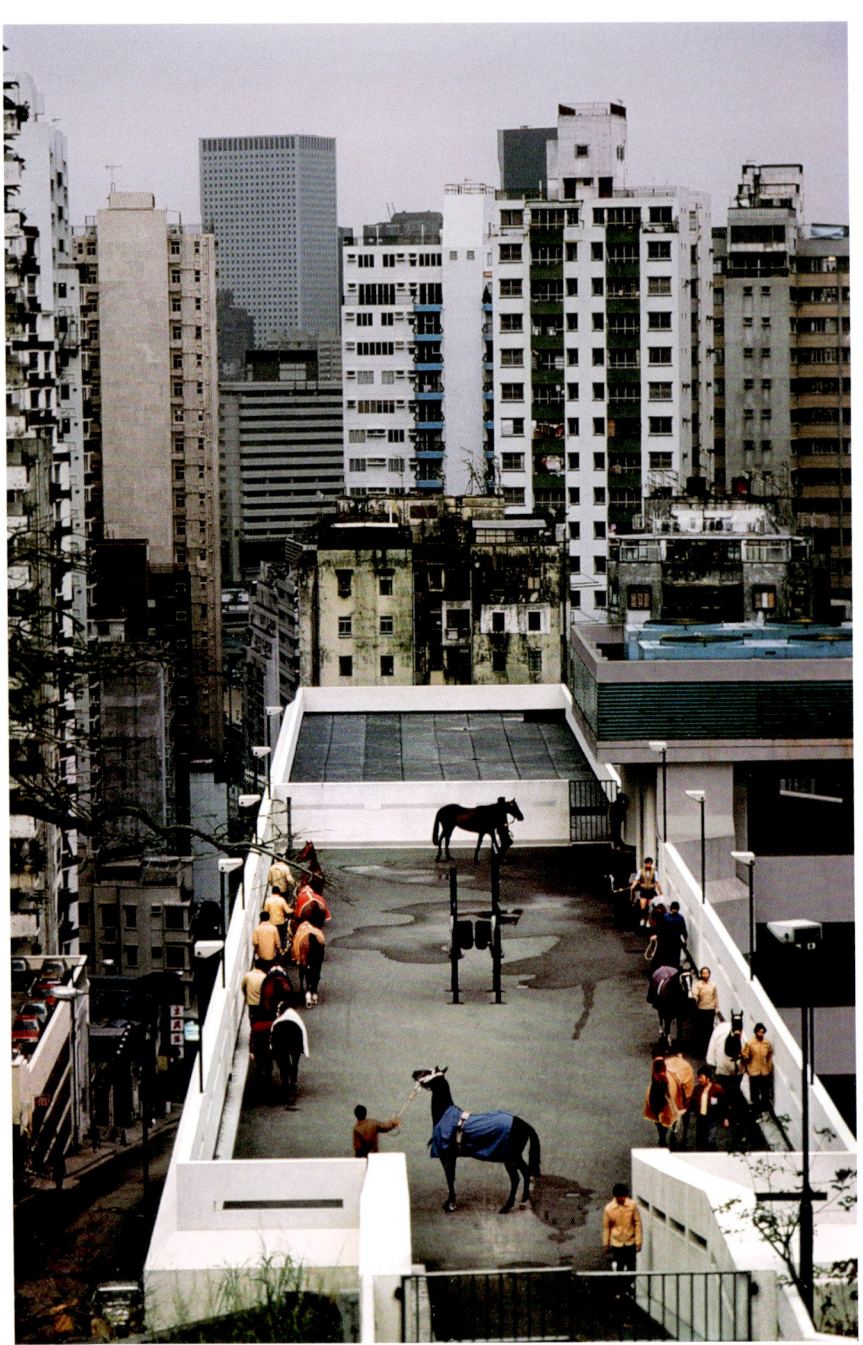

122   HONG KONG, CHINA, 1998

"When I bestride him, I soar, I am a hawk: he trots the air; the earth sings when he touches it; the basest horn of his hoof is more musical than the pipe of Hermes."

WILLIAM SHAKESPEARE

Trainers take thoroughbred horses out for exercise atop a building in Hong Kong because it is one of the few places with enough space. The Happy Valley racecourse is near the center of the city. Horse racing has been a fixture in Hong Kong since 1841.

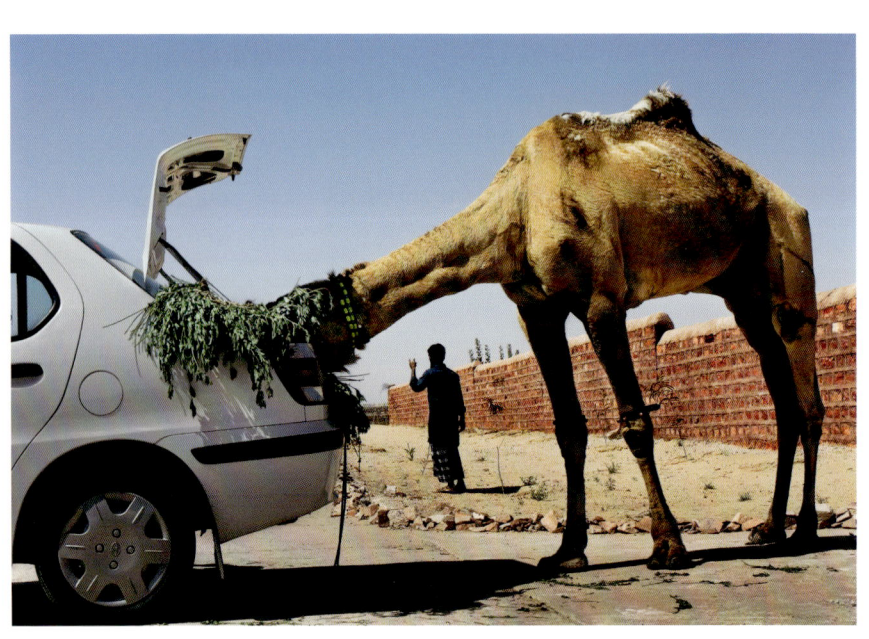

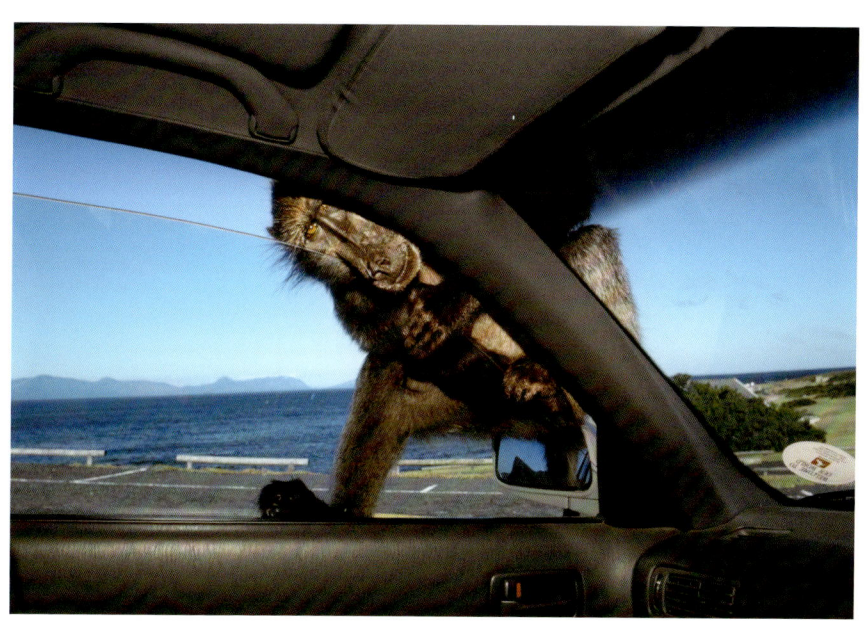

CAPE TOWN, SOUTH AFRICA, 1996

"You think dogs will not be in heaven?
I tell you, they will be there long before
any of us."

ROBERT LOUIS STEVENSON

Fred Hayman was known as the Godfather of Rodeo Drive.
He is photographed outside one of his stores with his true love:
his German shepherd.

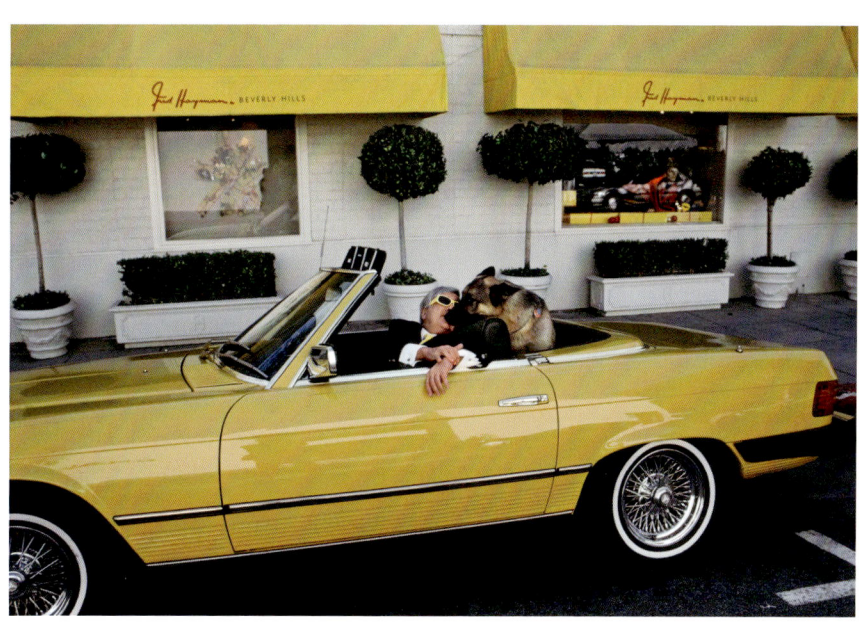

LOS ANGELES, CALIFORNIA, USA, 1991

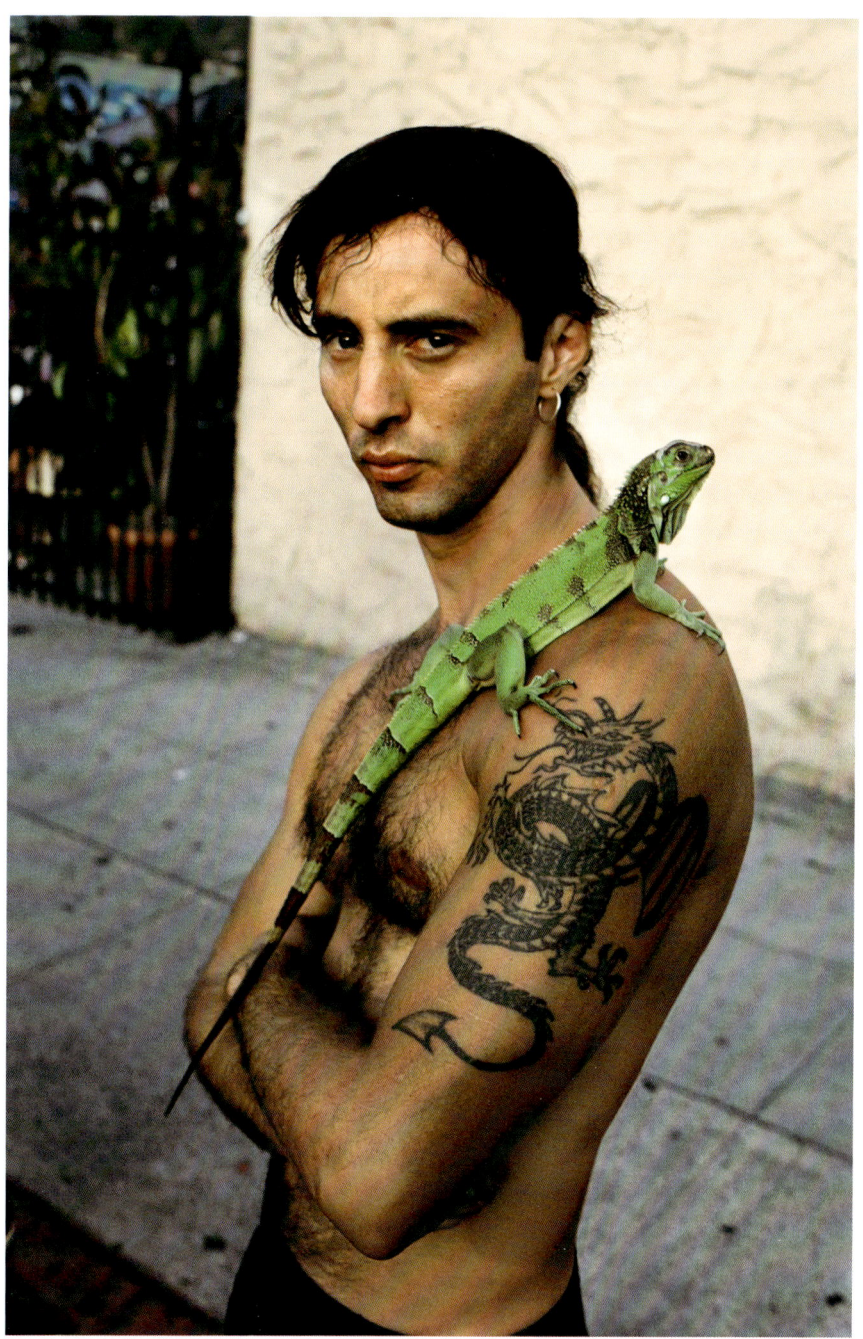

LOS ANGELES, CALIFORNIA, USA, 1991

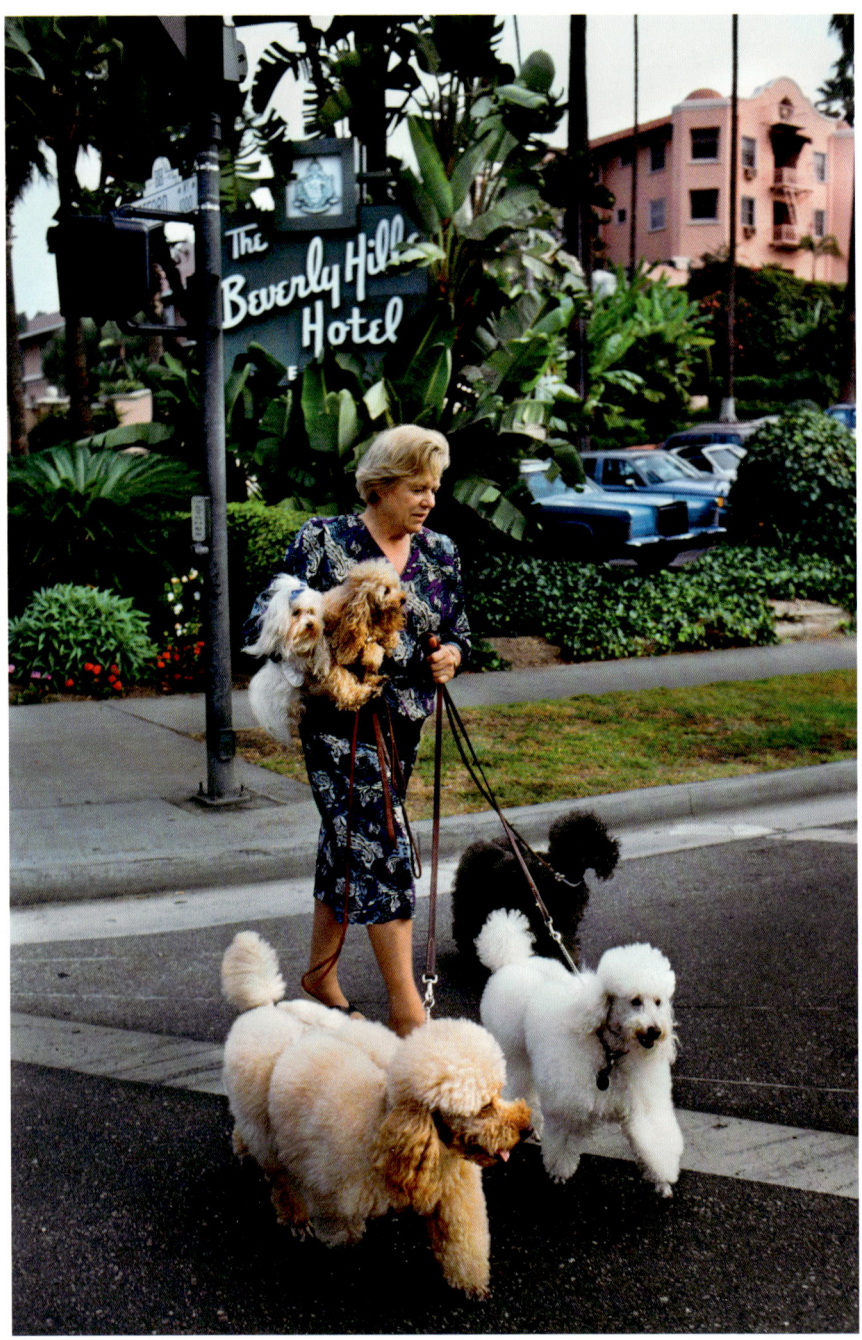

130   LOS ANGELES, CALIFORNIA, USA, 1991

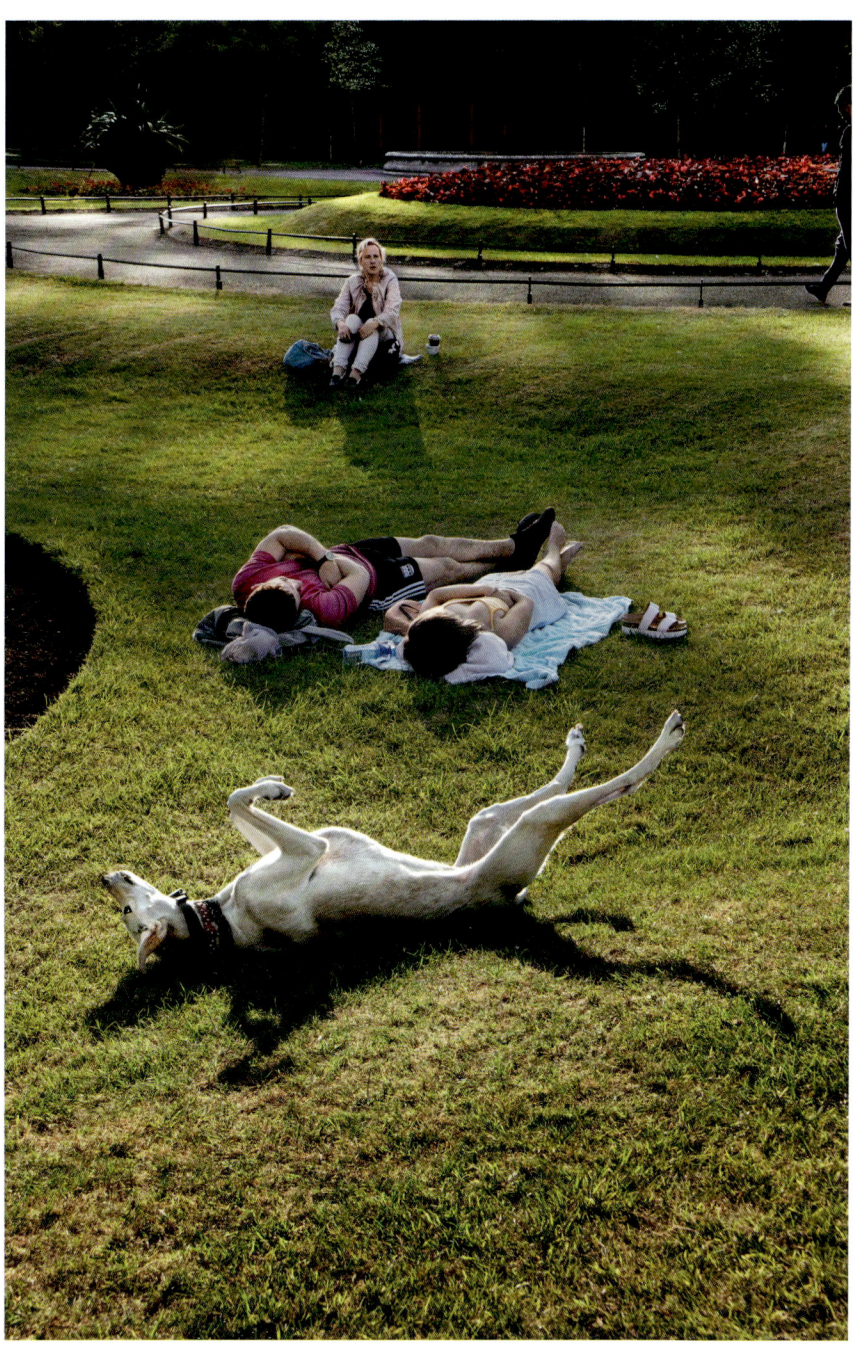

DUBLIN, IRELAND, 2018

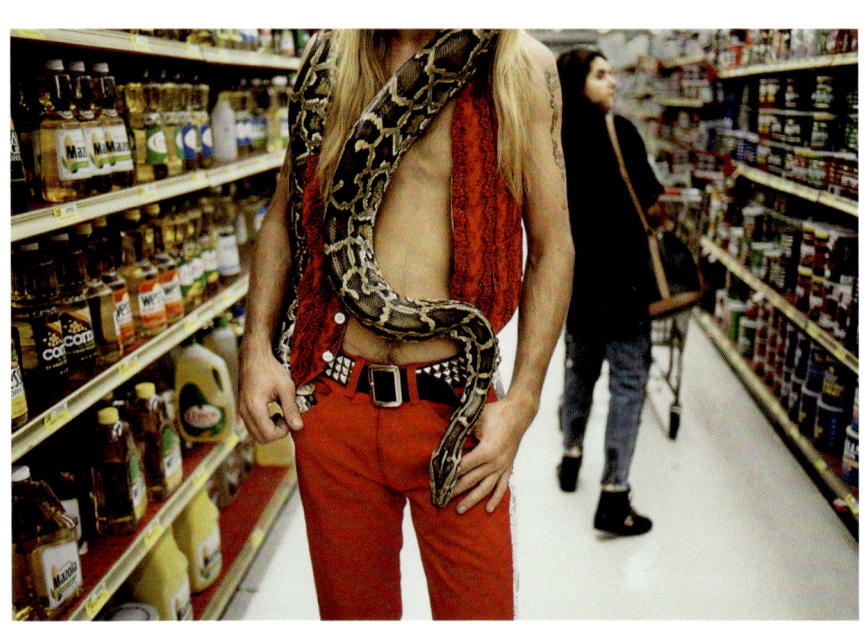

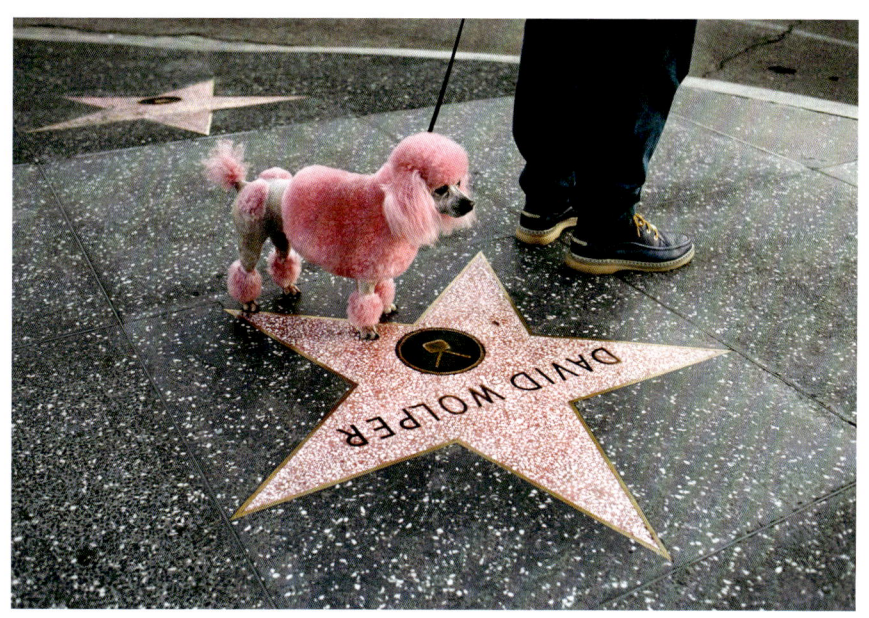

LOS ANGELES, CALIFORNIA, USA, 1991

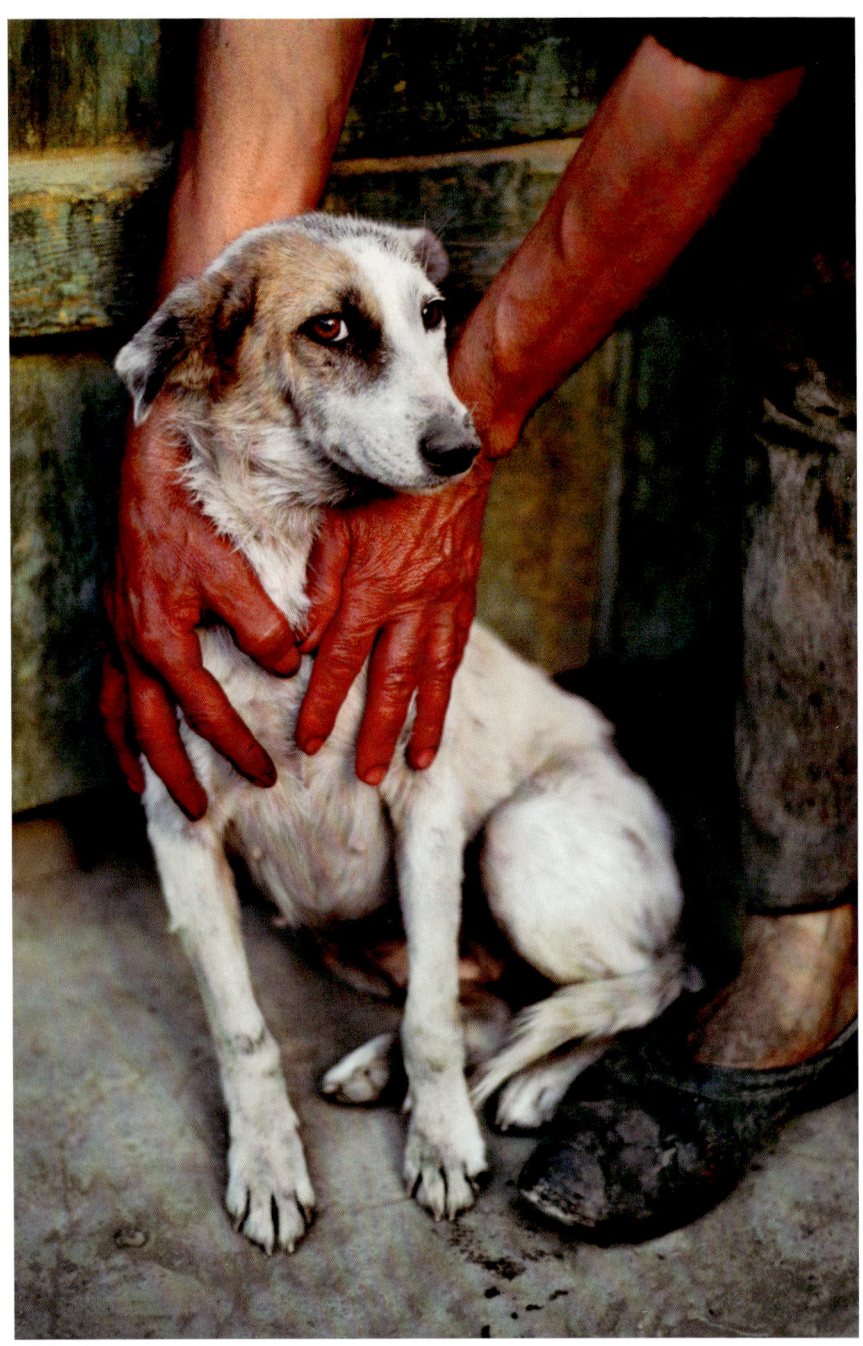

134   KABUL, AFGHANISTAN, 1992

At first glance, this image is jarring because the man's hands look like they're covered in blood, however, he was mixing up a batch of red dye for wool carpet making.

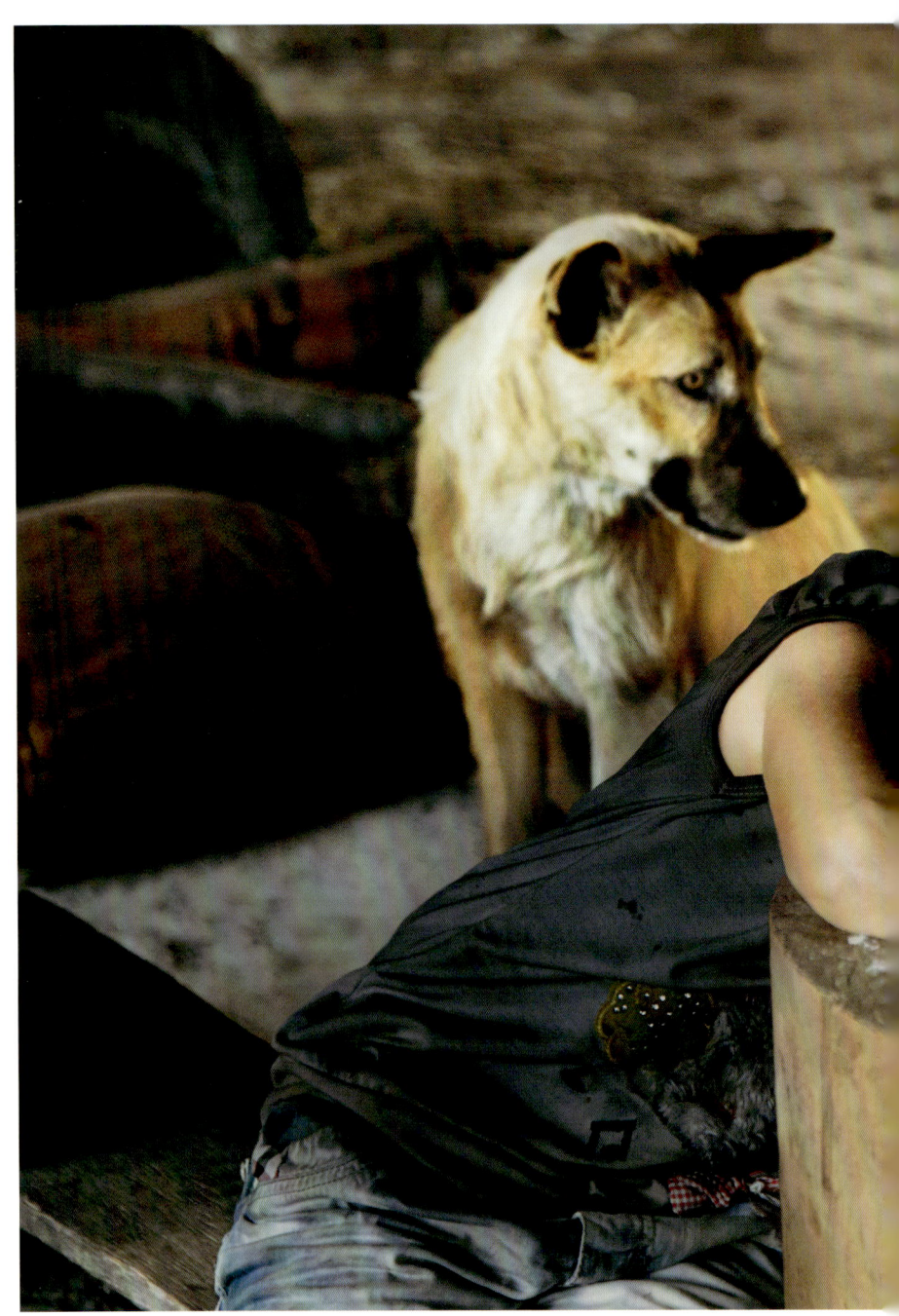

136   ĐẮK LẮK PROVINCE, VIETNAM, 2013

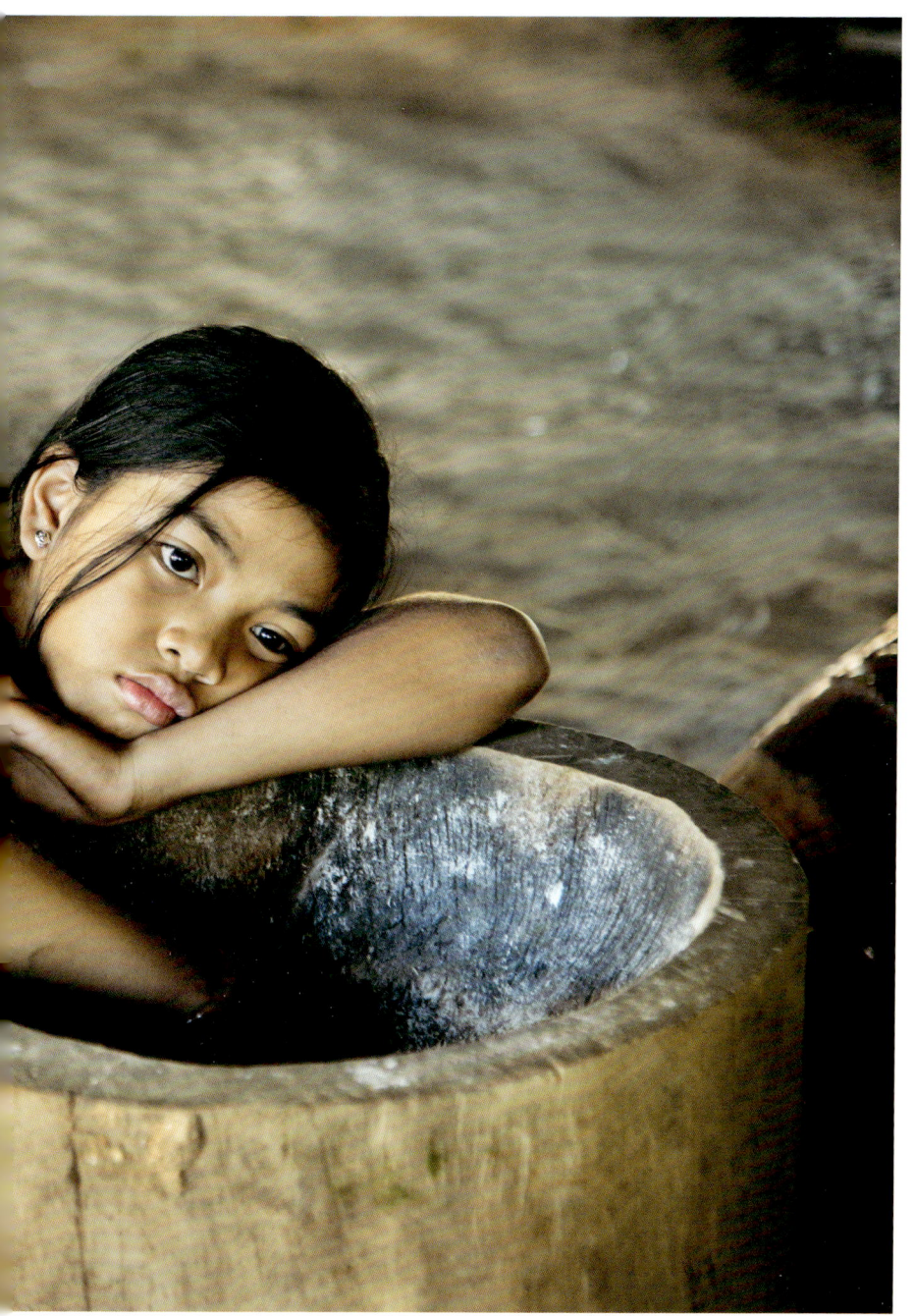

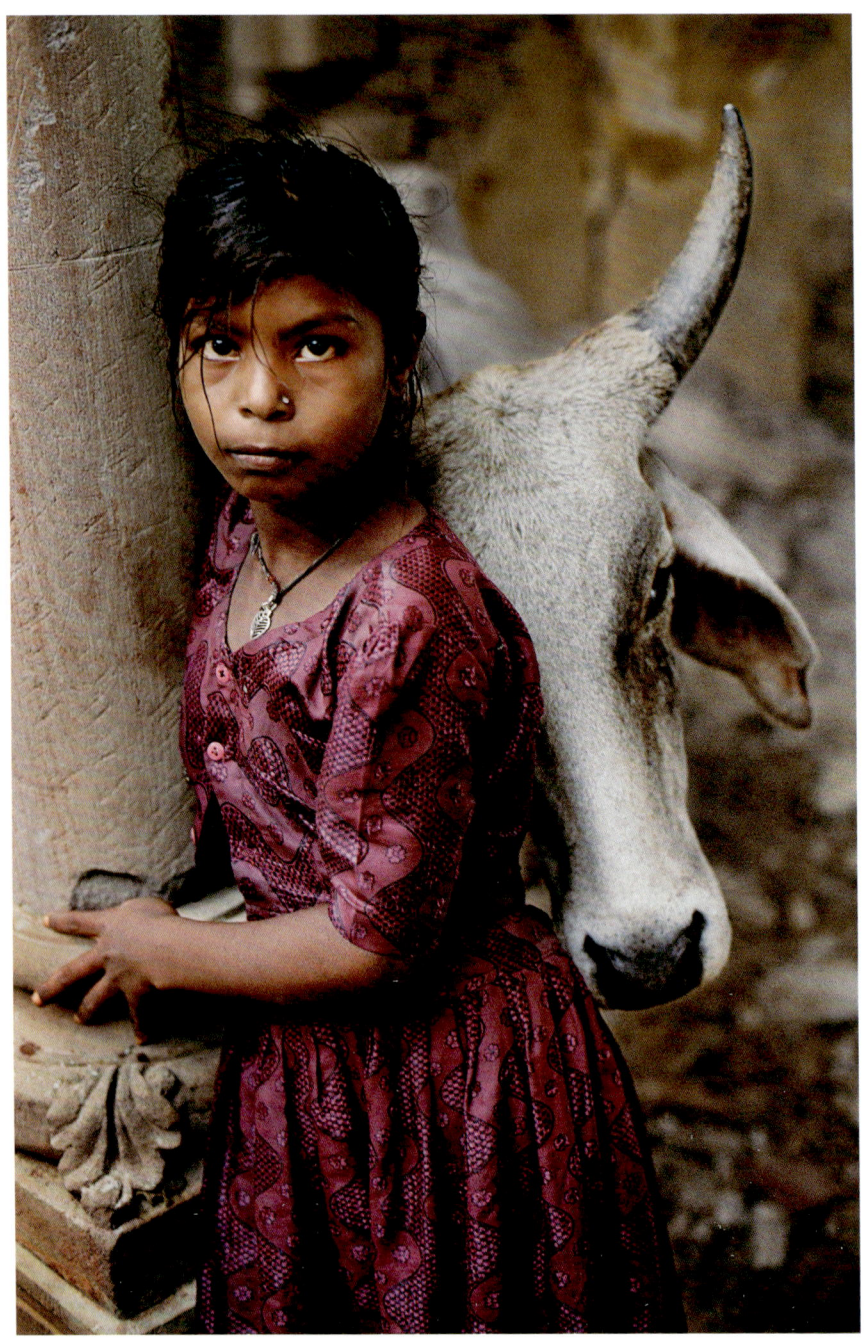

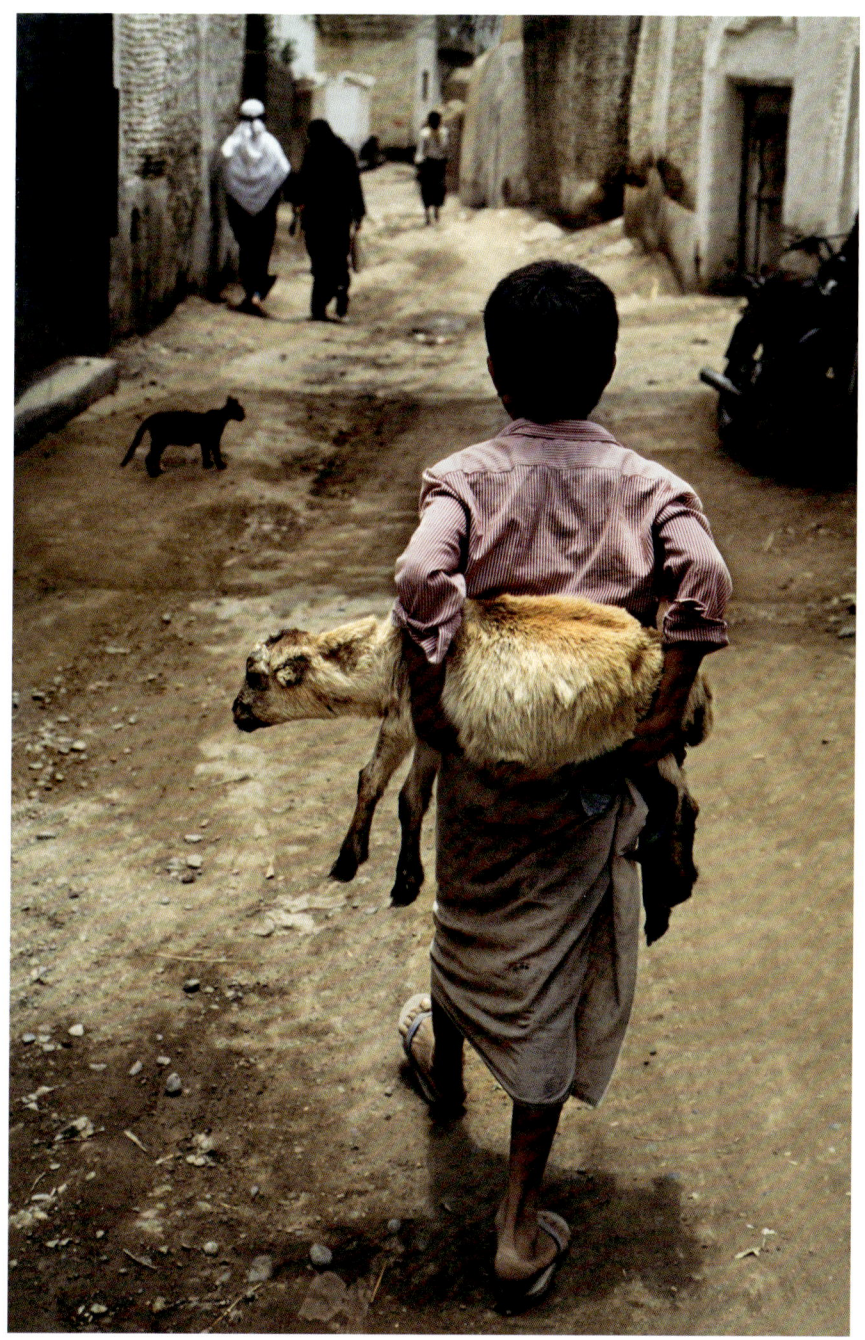

ZABID, YEMEN, 1997

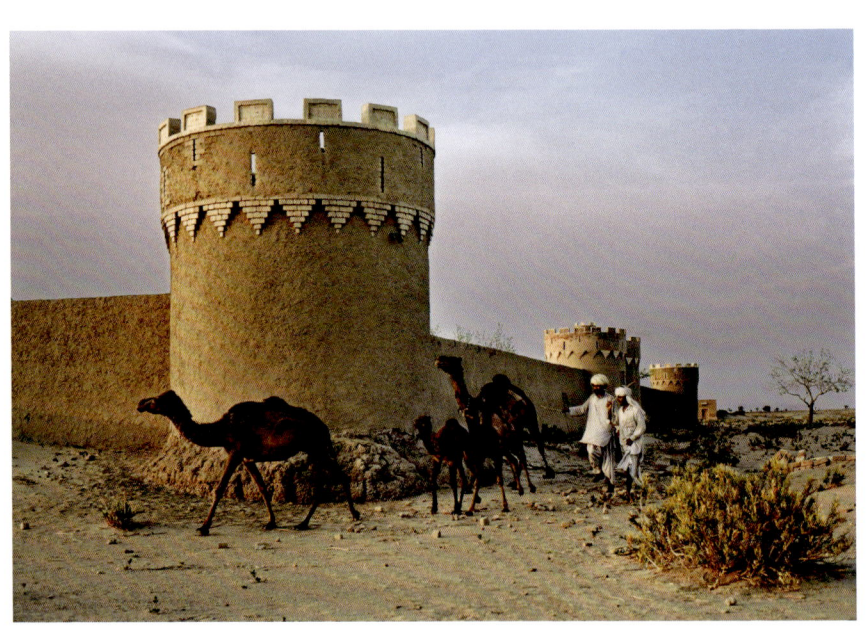

140   BALOCHISTAN, PAKISTAN, 1981

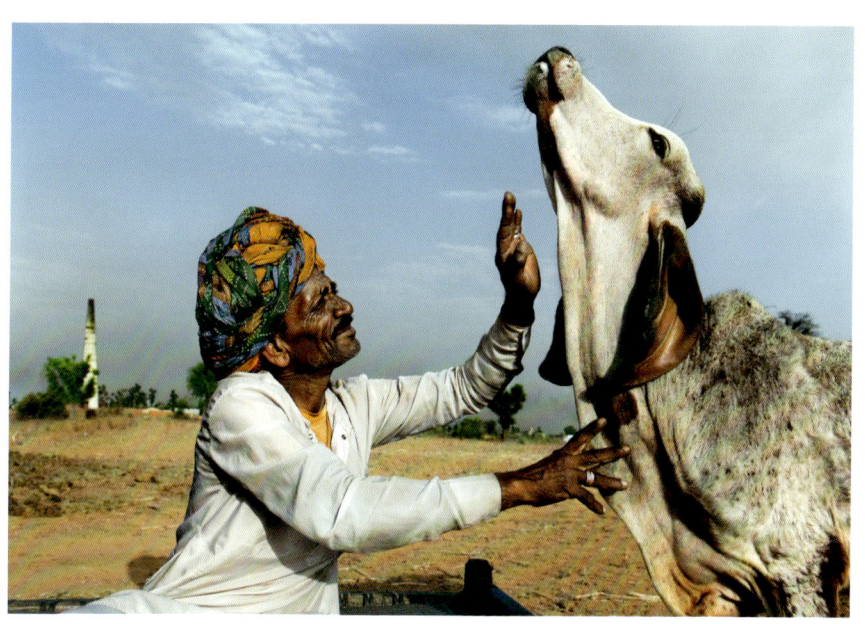

JAIPUR, INDIA, 2008

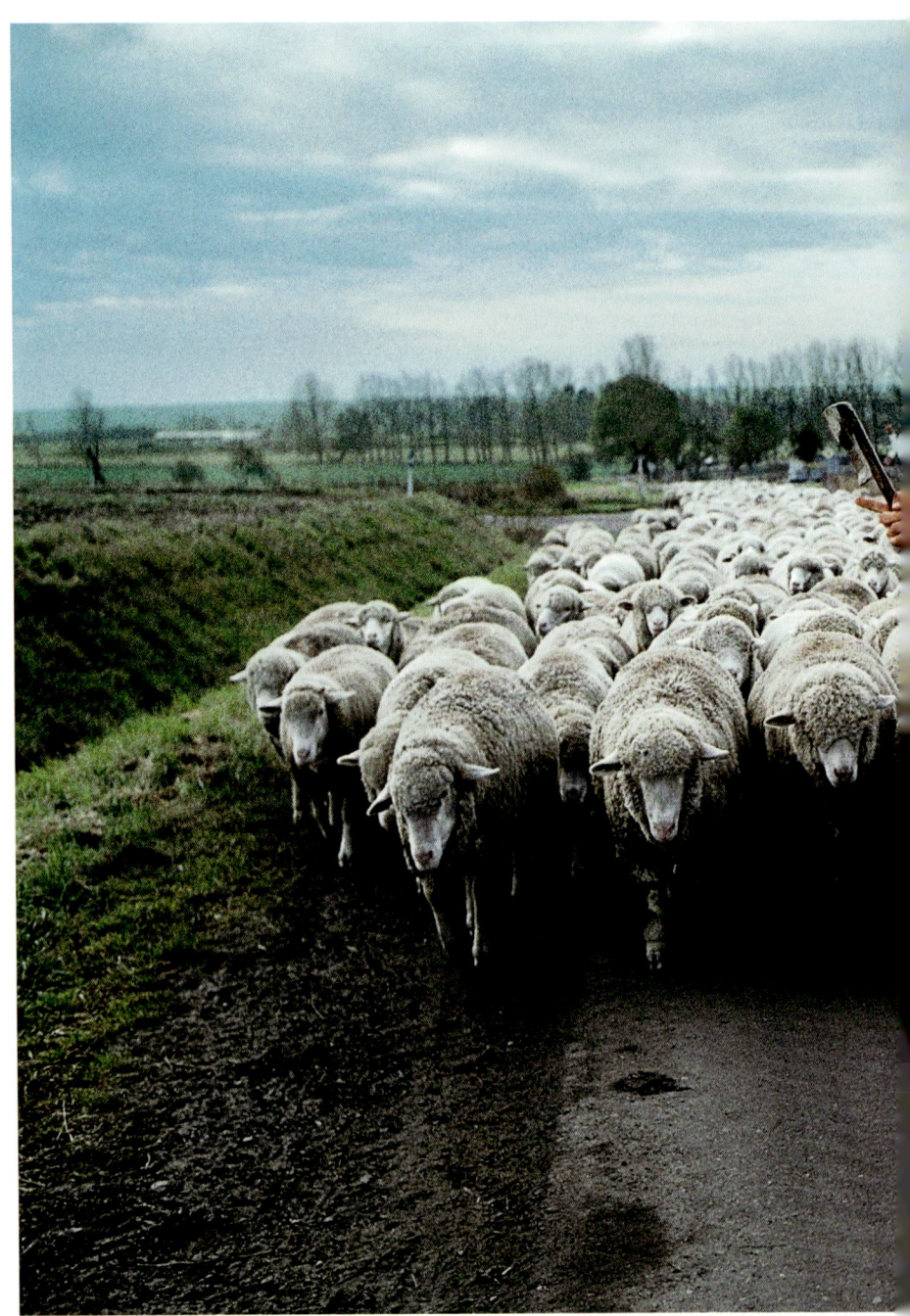

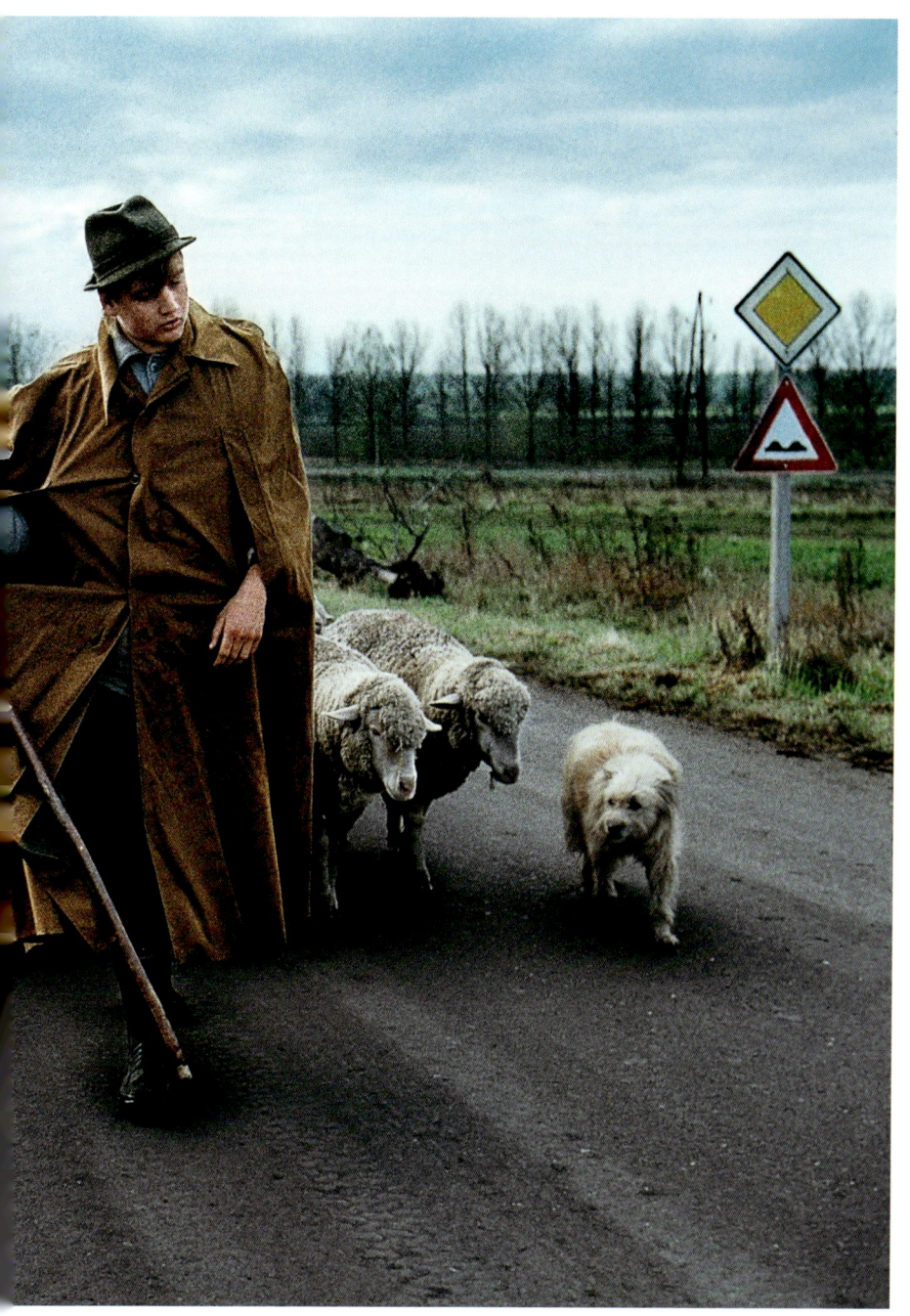

"The beast which passeth
all others in wit and mind."

ARISTOTLE

While in Sri Lanka during the monsoon season, I made this picture
of a man on an elephant with his umbrella. The young man next to
him picked a big leaf from the side of the road to serve as a makeshift
covering. The elephant and his handlers were headed to a Hindu
temple to participate in a wedding or blessing. Sri Lankan elephants
do not face the same level of threat as other elephants, because less
than 10% of males have tusks and therefore do not face ivory poachers.
Today, the Sri Lankan elephant is protected under Sri Lankan law
and killing one carries the death penalty.

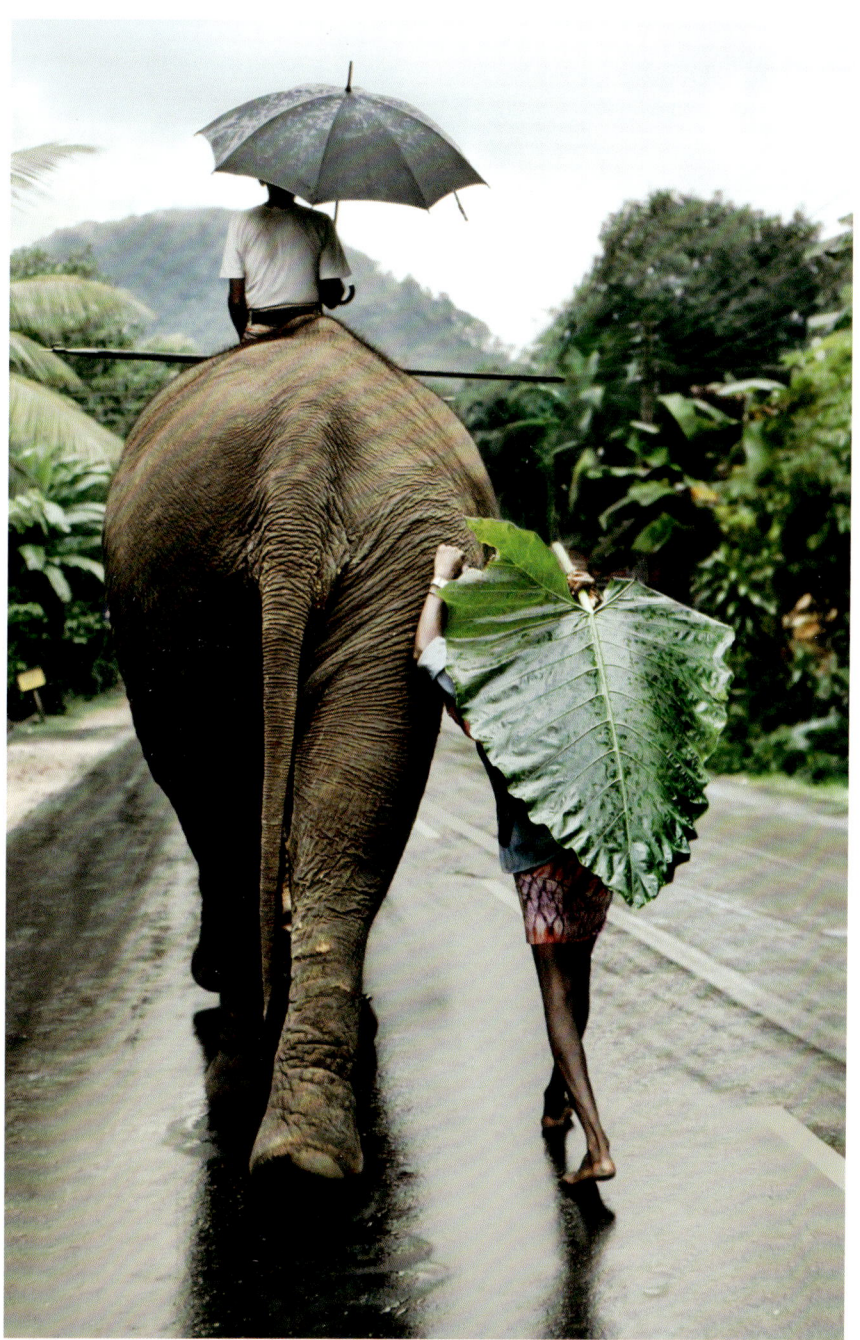

KANDY, SRI LANKA, 1995

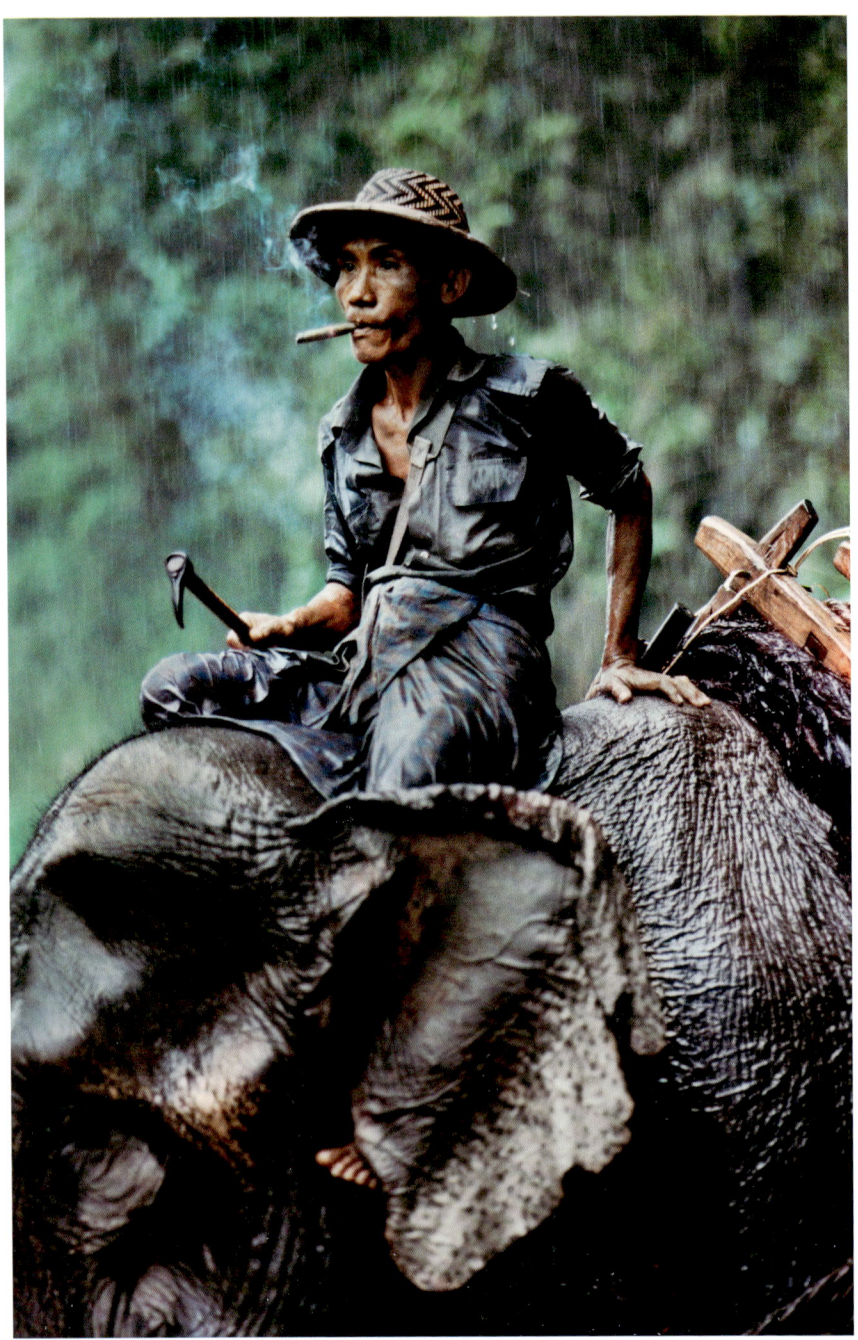

146   BAGO REGION, MYANMAR, 1994

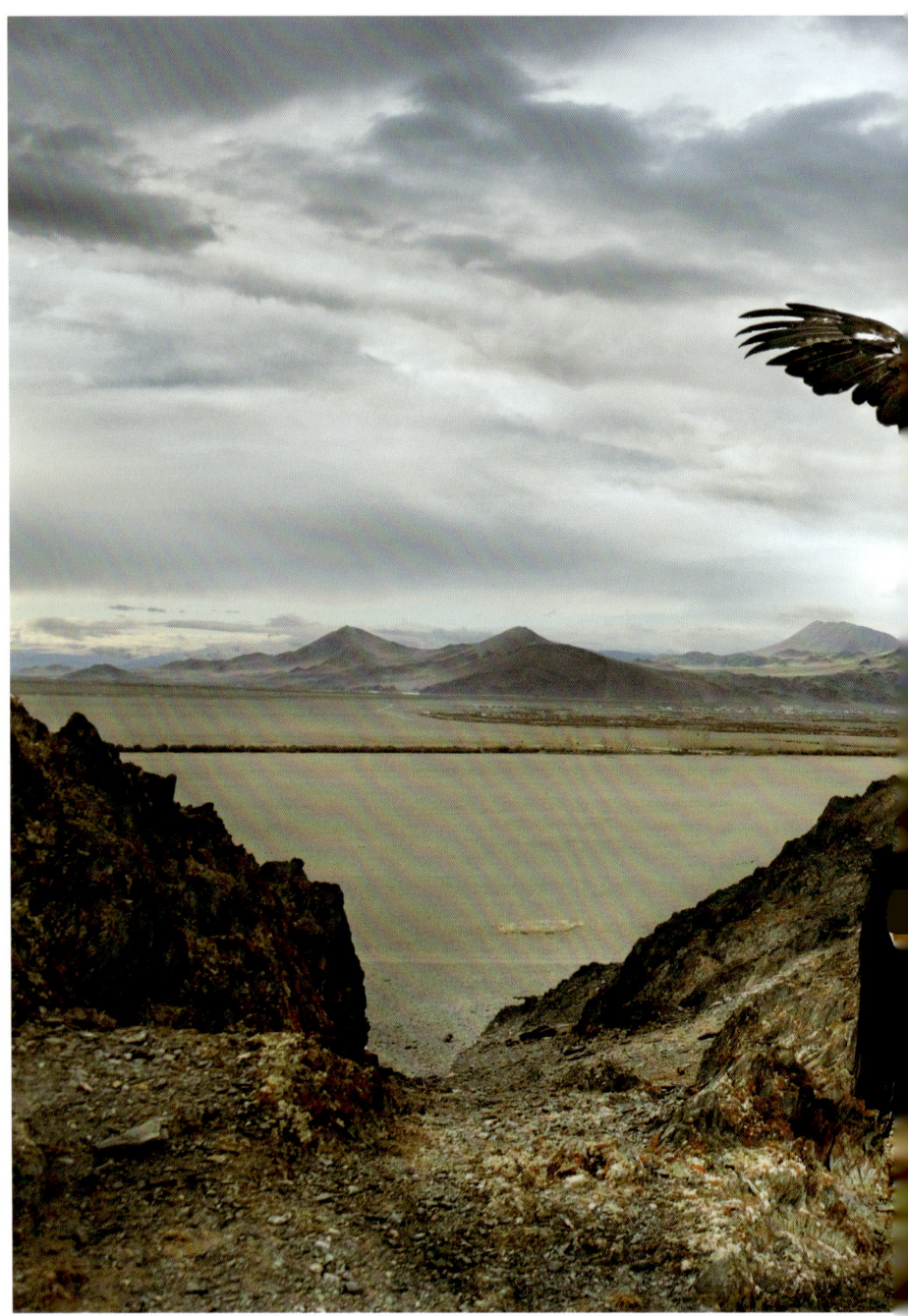

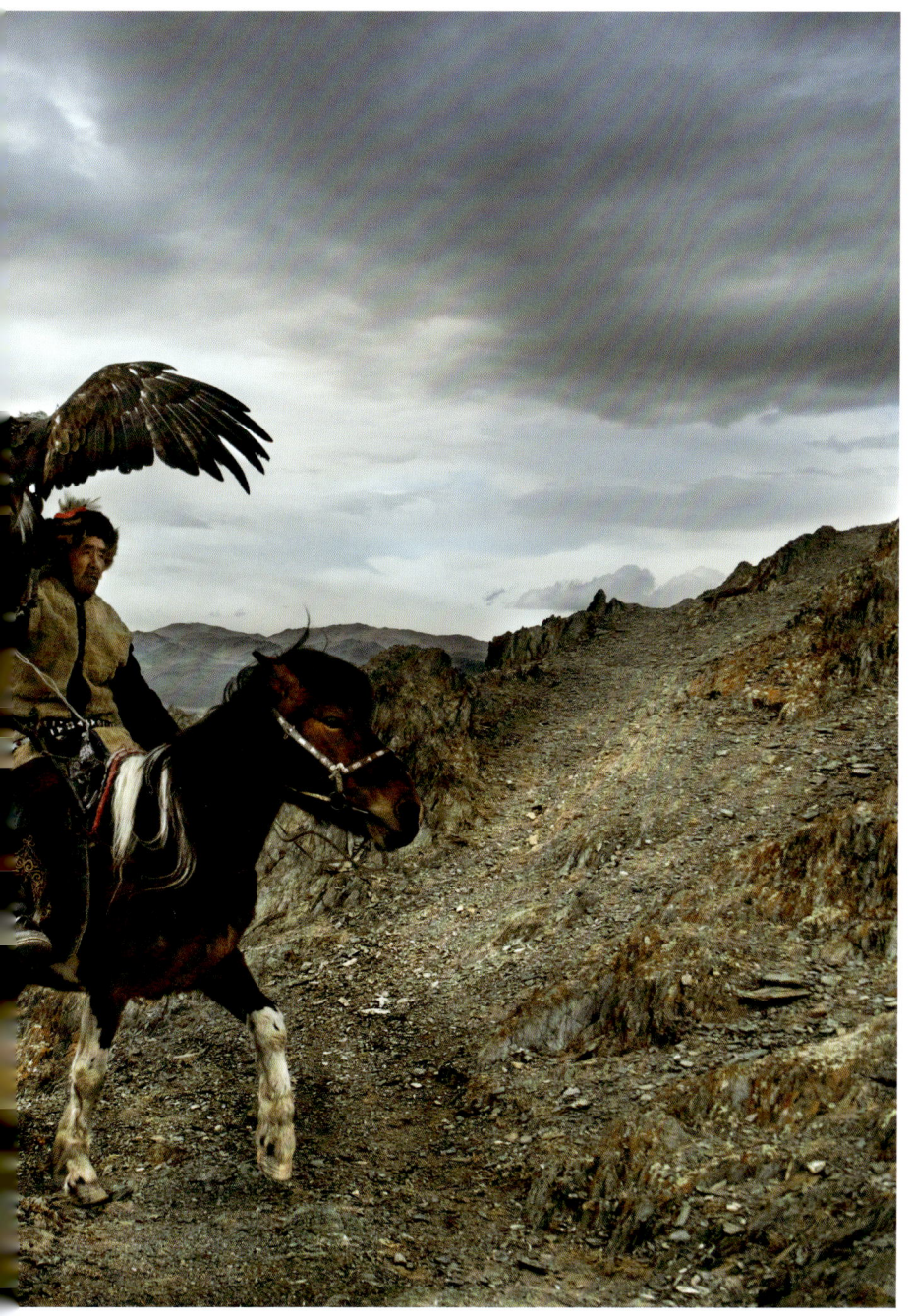

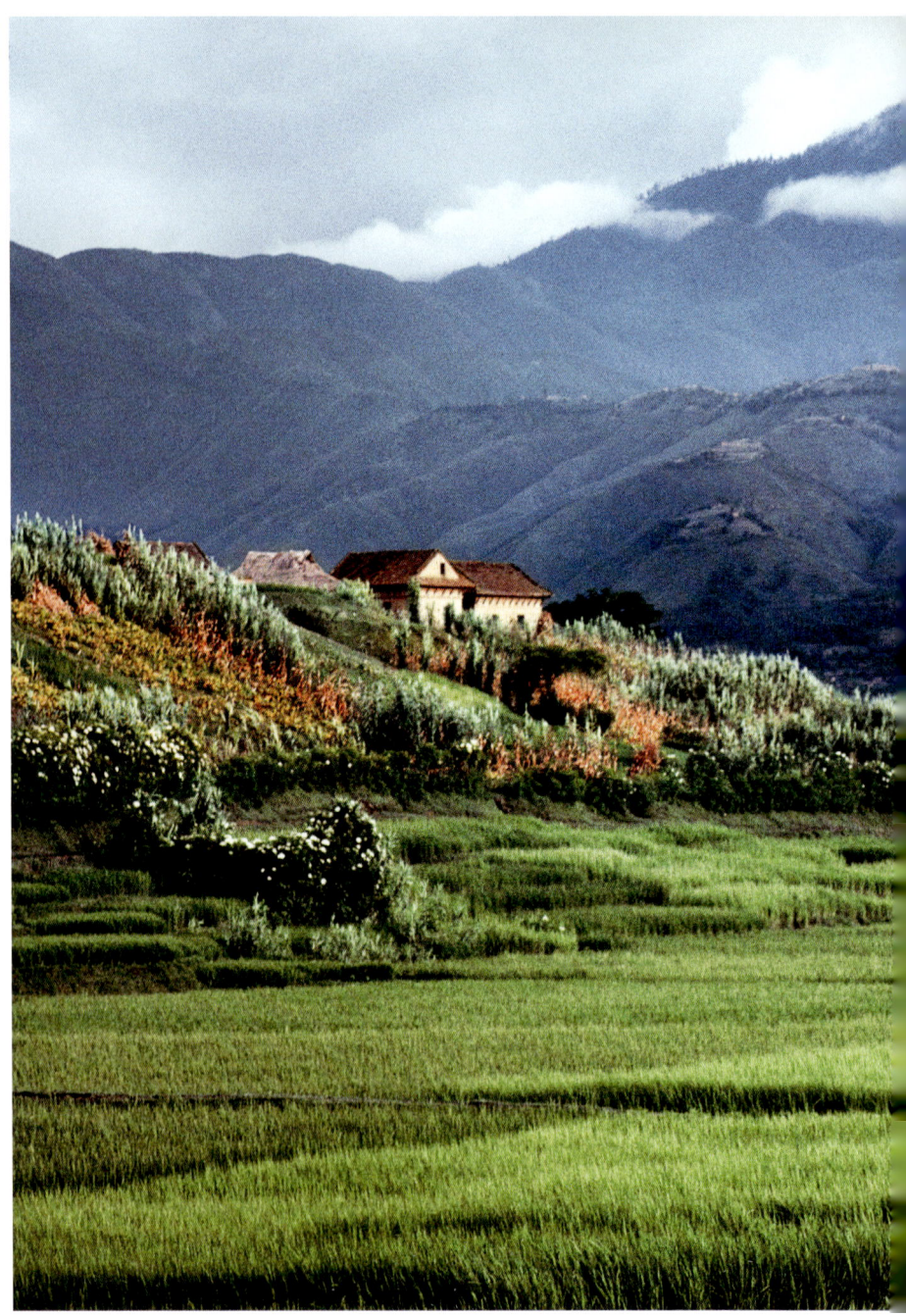

150   KATHMANDU, NEPAL, 1983

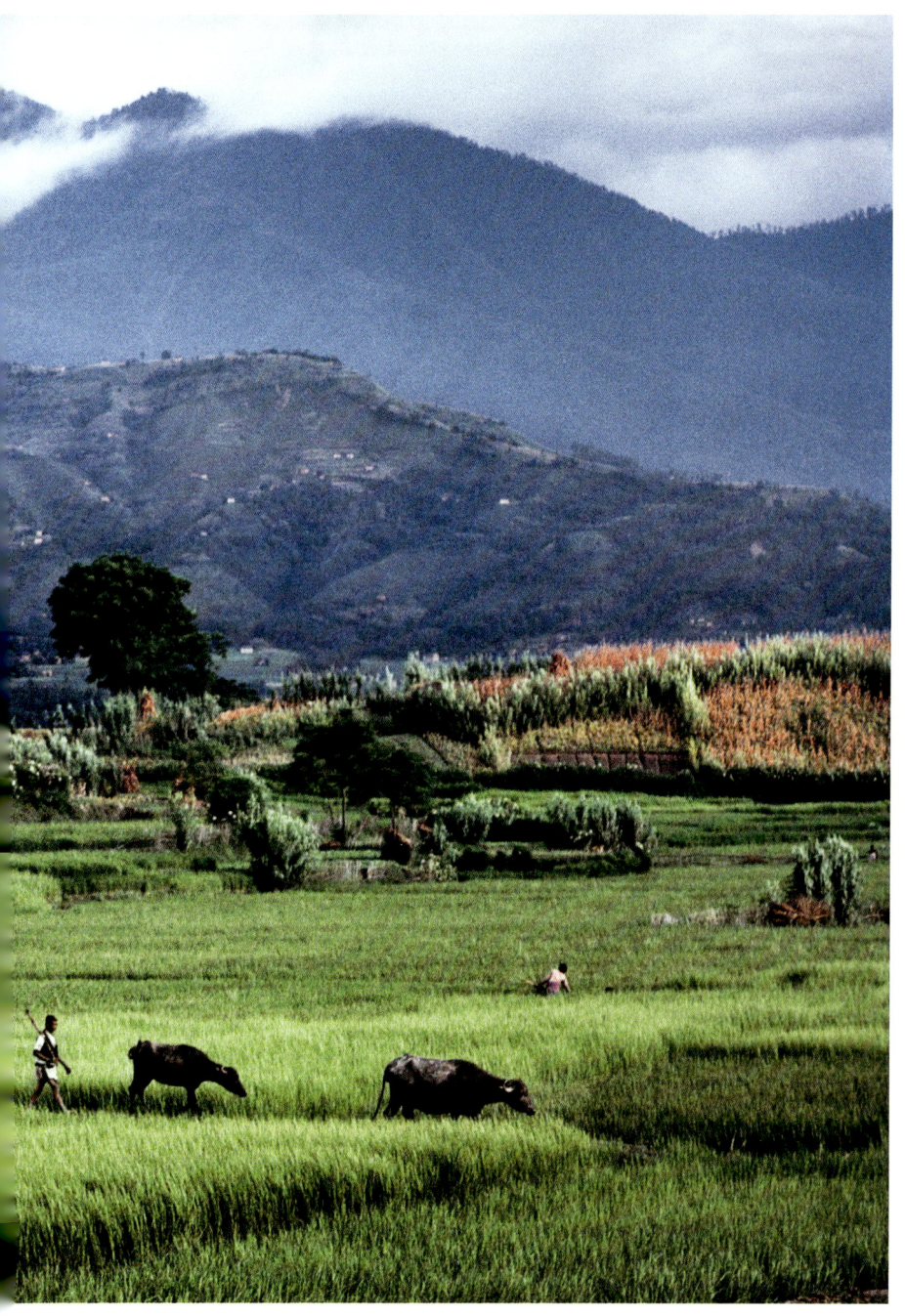

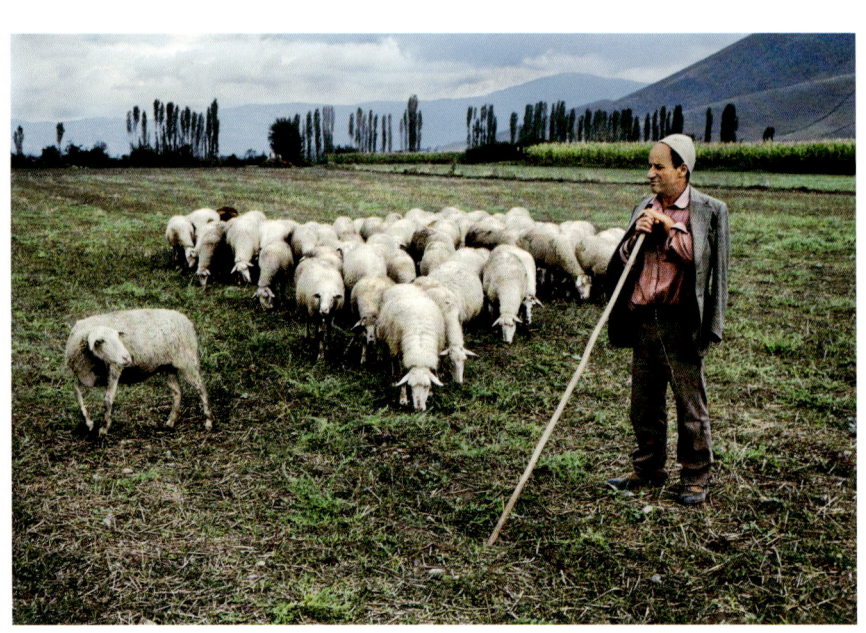

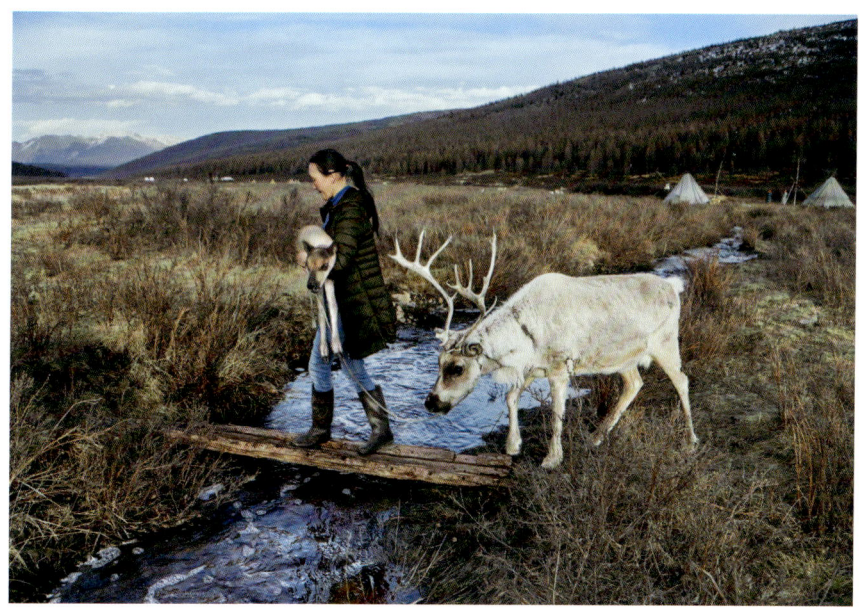

People in Mongolia have a special relationship with reindeer;
they raise their animals for milk and cheese and even use their hair
for textiles, but they rarely eat the meat. It was intriguing to witness
their rituals and customs.

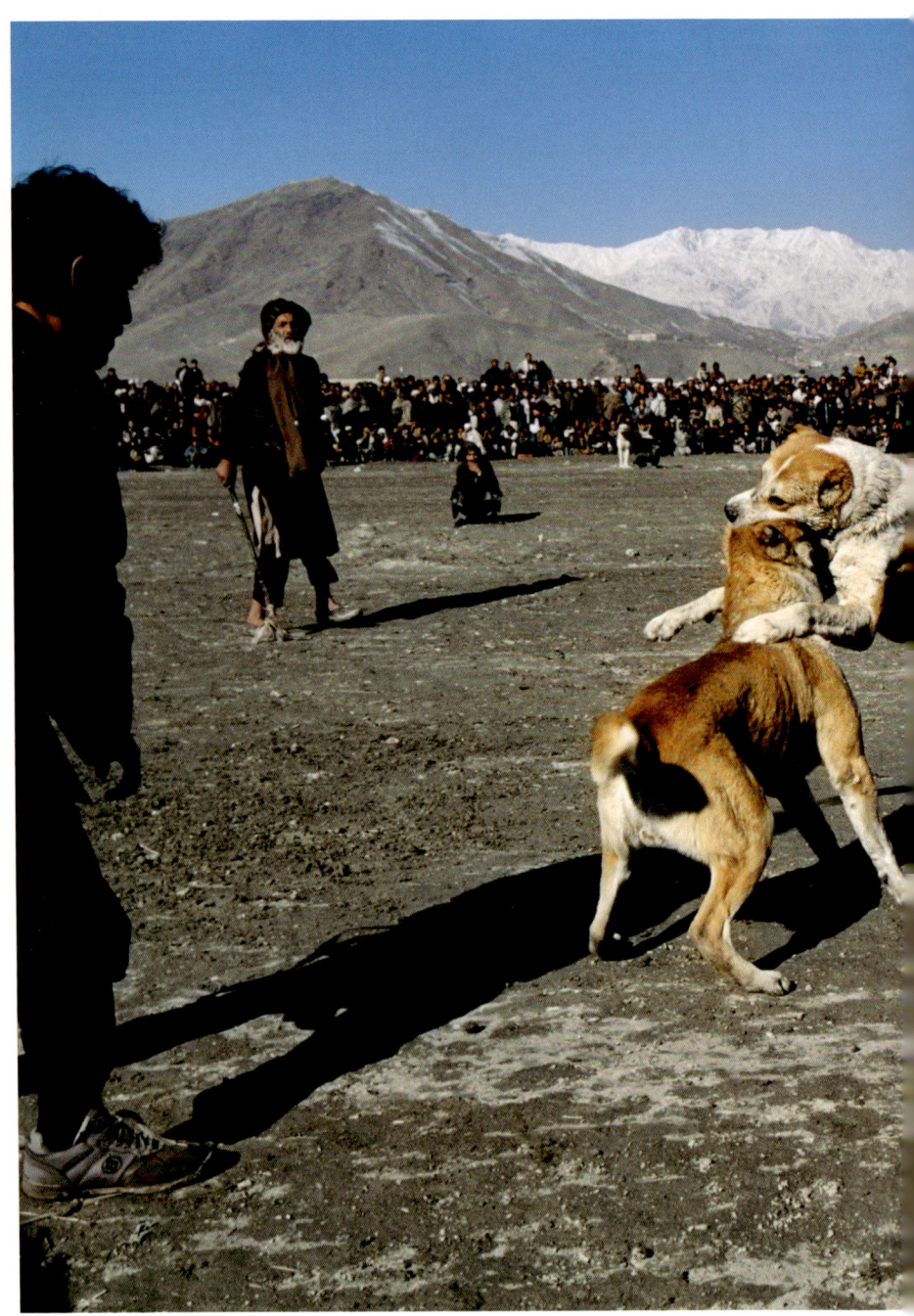

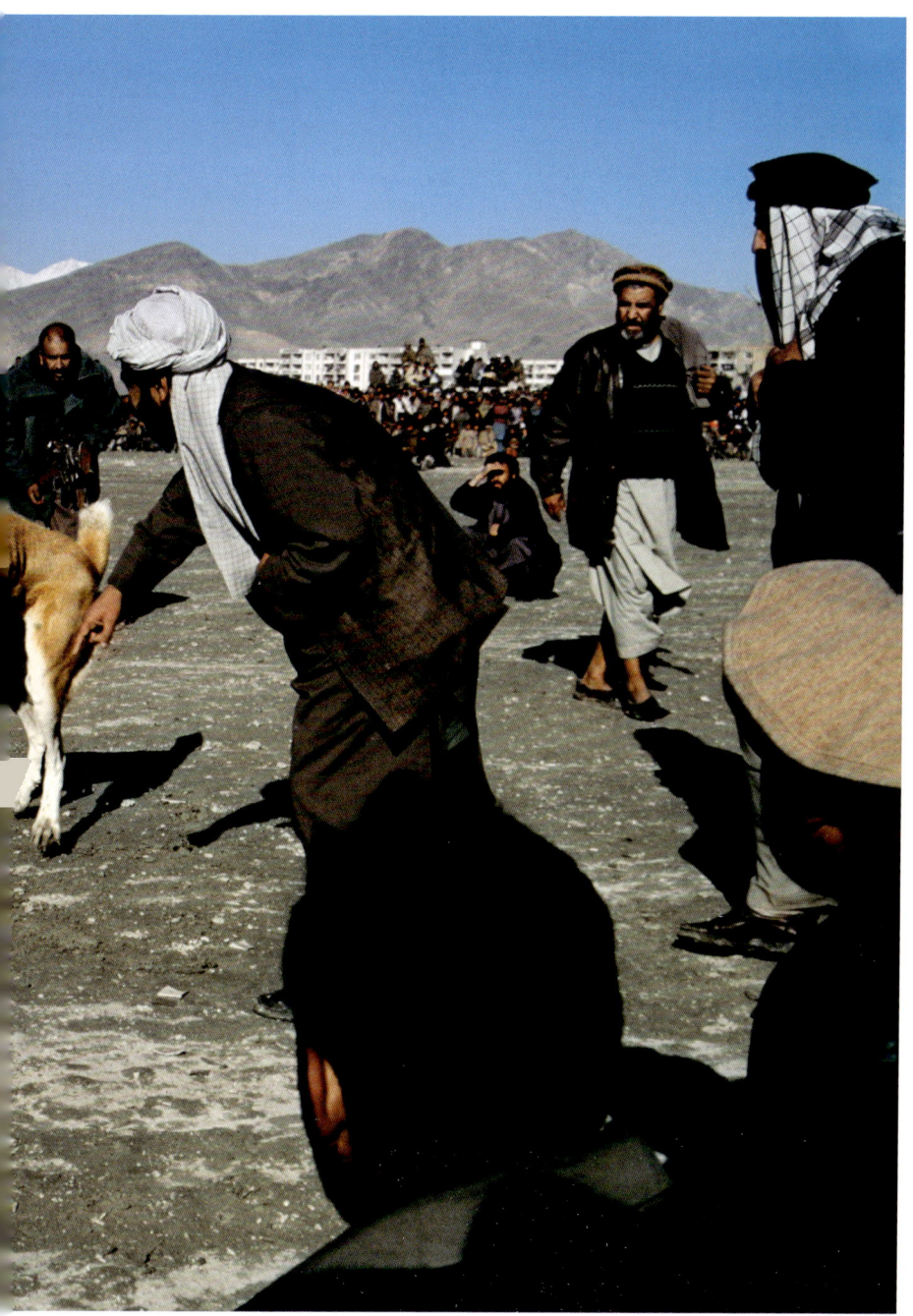

155

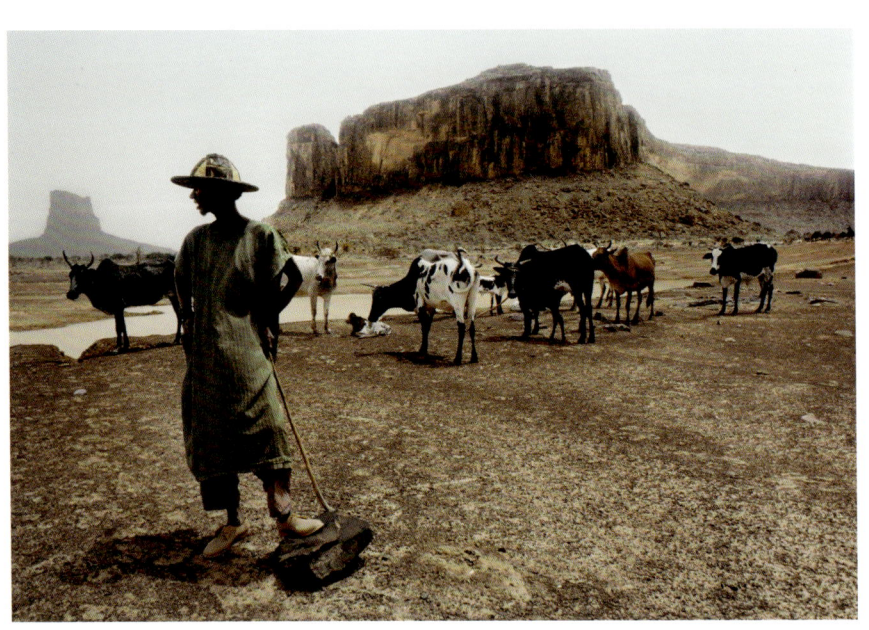

156   NEAR DOUENTZA, MALI, 1985

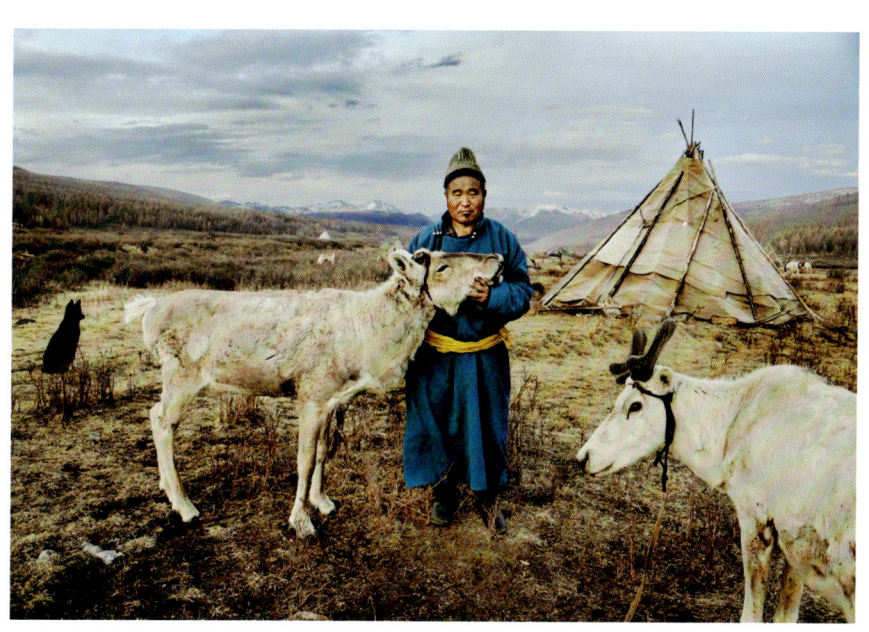

KHÖVSGÖL, MONGOLIA, 2018

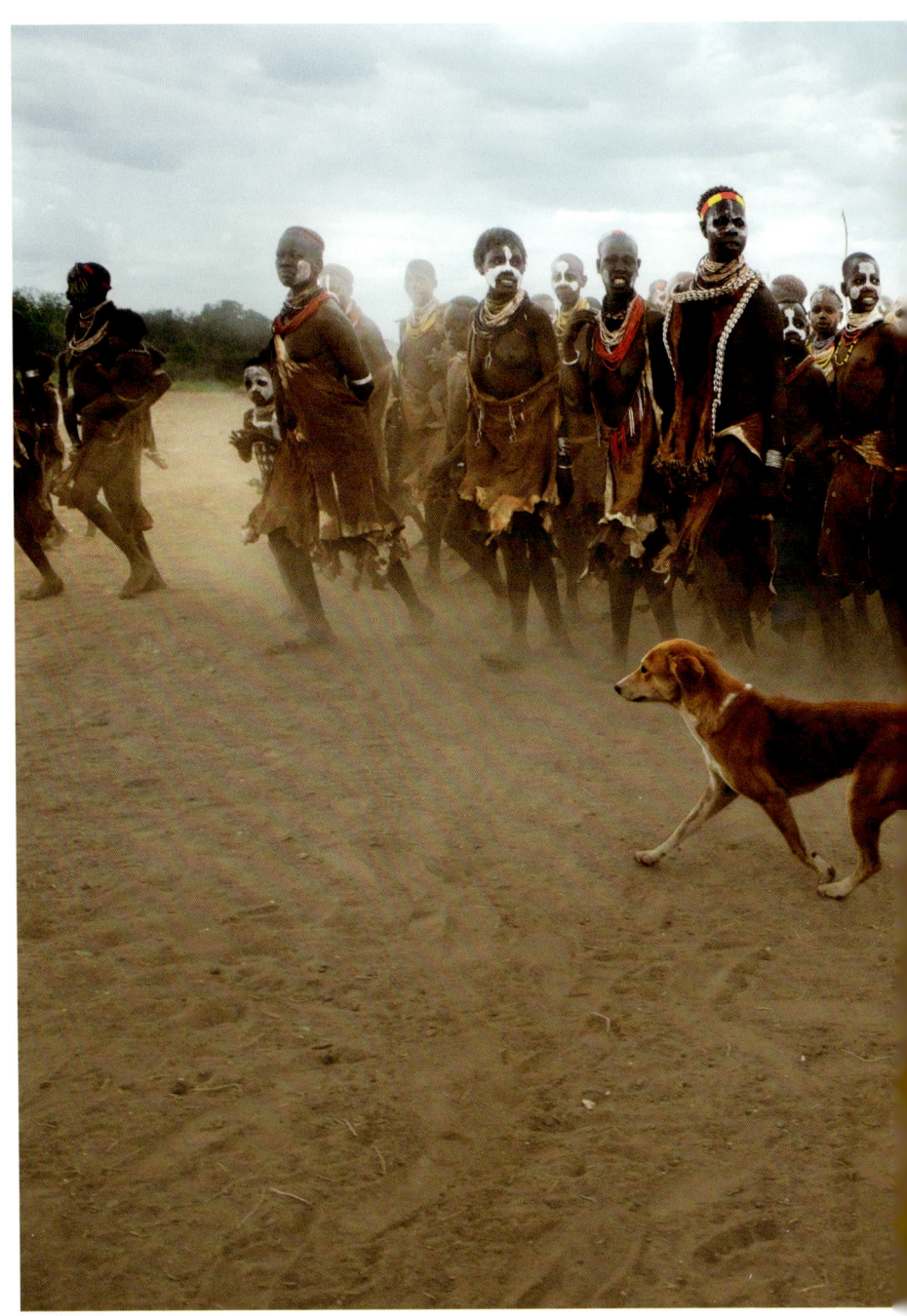

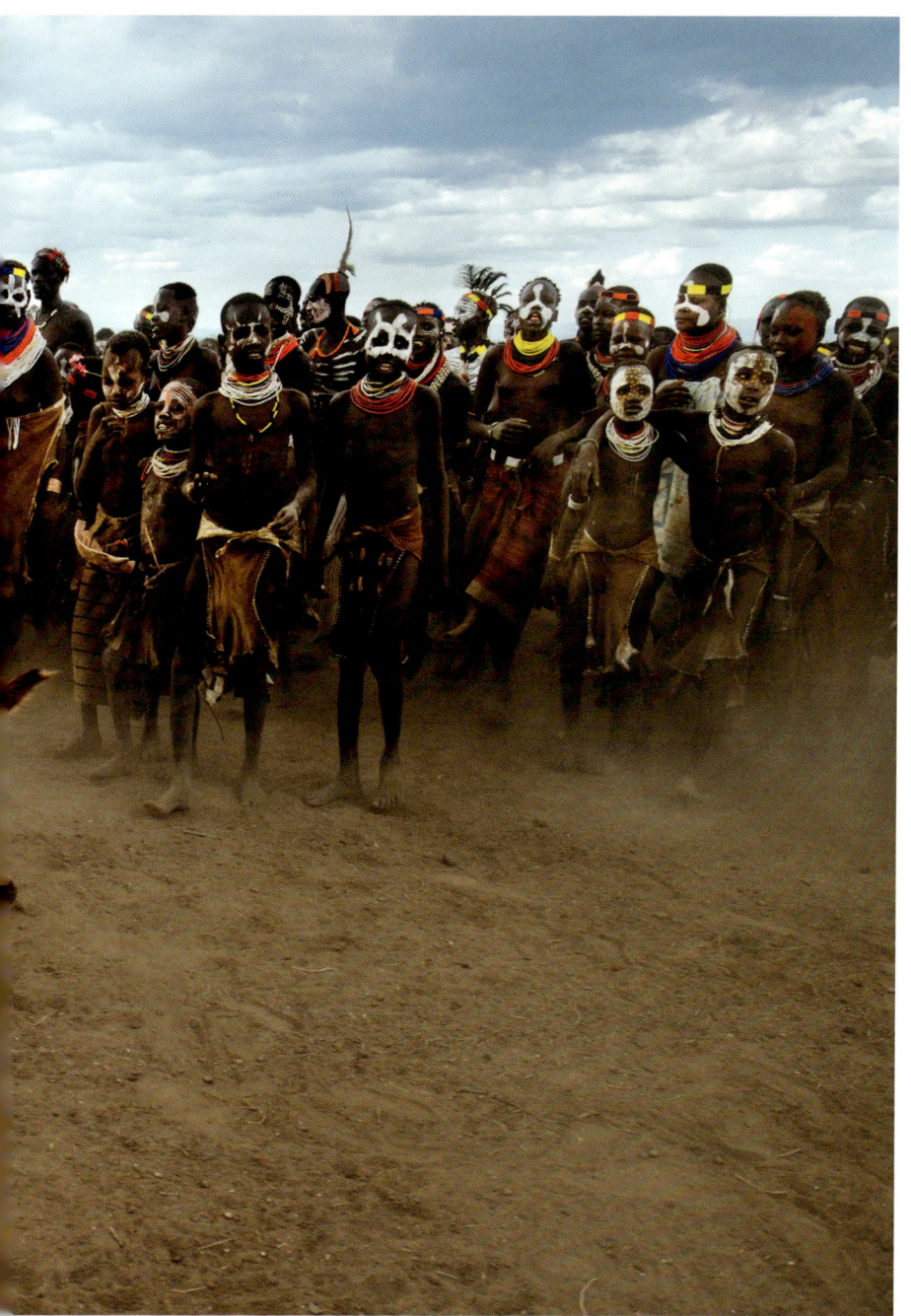

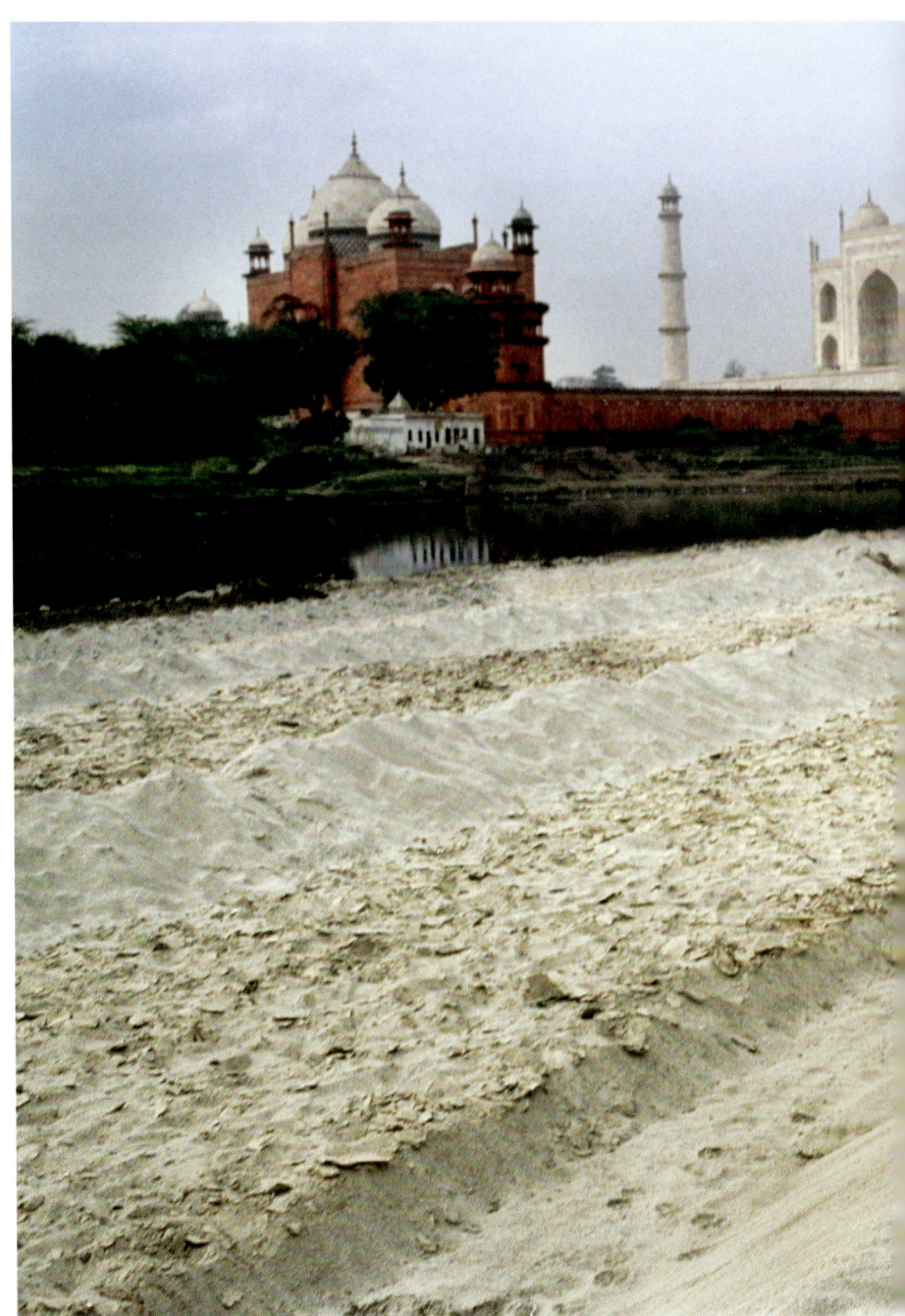

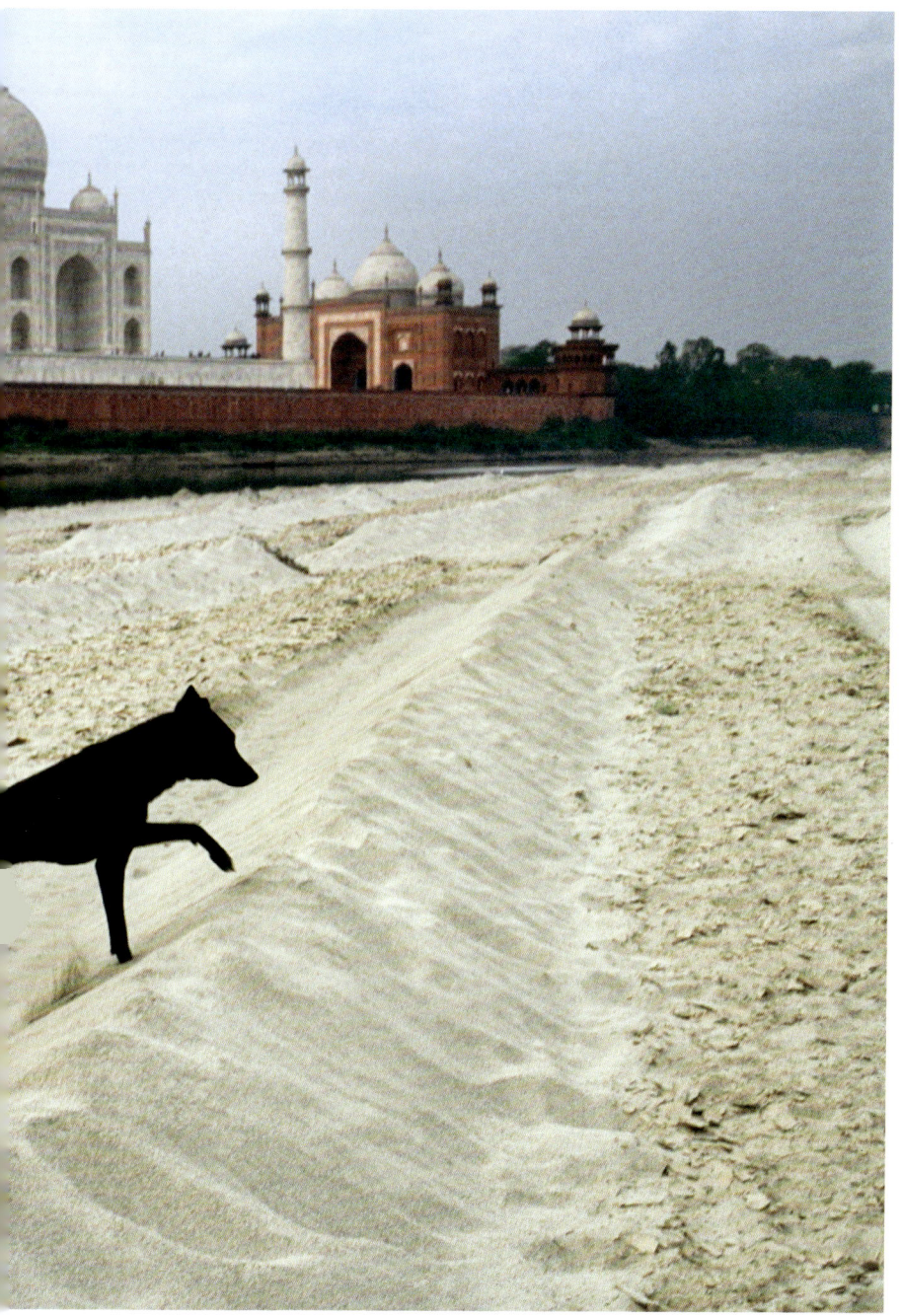

"Until one has loved an animal, a part of one's soul remains unawakened."

ANATOLE FRANCE

This woman was feeding doves in front of the Blue Mosque in Mazar-i-Sharif. Legend says the mosque is so sacred that any dove with a speck of color on its feathers will instantly become pure white after entering the mosque's vicinity.

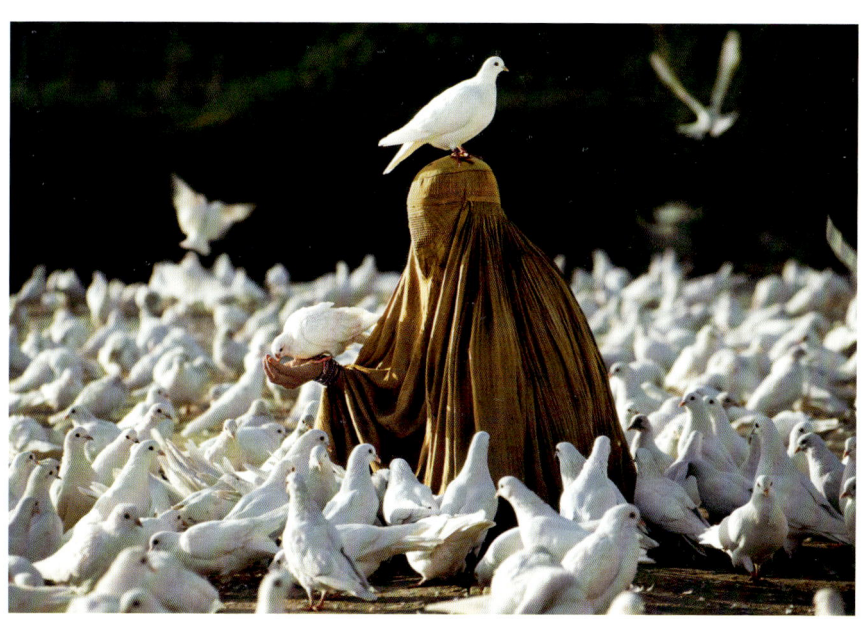

MAZAR-I-SHARIF, AFGHANISTAN, 1991

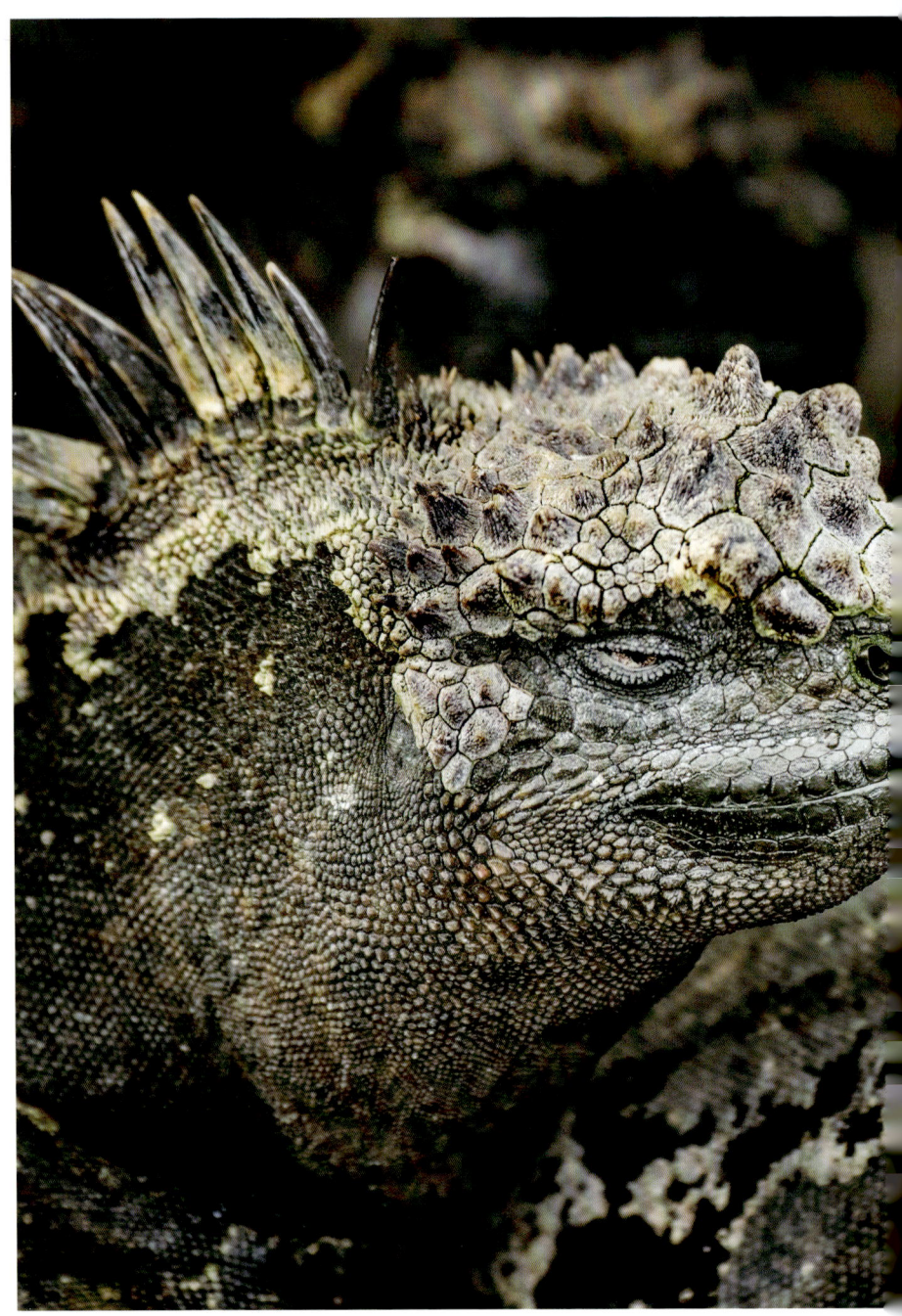

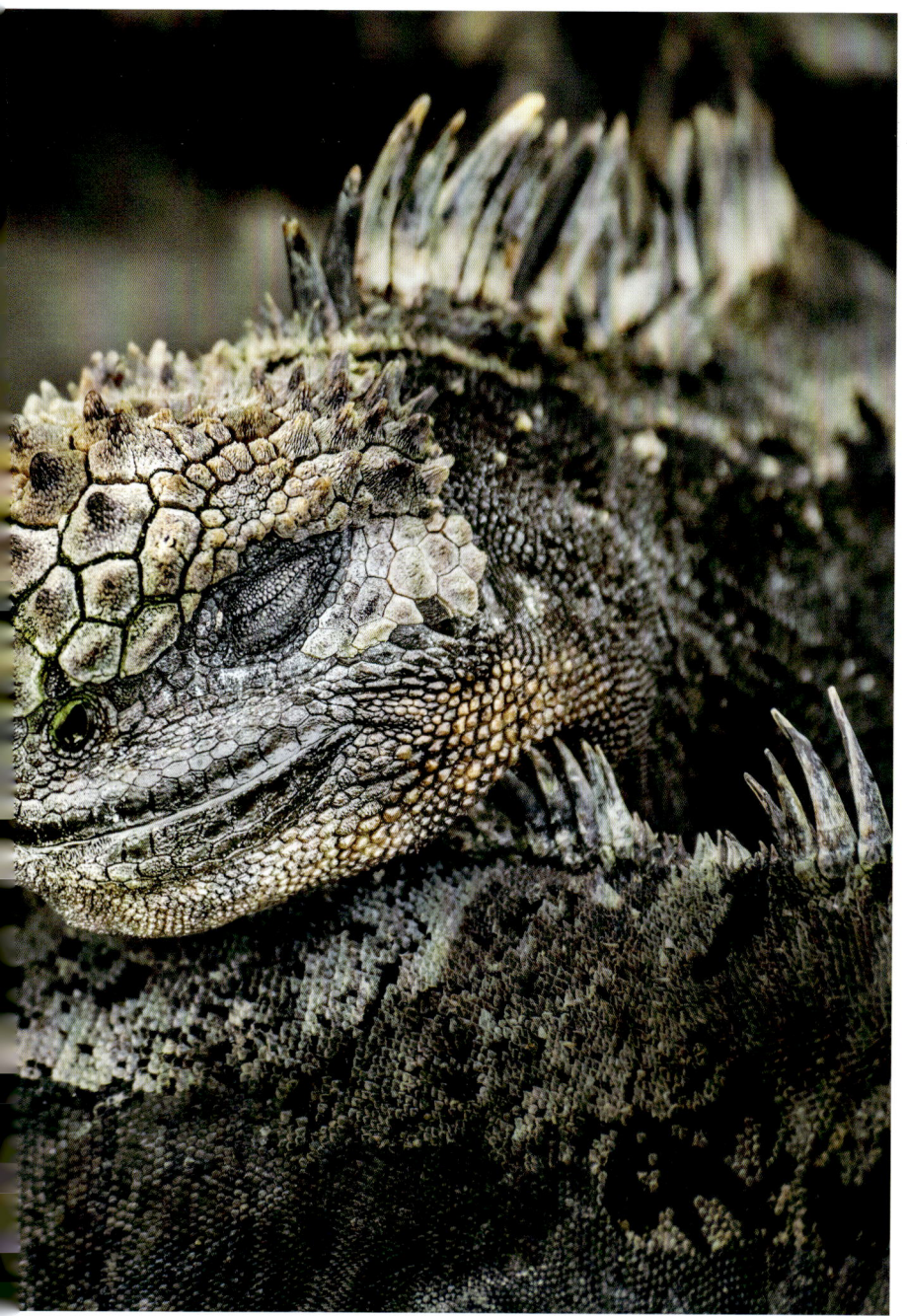

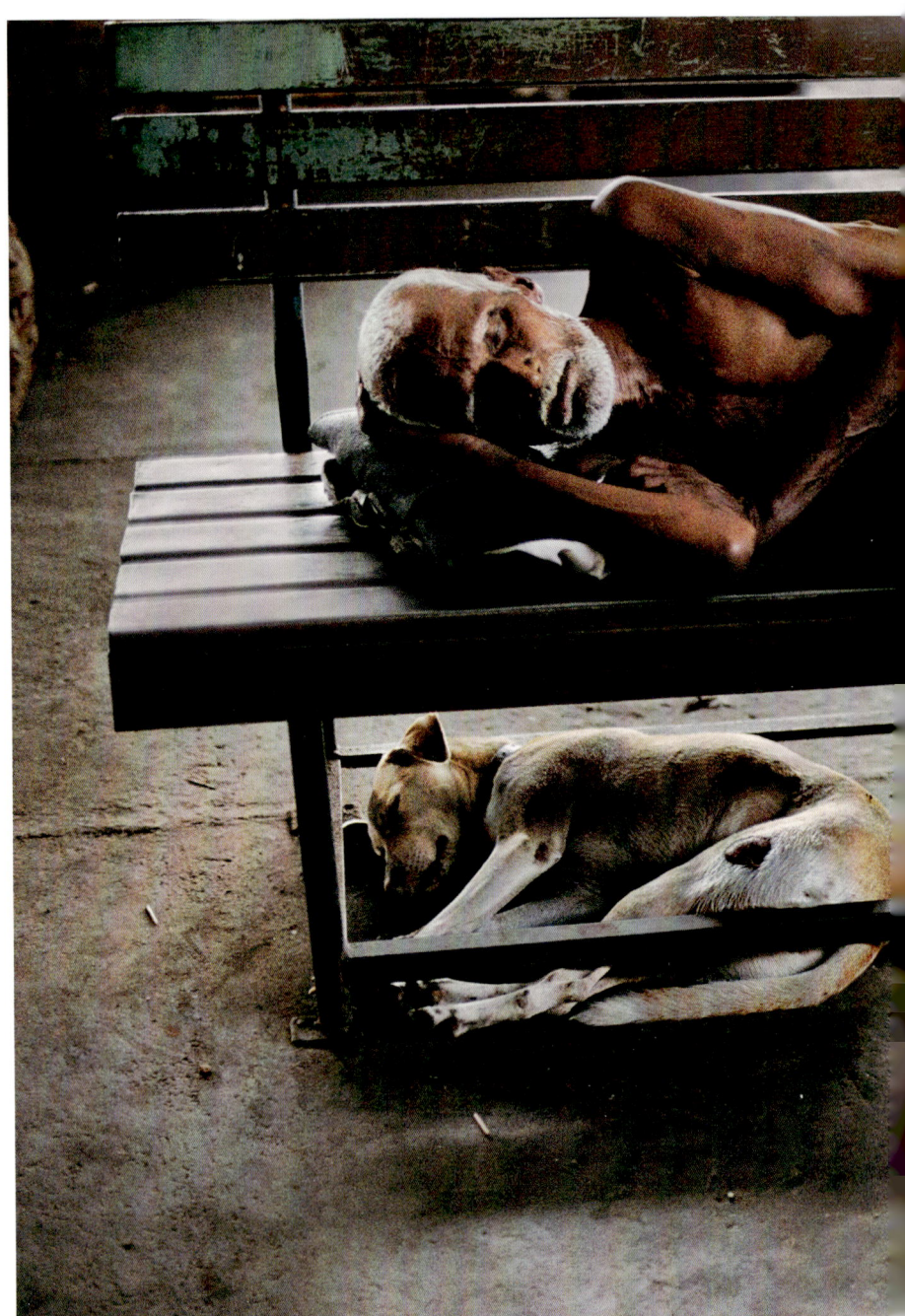

166   MUMBAI, INDIA, 1996

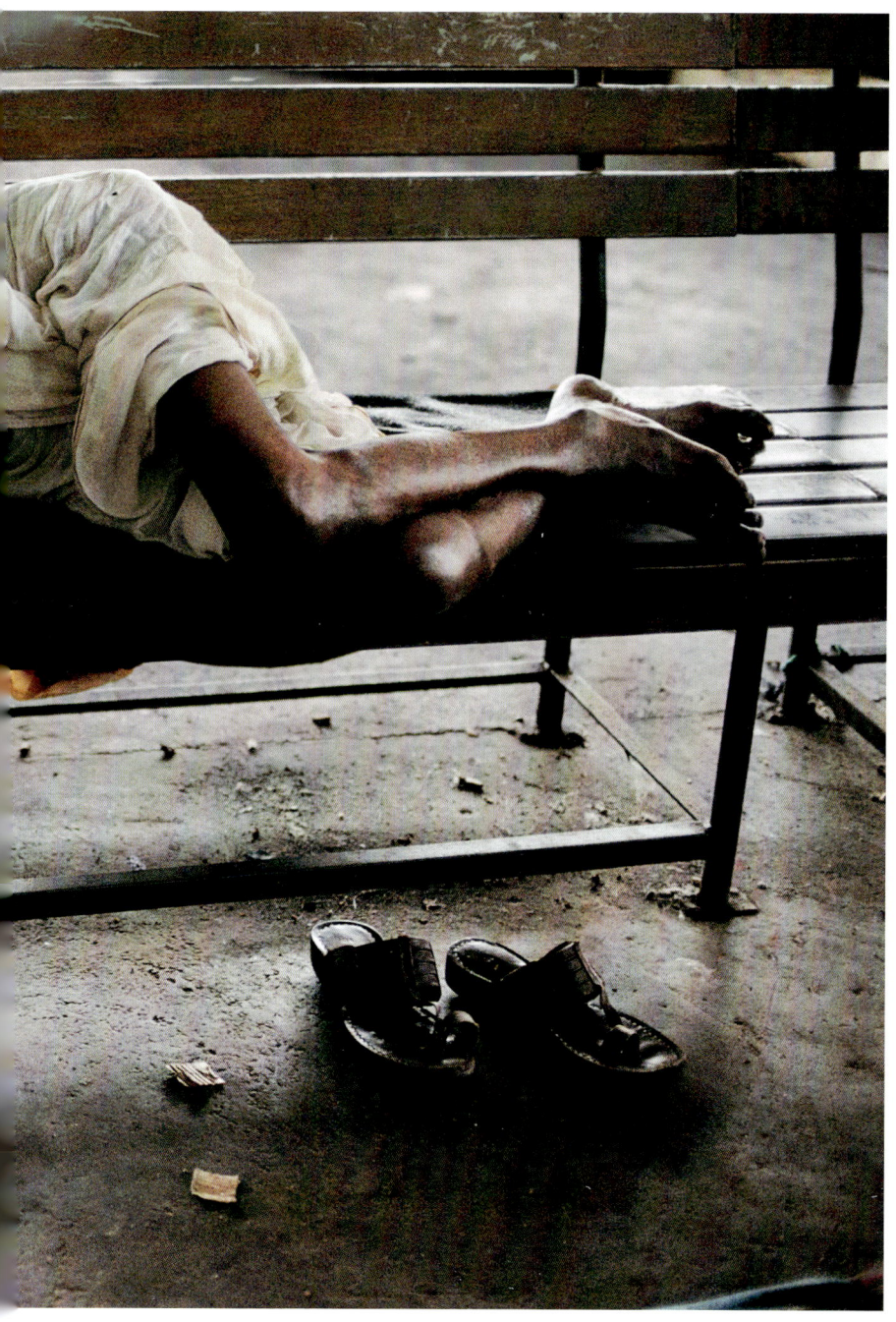

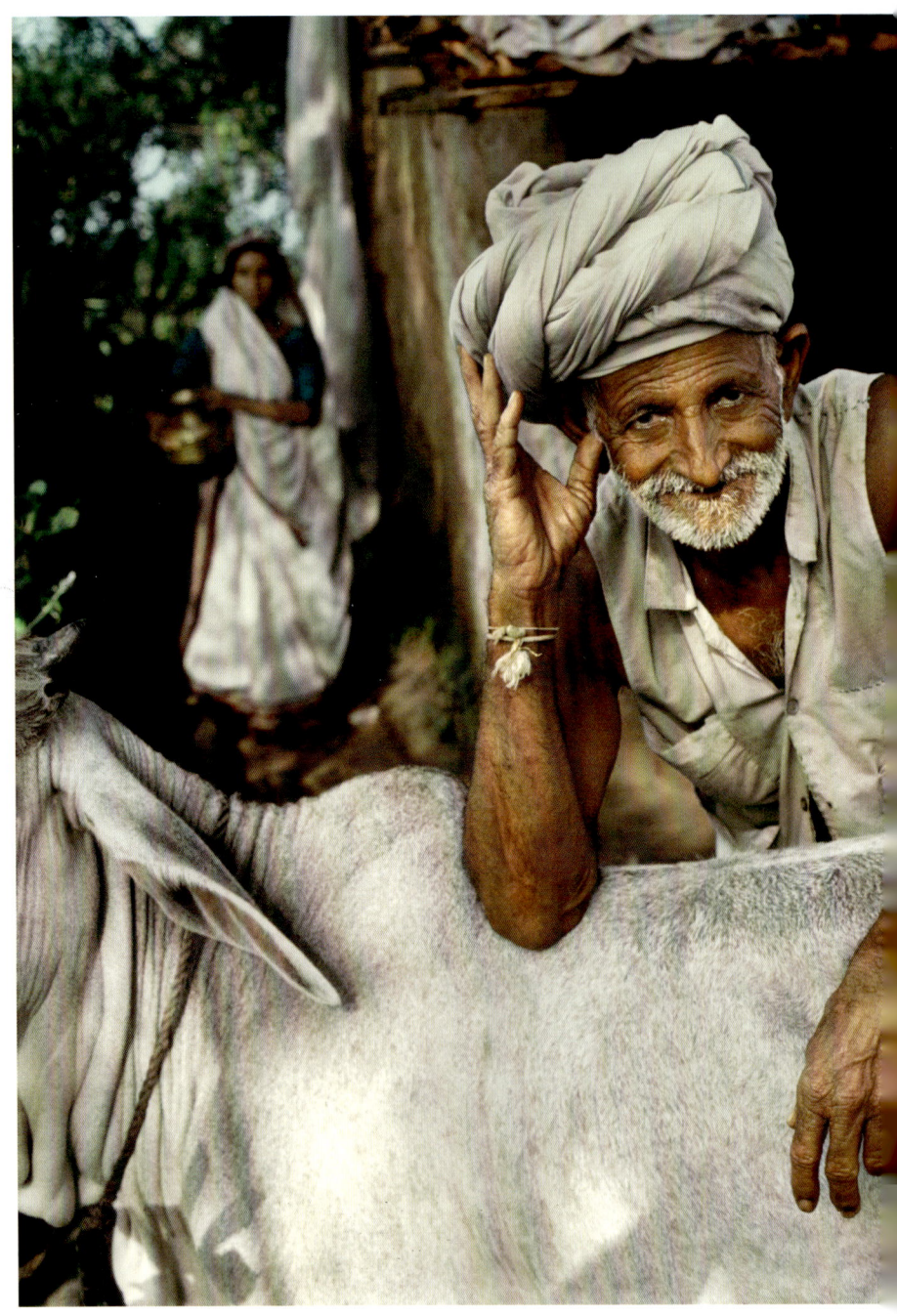

168   RAJASTHAN, INDIA, 1996

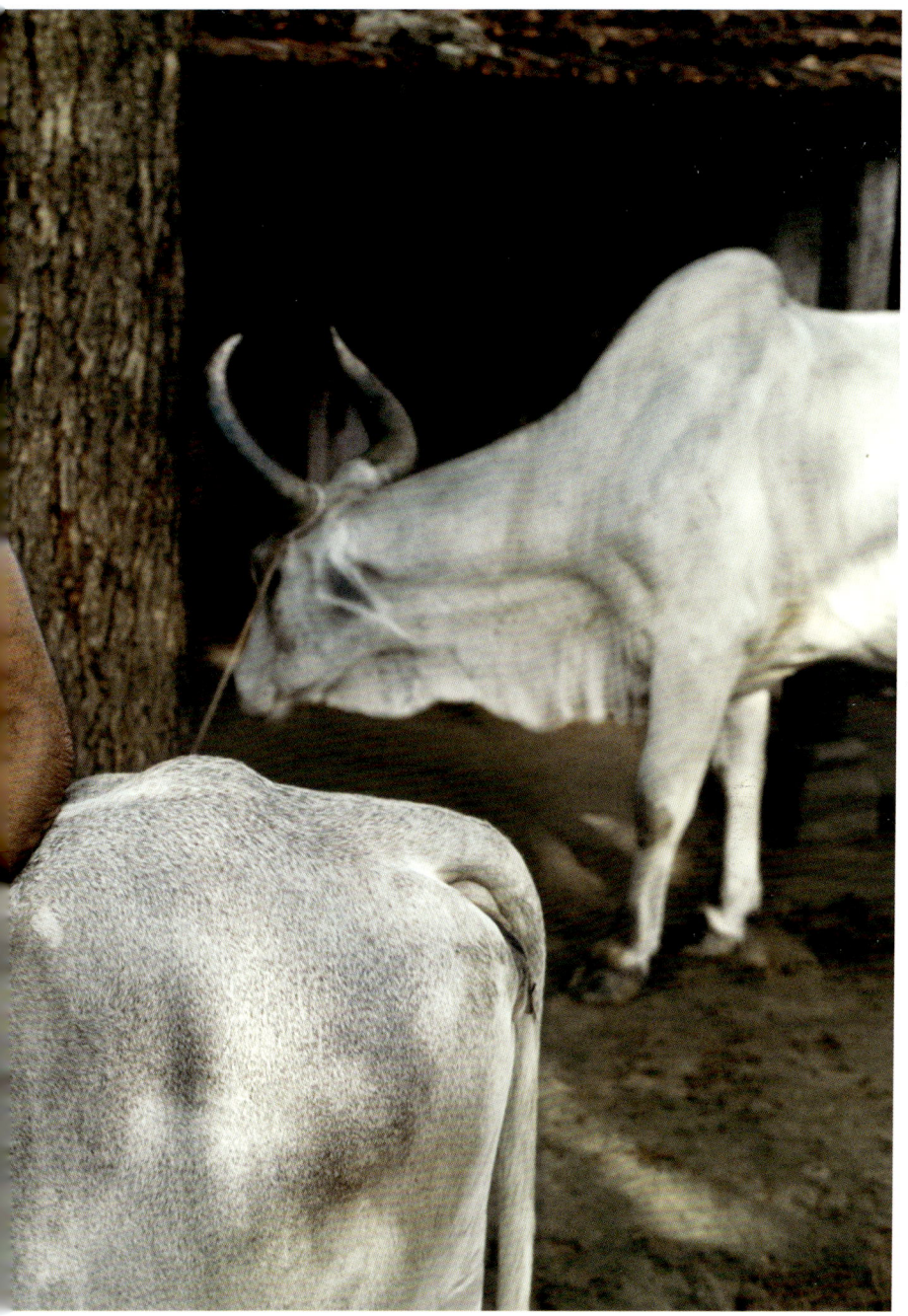

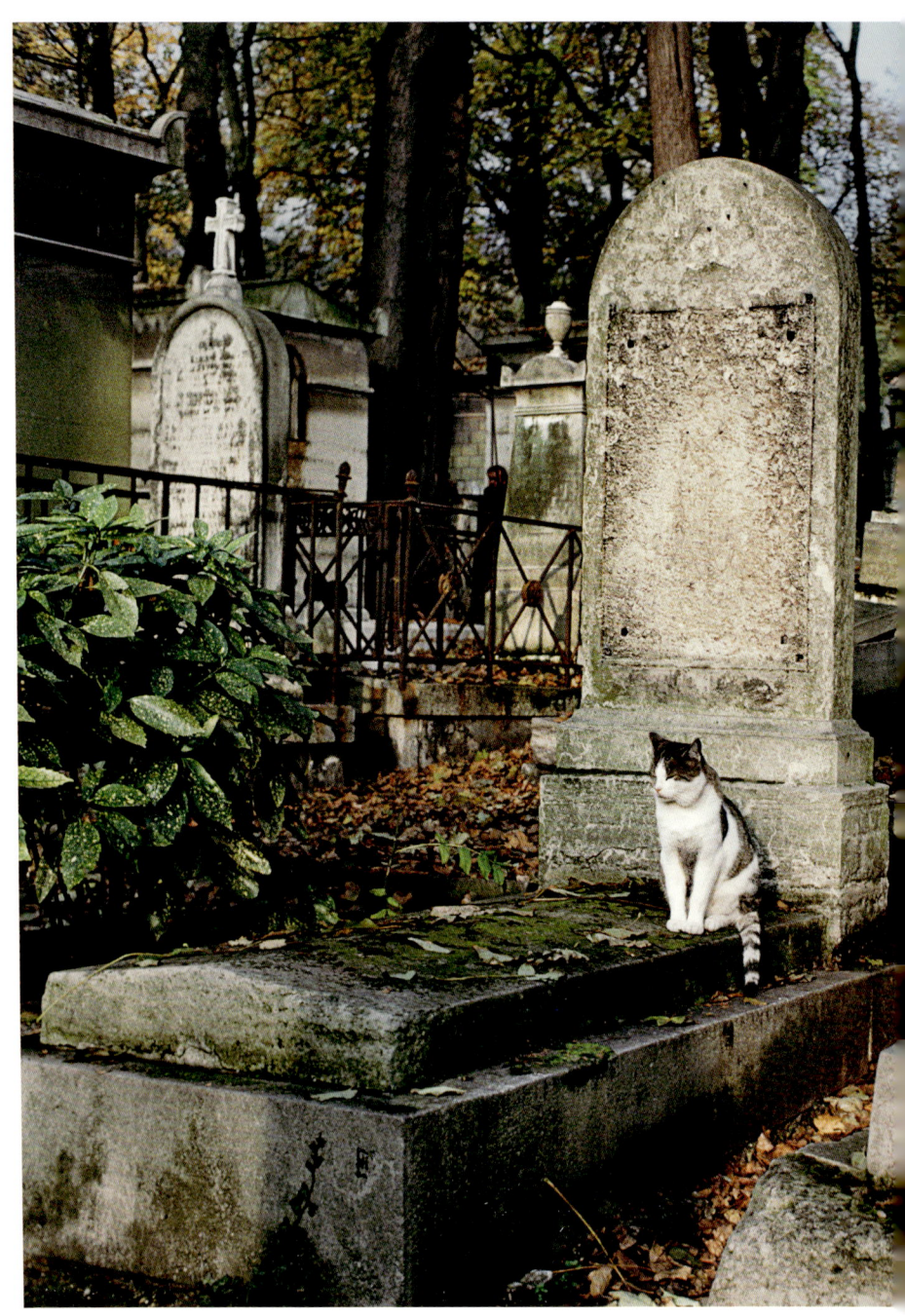

170   PÈRE LACHAISE CEMETERY, PARIS, FRANCE, 1988

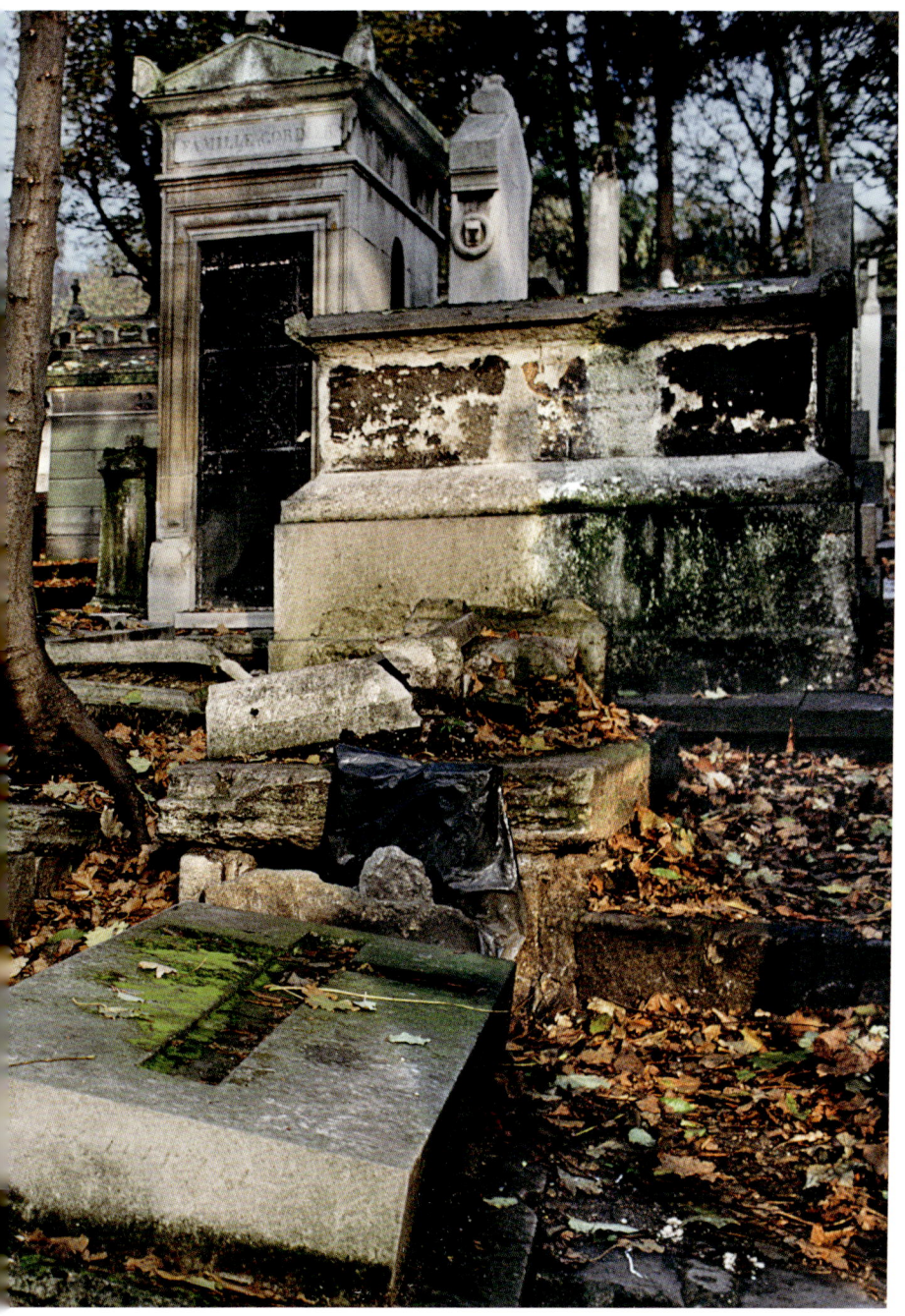

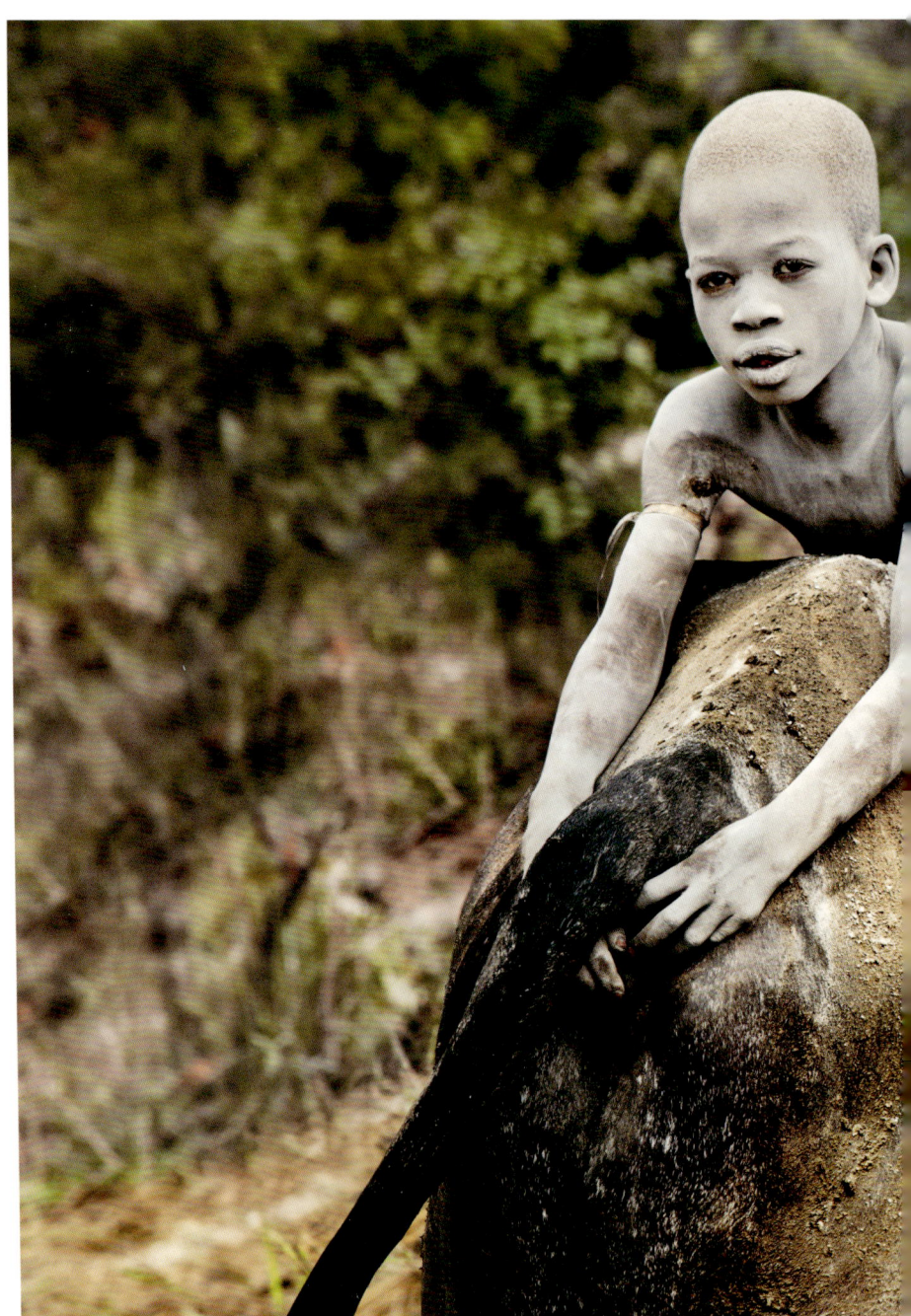

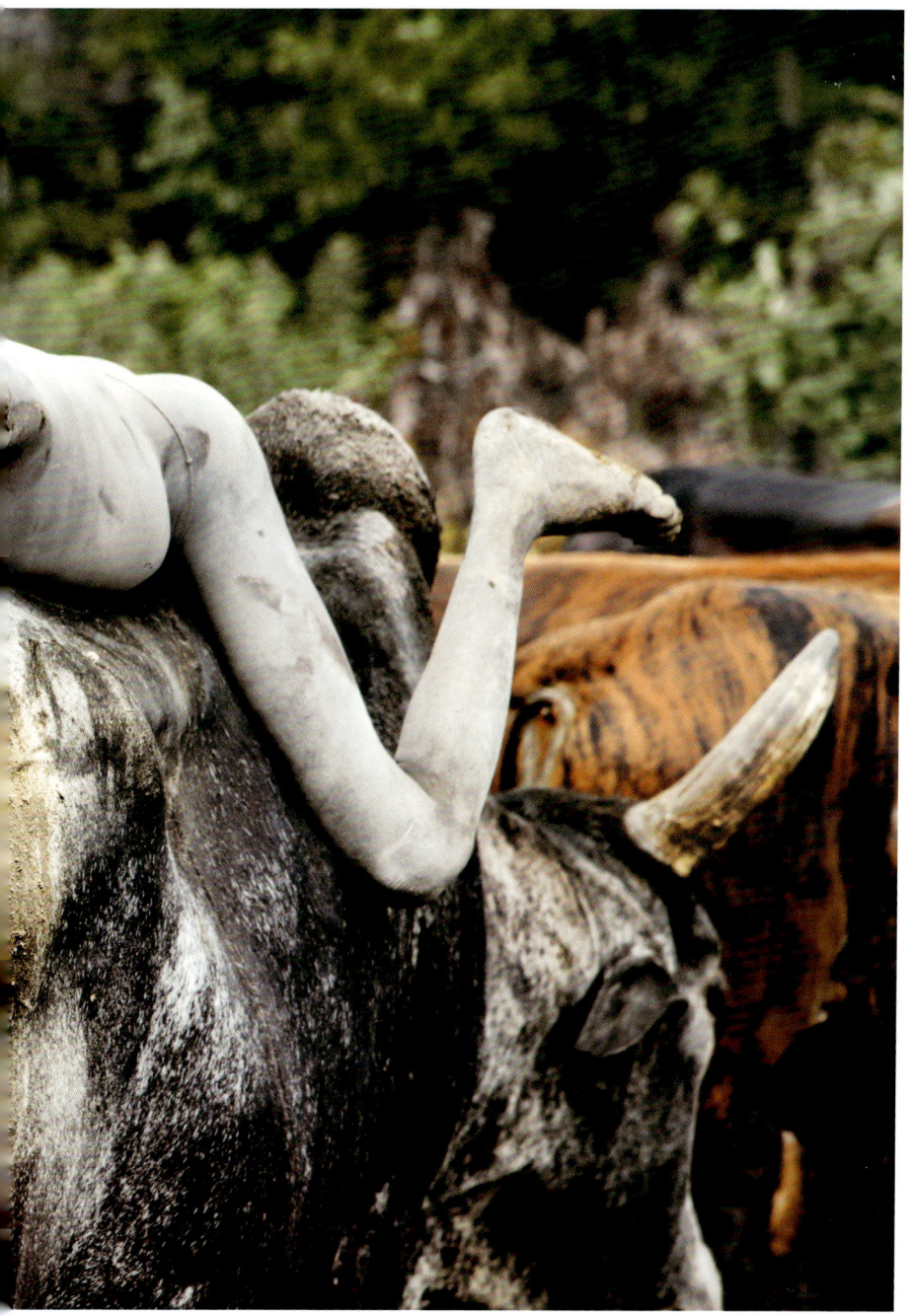

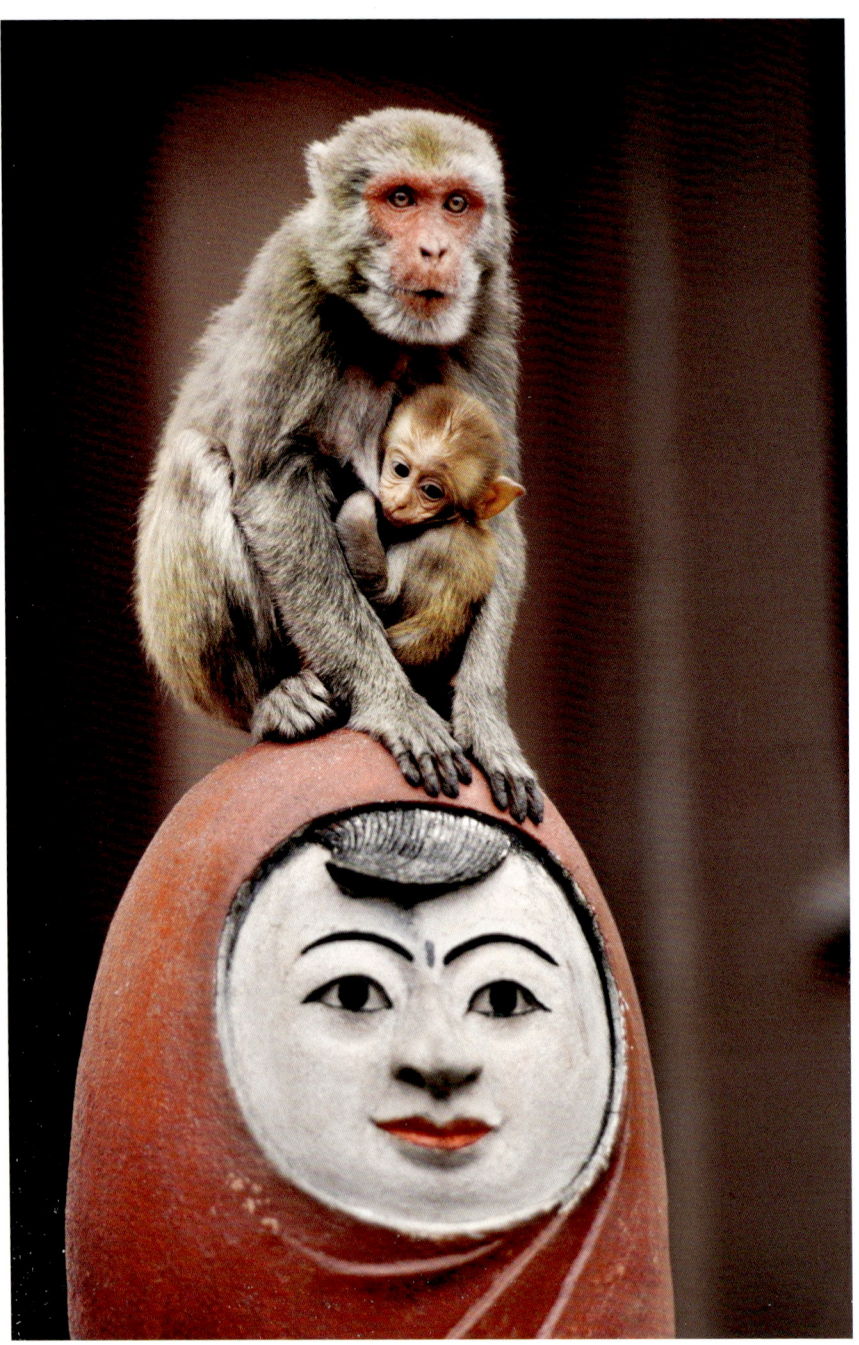

MANDALAY, MYANMAR, 1994

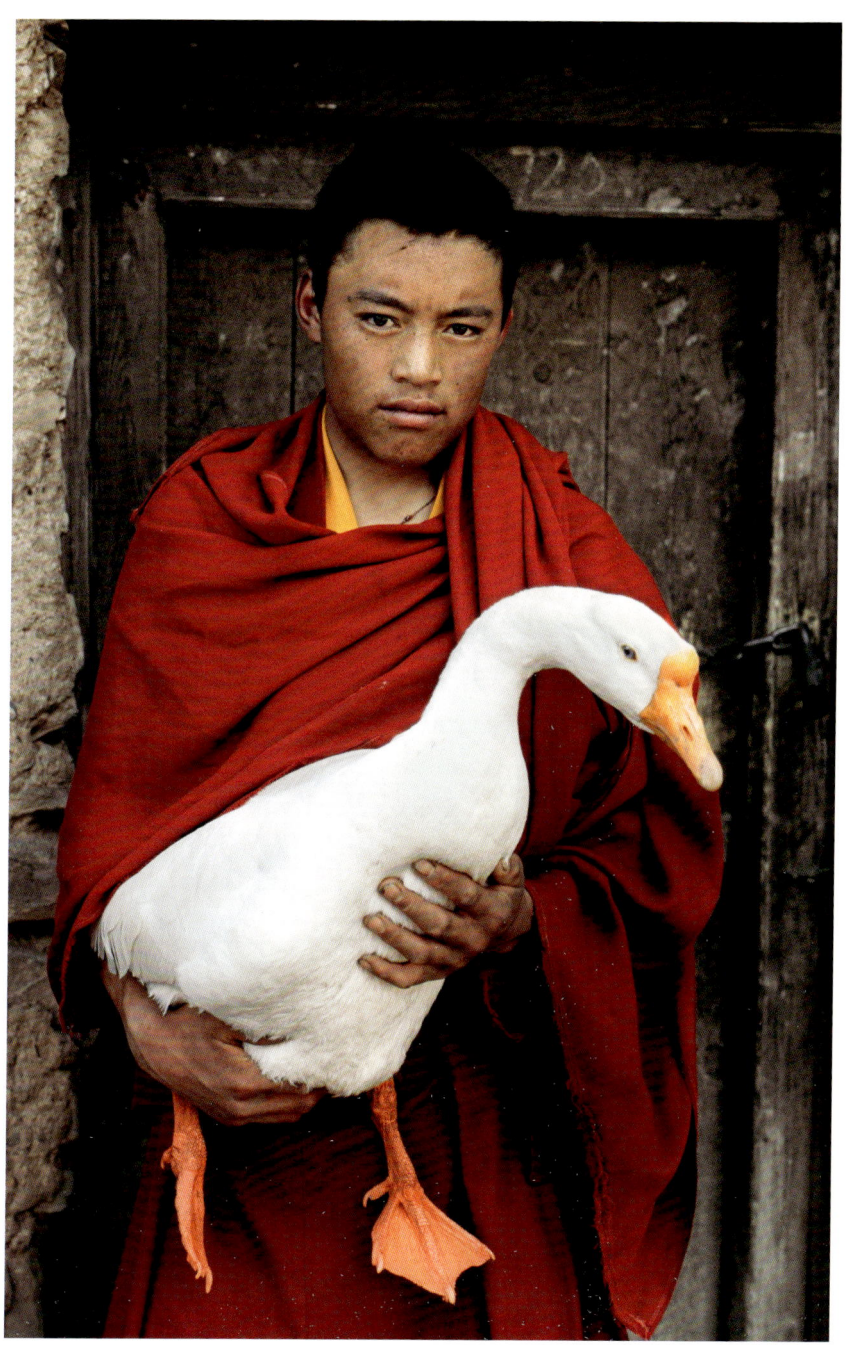

LITANG, TIBET, 2000

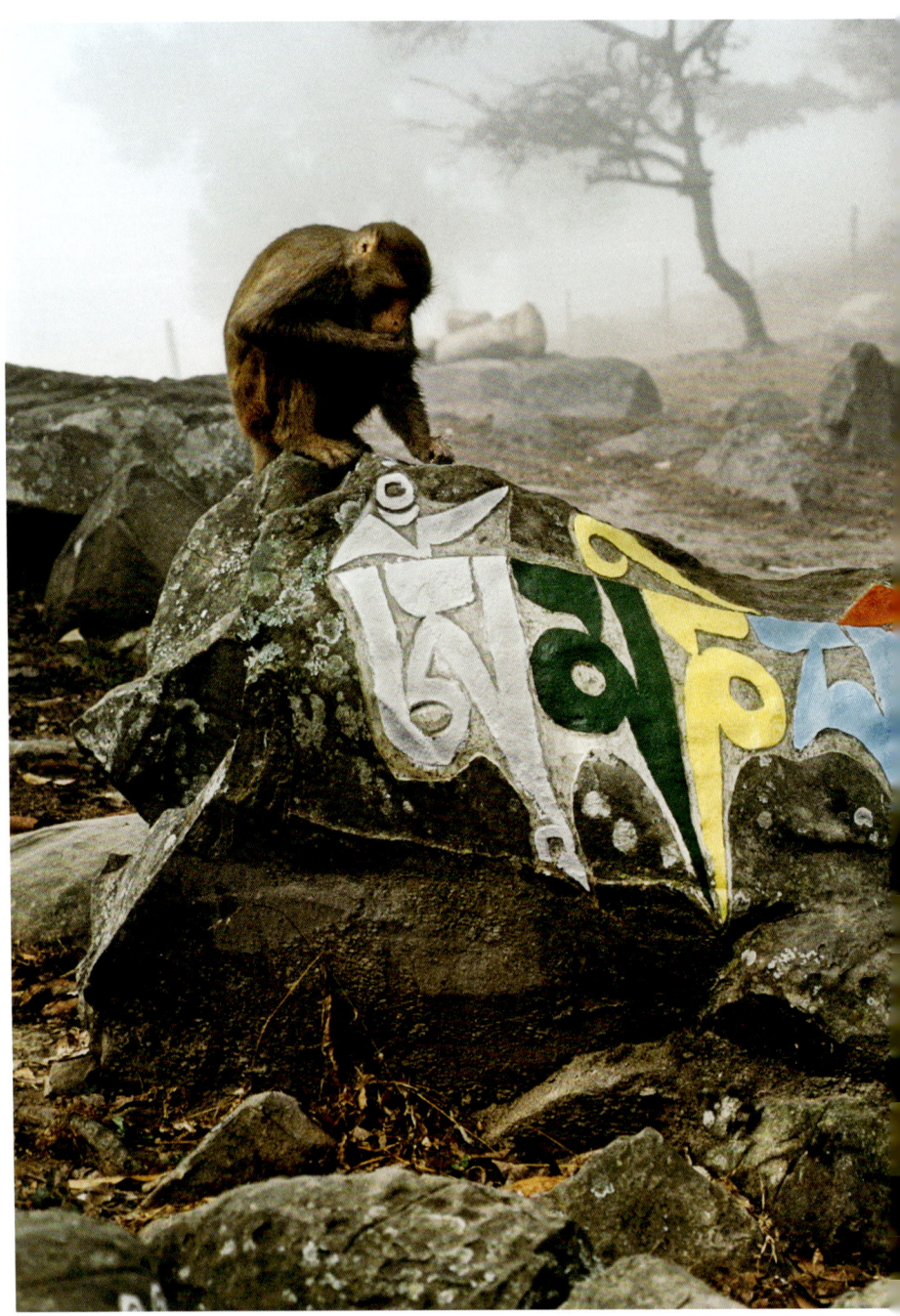

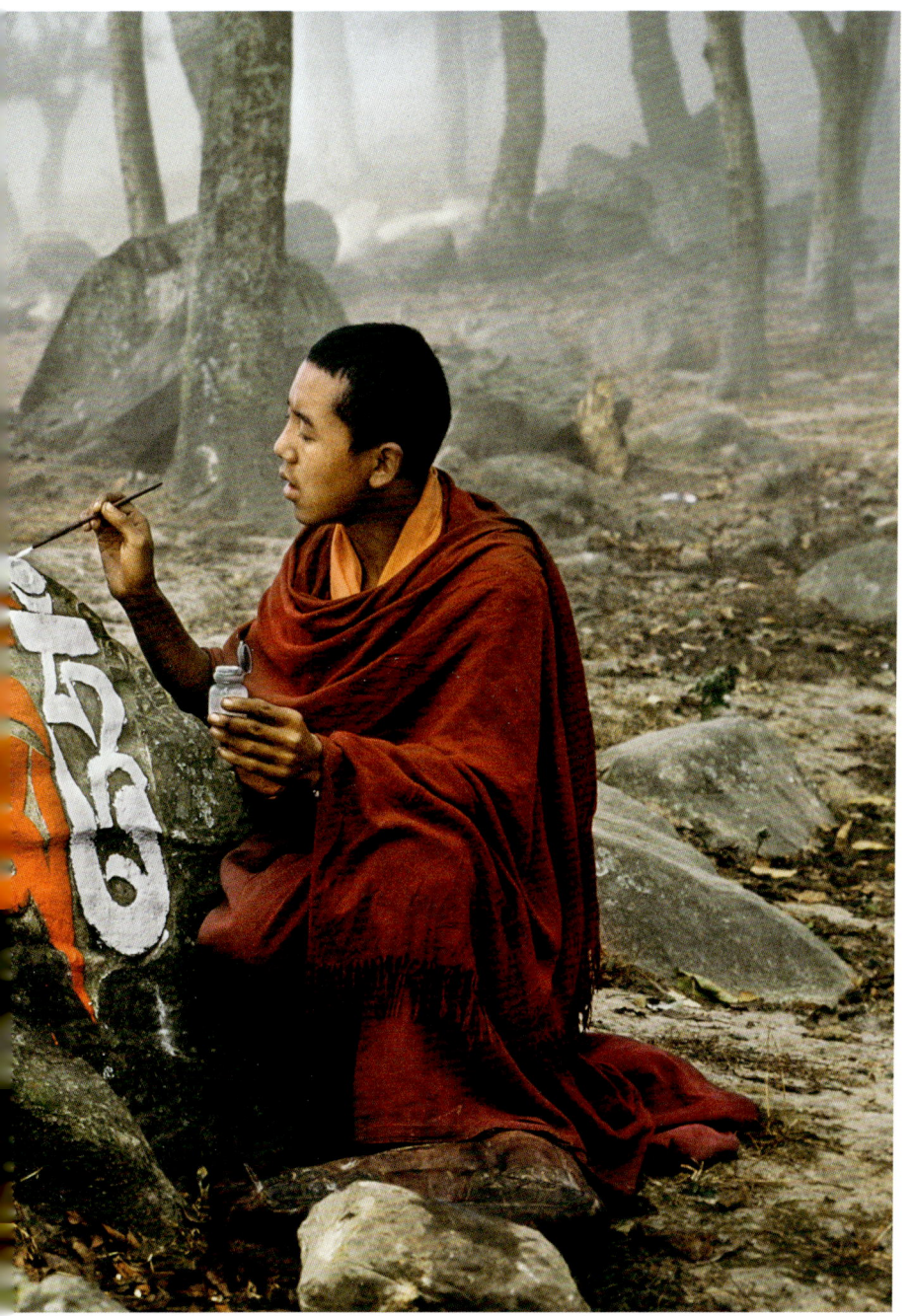

PAGES 176-177 Kathmandu, Nepal, 1998. This monkey is observing a monk painting a "mani stone." Inscribing stones and rock faces with sacred Buddhists texts, mantras, and images is an ancient and widespread practice in Tibetan Buddhism. The man is painting the six syllable mantra of compassion: "Om mani padme hum."

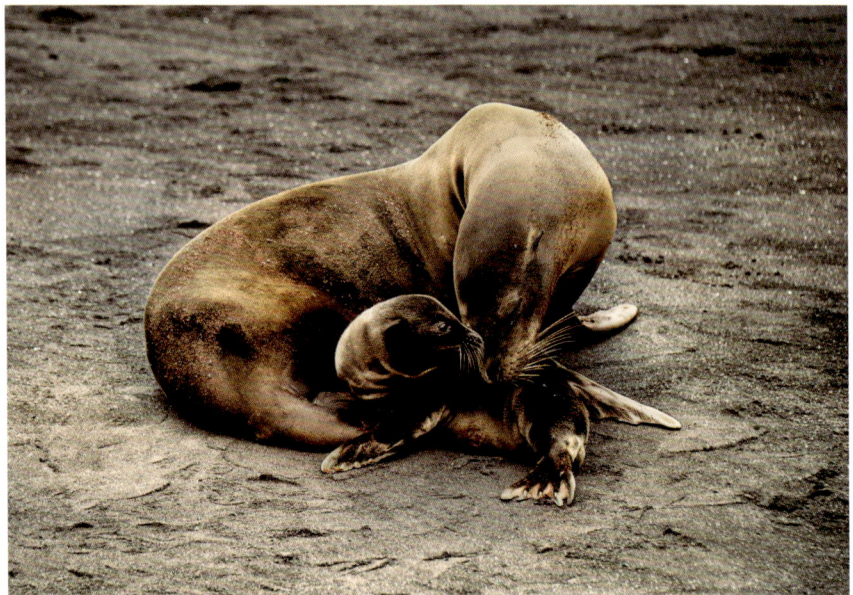

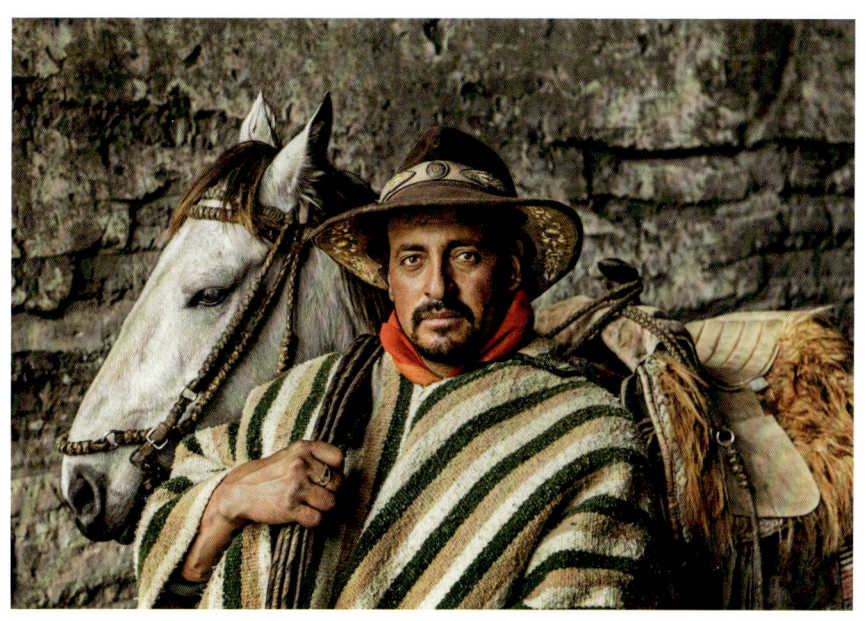

ALOAG, ECUADOR, 2017

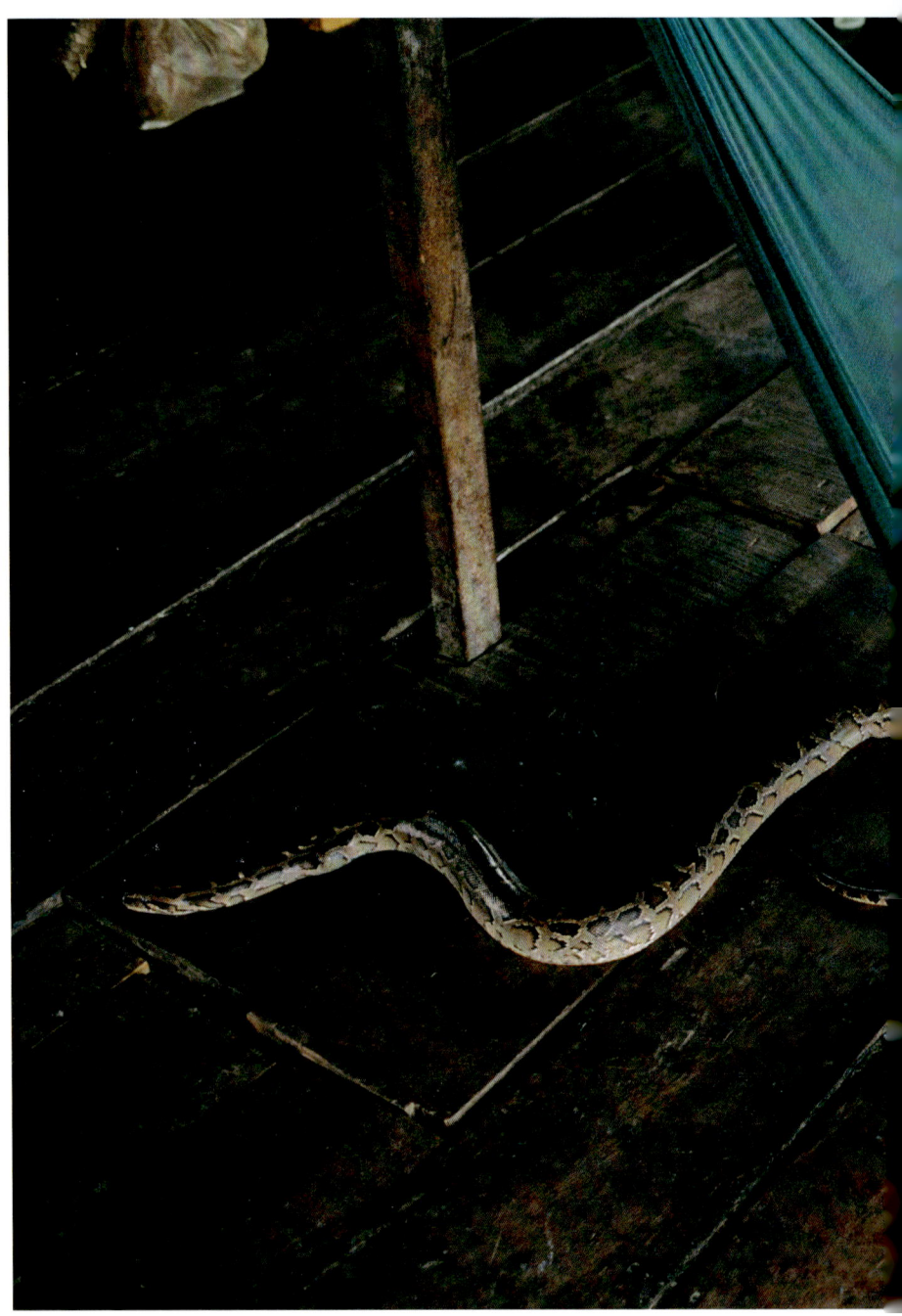

180   TONLÉ SAP, CAMBODIA, 1996

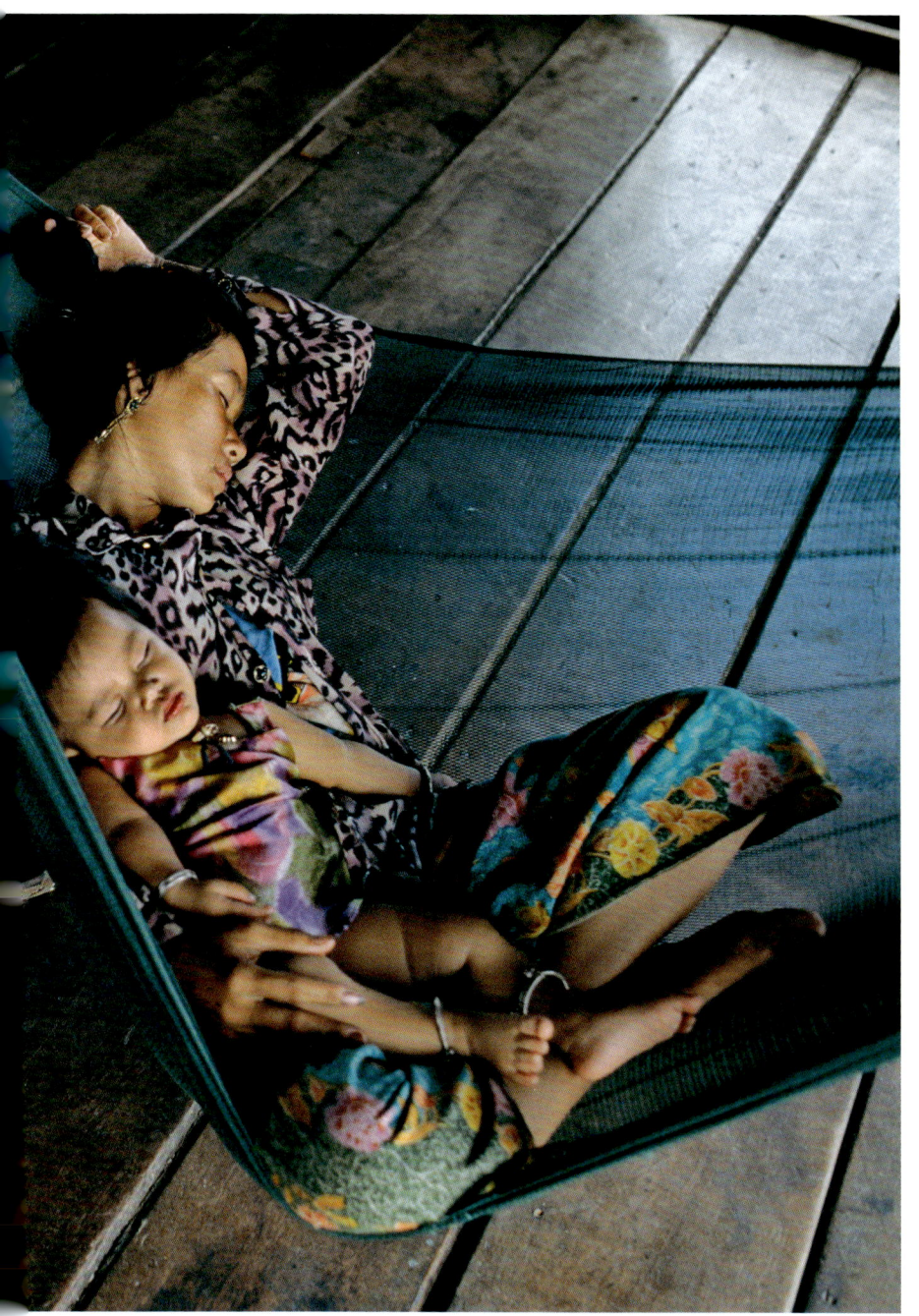

"Cows are amongst the gentlest of breathing creatures; none show more passionate tenderness to their young when deprived of them."

THOMAS DE QUINCEY

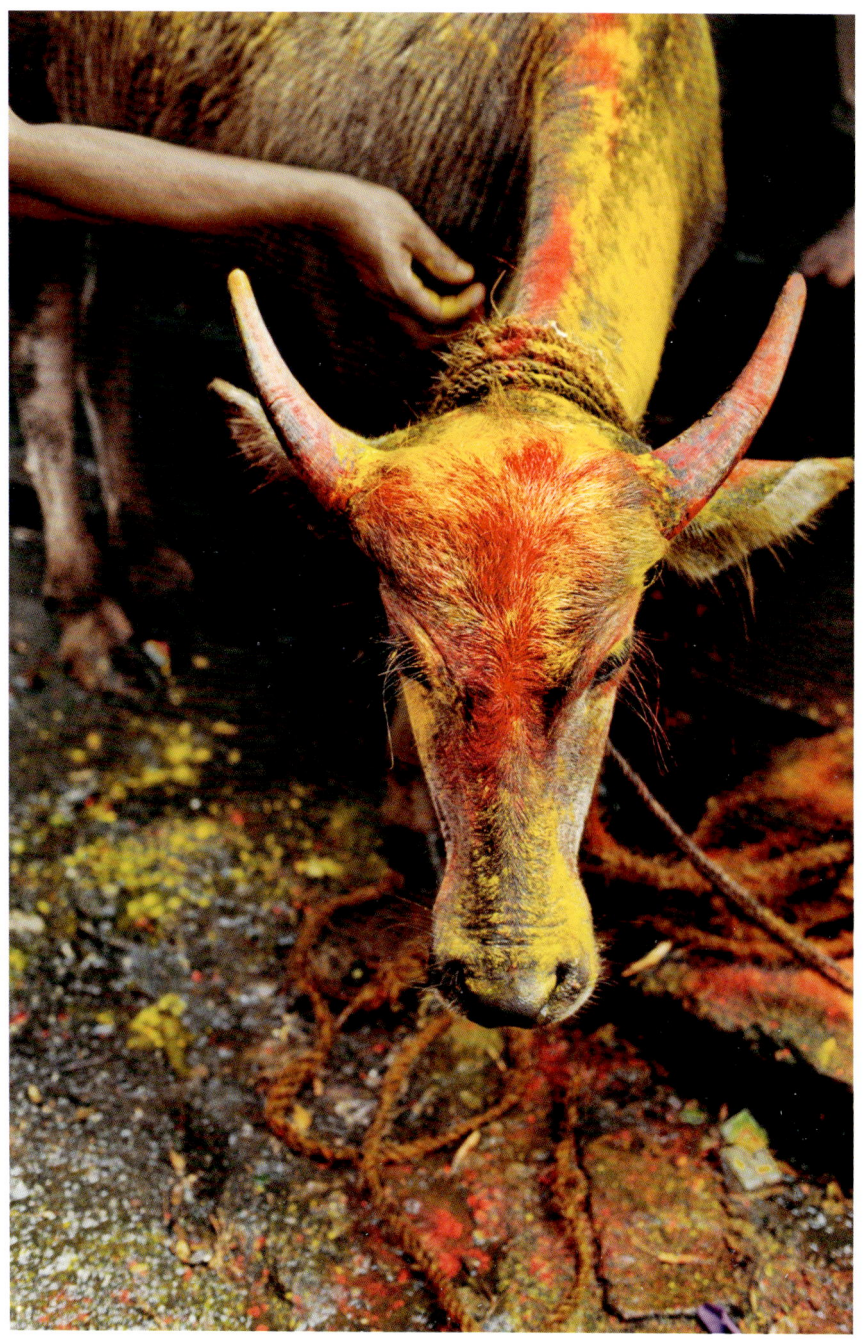

ASSAM, INDIA, 2007

183

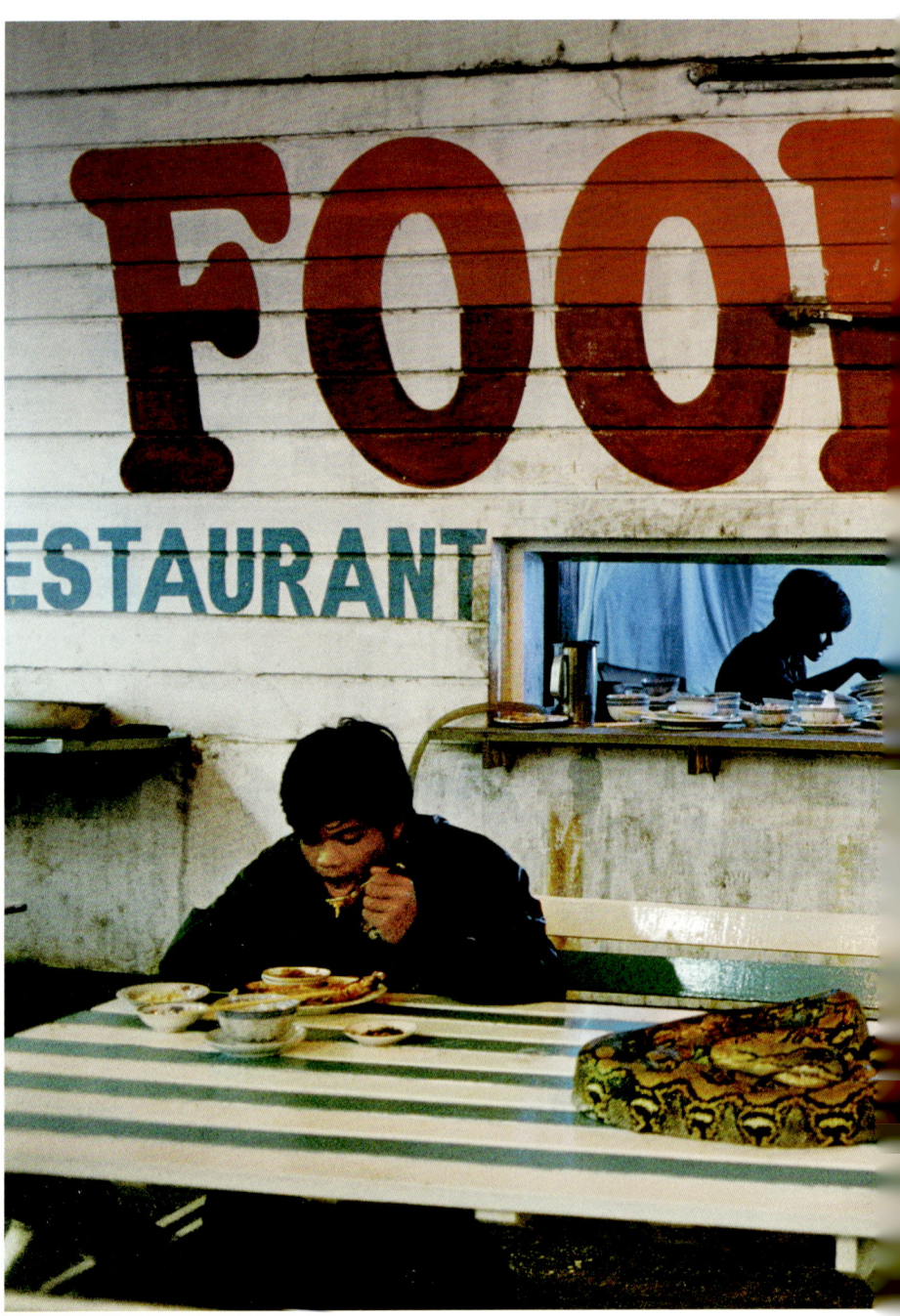

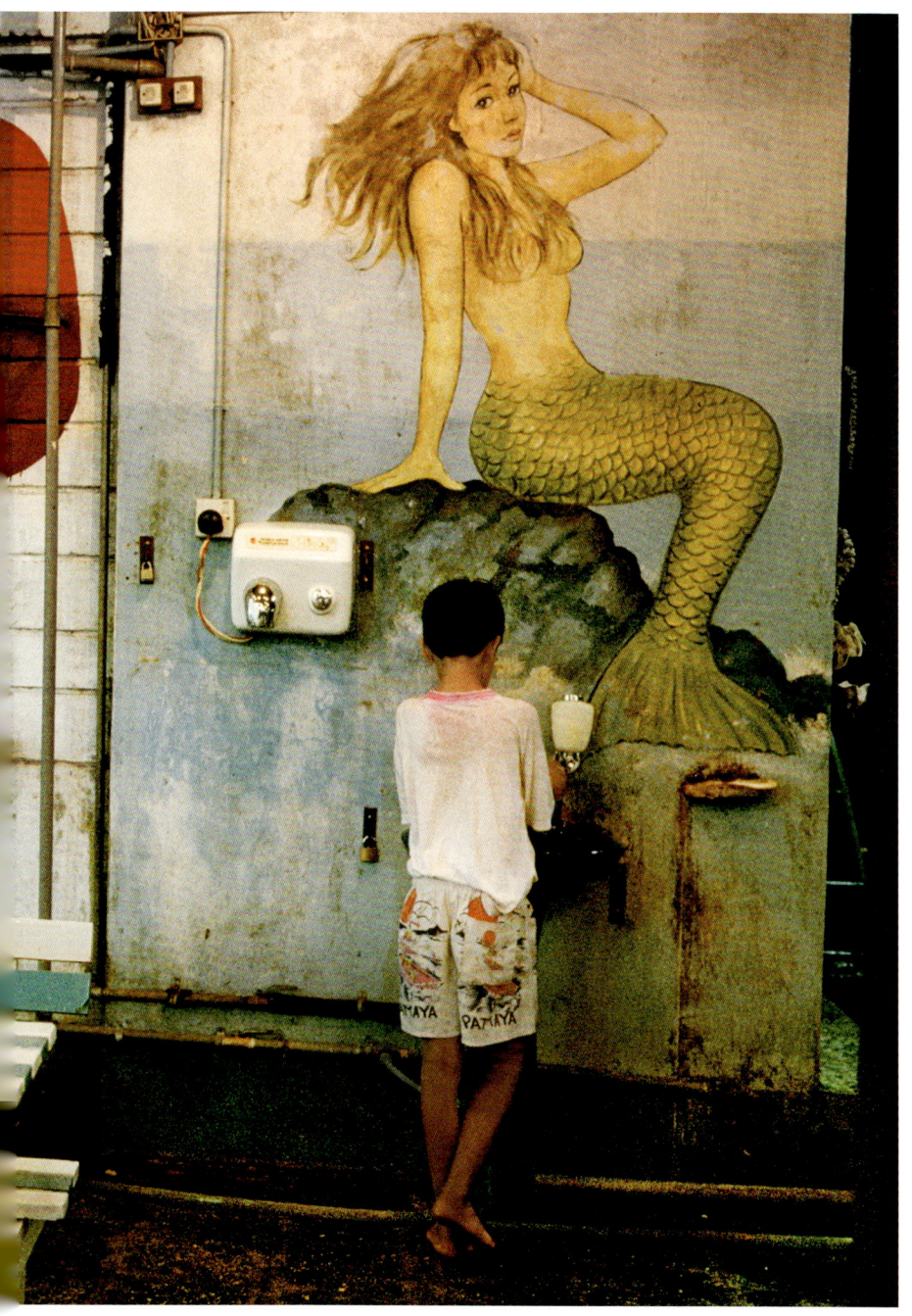

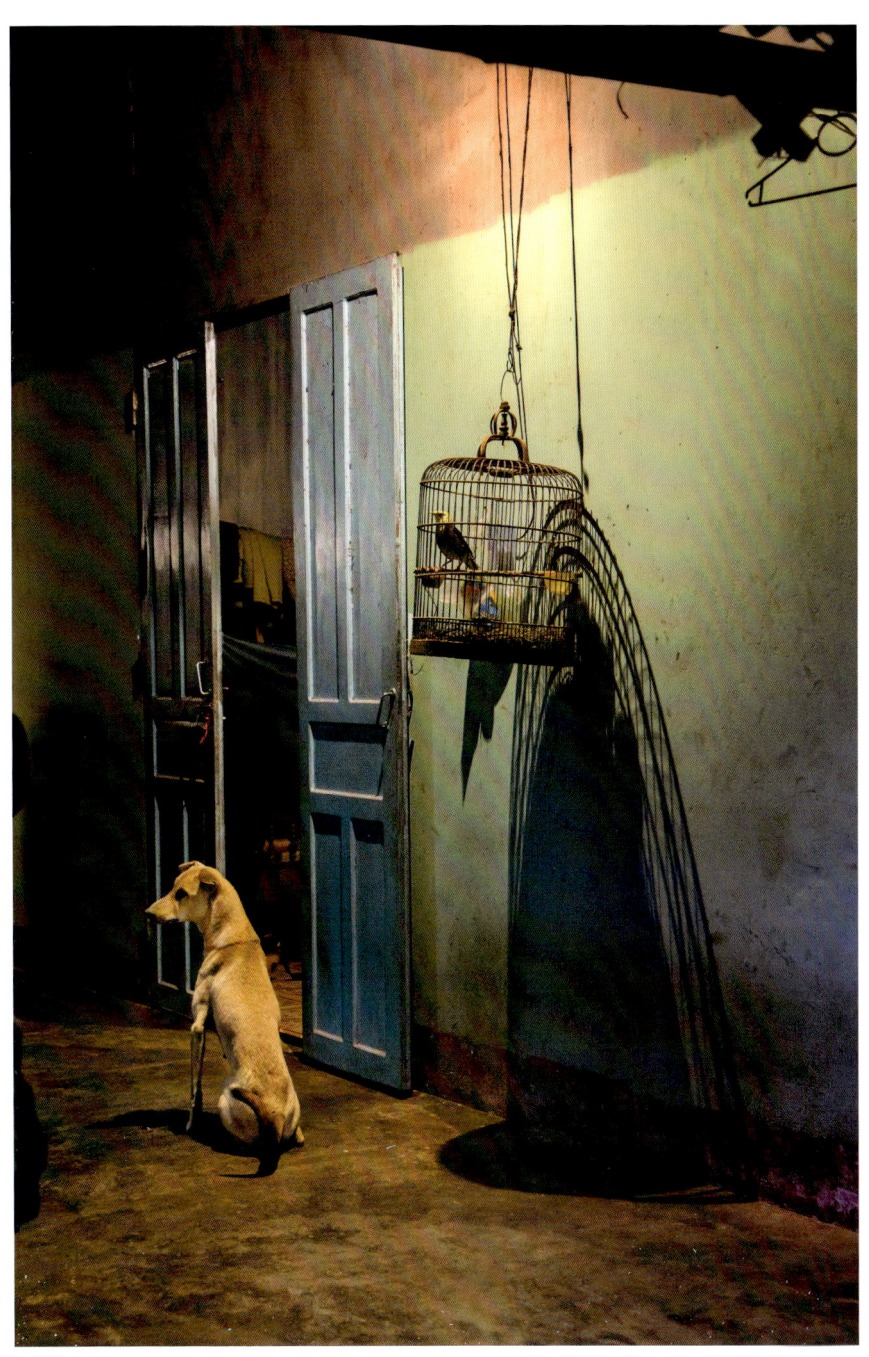

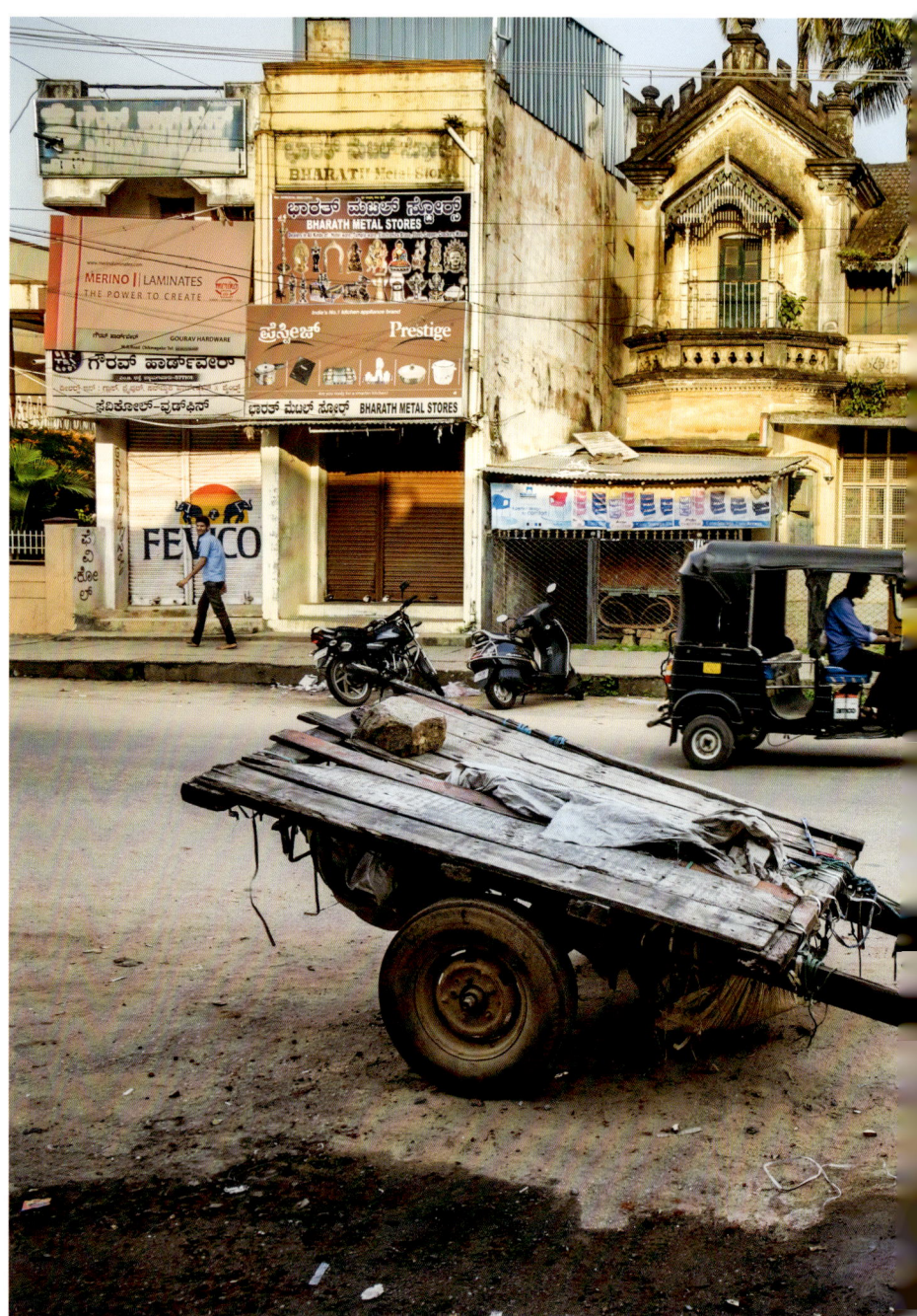

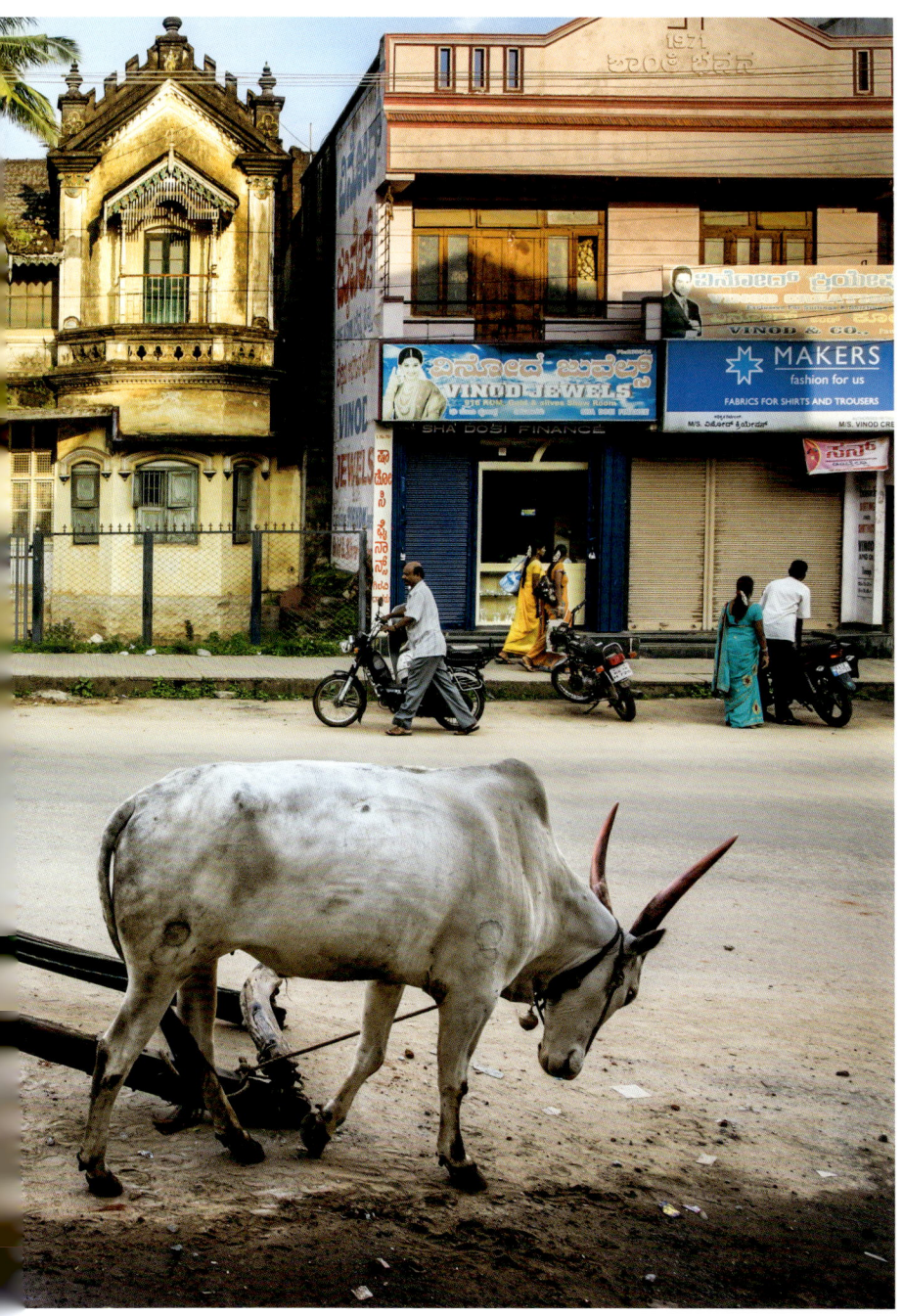

To Andie, Lucia, Bonnie, and
Doris Mae with love

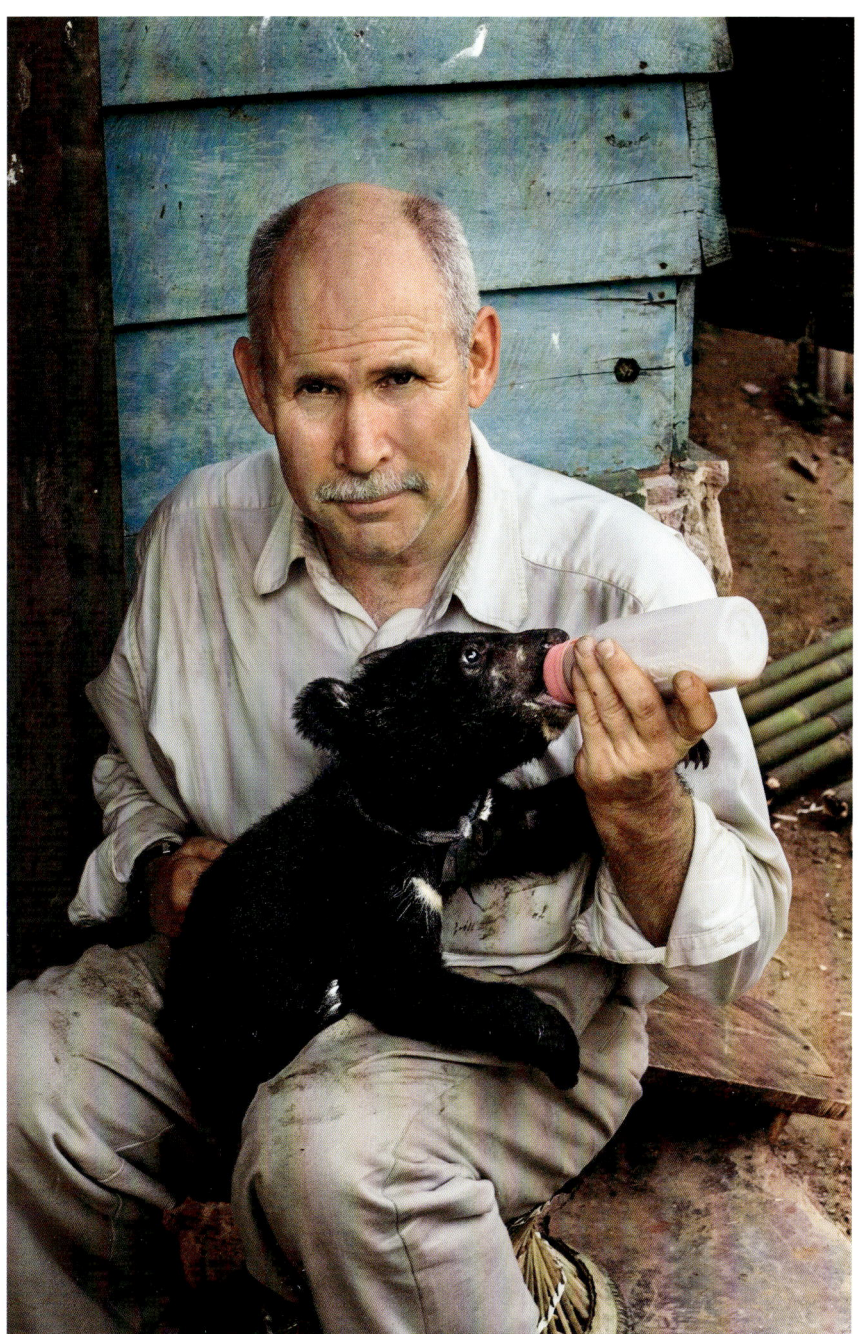

MIZORAM, INDIA, 2006

ACKNOWLEDGMENTS

Qais Azimy, Anthony Bannon, Giuseppe Ceroni, Dolores Clark, Bob Dannin, Bruce Duffy, John Echave, Elliott Erwitt, Peter Fetterman, Diane Fortenberry, Biba Giachetti, Frank Goerhardt, Jonna Golbach, Reuel Golden, Giles Huxley-Parlour, Jackie Ko, Francesca Lavazza, Giuseppe Lavazza, JeanE McCurry, Barbara Muckermann, Deepak Puri, Matthieu Ricard, Elie Rogers, Stuart Smith, "Dano" Steinhardt, Benedikt Taschen, Paul Theroux, Charlene Valeri, Jose Vuolo, Andrew Wylie, William Wegman, Phil Cifone, Camille Clech, Ashley Crabill, Kacy Edelmayer, Gemma Gerhard, Claudia Paladini, Eolo Perfido, Magnum Photos, Emily Rogers

FRONT COVER
Chiang Mai, Thailand, 2010

BACK COVER
Rome, Italy, 1994

EACH AND EVERY TASCHEN BOOK PLANTS A SEED!
TASCHEN is a carbon neutral publisher. Each year, we offset our annual carbon emissions with carbon credits at the Instituto Terra, a reforestation program in Minas Gerais, Brazil, founded by Lélia and Sebastião Salgado. To find out more about this ecological partnership, please check: www.taschen.com/zerocarbon
Inspiration: unlimited. Carbon footprint: zero.

To stay informed about TASCHEN and our upcoming titles, please subscribe to our free magazine at www.taschen.com/magazine, follow us on Instagram and Facebook, or e-mail your questions to contact@taschen.com.

Design
SMITH, London

Editor
Reuel Golden, New York

Printed in Italy
ISBN 978–3–8365–9703–6